CONTENTS

ACKNOWLEDGEMENTS

Many people have assisted in different ways in the writing of this book. Some have produced chapters; others have been there when small pieces of information have been needed. However, it was the support of people all across the live music industry who were so interested in the project that enabled us to collate all the information necessary and our thanks goes out to them.

HEALTH AND SAFETY ASPECTS IN THE LIVE MUSIC INDUSTRY

PART I
THE THEORETICAL CONCEPTS:
THE MANAGEMENT AND PLANNING OF AN EVENT

1 INTRODUCTION TO THE CONCEPT OF HEALTH AND SAFETY AT LIVE EVENTS
Chris Kemp

Managing an event and providing the audience with an environment, which is both safe and risk free, is an extremely complex undertaking. Injuries or deaths arising at concerts are no longer perceived as chance happenings resulting from the concert attendee being in the wrong place at the wrong time but as a vehicle through which blame is sought. The compensation culture pervading society today enables those involved or those associated with those involved in such accidents to seek compensation from those liable.

Such liability manifests itself in many ways: personal, public and criminal liability all impact on those responsible for events. It is the accountability for their actions that drives event promoters and managers to institute ever more stringent safety procedures at concerts to ensure that risks are minimised and that safety systems are set up to cover all possible eventualities. However, the impact of effective and efficient risk assessment and the validation of new safety procedures increases the cost of the event. Nonetheless, "It is a requirement of the Management of Health and Safety at Work Regulations, 1992, for employers to carry out a risk assessment of any significant hazards to their staff at work or to any visitors who may be affected by work activities". (Frosdick, S. Walley, L. 1999: 174). This impacts not only on the promotional costs but also on the cost of the individual tickets. The increased cost of highly trained personnel and equipment that has to meet ever increasing safety standards often make promoters think twice about staging events.

As John Huntington states "Safety is no accident". Unlike many clichés, this one is true.

Stage set up at GWR show, National Bowl, Milton Keynes.

Safety can only exist if considered for every situation, every action, from the top of a system, process, or design to the bottom. Safety should always override any other consideration: "If you can't afford the resources (time, money, etc.) to do it safely, you can't afford to do it." (Huntington, J. 2000: 248)

In the development, production and promotion of a live event there are many factors that need to be taken into consideration to ensure that the event itself runs smoothly. If any member of a live event team is asked which factor is the most important, the probable answer will be in some way connected to the health and safety of the artistes, the event team and the audience.

To define the exact nature of health and safety as a concept is difficult as it impinges on or is inherent at many levels within the general development of the live event. However the aim of health and safety legislation and guidance is to enable a safe and risk free environment for those watching, working on or appearing at a live event. The delivery of health and safety is not a one-off institution of protocols; it is a continuum where review, revalidation and change are all part and parcel of its development. With every event new challenges, risks and dangers become apparent. This is why planning is the key to all event development. The Event Safety Guide states that 'In order to protect the health and safety and welfare of people attending a music event, as well as the employees, contractors and sub-contractors working on the event, health and safety has to be managed. It is of fundamental importance to appreciate that planning for effective health and safety management should start at the same time as the planning for all other aspects of the proposed event'. (HSE 1999: 3).

A plethora of both tangible and intangible elements fluctuate creating unpredictability, which is ultimately dependent on the internal and external factors directly and indirectly affecting the promotion. It may be the case that one seemingly innocuous element that may have been perceived as safe for a number of years at a particular event suddenly becomes the focus of risk and safety planning at the same event, owing to a change in the juxtaposition of this factor. This factor could be the weather at an outdoor event, for example. It may be the case that for the last six years the weather has been fine for the event, and this has enabled the promoter to rely on the same risk and safety measures instituted over the six-year period. However, on the seventh year the weather encountered includes storms and torrential rain. If the soil beneath the stage becomes saturated and subsistence is caused, there will be an immediate danger to the artiste, the audience and those working on the event.

Therefore a contingency plan has to be ready to institute with immediate effect to safeguard those working on, presenting or watching the show.

Take the example of 'Monsters of Rock 'at Donnington, where for a number of years the front of stage area was thought to be safe and therefore the promoters MCP and Leicester County Council felt it unwise to change their risk and safety planning. However, at the event a sudden crowd surge down the gentle slope at the front of the stage resulted in the death by crushing of two audience members. It was impossible to foresee the danger, but the tragedy fixed in the minds of all of those working on live events that even if an area has been safe for a number of years it is not beyond the bounds of possibility that a change in crowd behaviour, or a change in the weather, could cause a change in the reliability of the risk and safety plan instituted. Assessment and planning are vital to all event strategies. Vasey states that

"Workers in the live music industry are exposed to hazards and risks. To ensure safety and reduce risk to vanishing point, a safety assessment has to be conducted as a matter of routine before any task is begun. Most safety regulations entail reasonable and practical precautions. Your safety and that of your artistes and the paying public have to be considered all the time. Safety ultimately is a matter of using caution with common sense. Learn first aid." (Vasey, J. 1999: 179)

It is therefore important to recognise that health and safety legislation and guidance are constantly in flux, and elements within both indoor and outdoor promotion need to be constantly reviewed and revalidated to take into consideration the changing factors surrounding each individual and unique concert performance. The prevention of risk rather than the post mortem enquiry is always preferable and in fact essential. Owing to the nature of those involved with concert promotion it is often difficult to identify constant and fluctuating risk possibilities prior to an event. The myth that events are easy to put on and that the rewards are enormous still pervades. Those who try to cut corners in areas such as health and safety to make bigger profits risk the failure of systems or human resource

Concrete used as ballast for delay towers at Glastonbury 2002.

elements which can lead to injury or death and as such cannot be allowed to happen. Those involved with health and safety try to do everything possible to obviate risk but owing to the constant repositioning of those involved, for example new promoters taking over festivals and promotions, unscrupulous promoters or a changing concert audience profile, this is often not possible.

The indoor concert scenario, although having risk and safety problems of its own, does not have the plethora of other elements involved with the health and safety of an outdoor event. Indoor concert venues are relatively stable, usually comprising a stage constructed in situ, in-house lighting and PA. The venue has four solid walls and a finite space with a pre-ordained capacity, which allows those involved with the concert process to focus on a smaller number of elements in flux rather than those elements which are of a fixed nature. In an outdoor scenario most of the structures have to be constructed in a non-concert environment and with the accompanying hazards of possible adverse weather conditions and other influences from macro environmental factors. The risk and safety factors involved in outdoor event promotion are significantly increased. An increase in heat or an increase in rainfall both have their problems. Increased heat and sun causes heat and sunstroke in an audience, which in turn causes problem for stewards, doctors and medics at an outdoor event. Heat also causes a change in the behaviour of sound as well as adding to the temperature of electrical installations at the site including PA and lighting systems and fridges causing food preservation problems. A wide range of such elements are discussed later in this book.

The issue of health and safety at concerts is one which has incurred a great deal of media coverage over the years which has usually centred on the various deaths and injuries caused by crowd surfing, surges and violence. However it is a truism that more people are killed and injured at concerts during access and egress from the venue rather than through crowd surfing or stage diving. Although the safety of the crowd at the front of the stage is an important issue within this book, the main part of the text concentrates more on the application of the Event Safety Guide issued in its first format in 1993 and updated in 1999. The Guide was commissioned by the HSE after deaths at the 'Monsters of Rock' festival at Donington and the book stipulates recommendations for health and safety at concerts and is a crucial *aide memoir* for those staging events. Another useful publication is the Green Guide for health and safety at sports grounds, which again details health and safety guidance for sports grounds in the aftermath of Hillsborough.

This book should be used in conjunction with the Event Safety Guide as it attempts to show the recommendations of the Guide in practice and any developments that have come about as a result of this initial guidance. So important is the aspect of health and safety that it is very difficult for an event to proceed unless the stipulated legal elements and regulations laid down in the entertainment licence have been met. Hawkins and Menear state:

"The starting point in matters of safety will be the licence. It will stipulate conditions to do with the provision of exits, the width of gangways and their obstruction, and emergency lighting. Whoever actually provides these features - the lighting person or the production/stage manager - the house manager is legally responsible for ensuring that they accord with the terms of the licenCe. Especially in an unconventional venue the licensing authorities will have made a special visit before granting a licence and will have made their conditions very clear. So if you are the house manager but not the licence holder make sure that you know exactly what these conditions are. Although you will hope never to have to do so, the ability to evacuate the theatre quickly in case of fire or other emergency is a vital element in the safety of the audience".

Remember, ignorance of the law is no defence. (Hawkins, T. Menear, P. 1988: 116). There are still a number of illegal events within the UK but the number of large illegal gatherings has declined over the last decade as what was then underground music has become accepted into mass culture. If the letter of the law and regulations were scrupulously applied by everyone it would be a miracle, as health and safety regulations and recommendations would disallow many events in many clubs, pubs and theatres from taking place. This book does not aim to tell promoters and managers what to do; it aims to apply best practice to live music situations and discuss the pragmatic elements encapsulated within such applications. In the case of crowd management, for example, there is no right and wrong way to manage a crowd, but there are ways

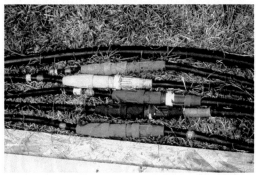

Cables from generator trucks to the stage – Big Day Out 2001.

which are safer than others and it is this type of review that is undertaken.

The macro and micro environmental factors associated with a concert are all inextricably linked together by health and safety legislation and recommendations. It is the way in which these factors are juxtaposed which affects the risk and safety at the concert.

Economic factors are key to the provision of adequate health and safety coverage at a concert. The amount of expenditure allocated to preventative action depends on a number of factors. The employment of efficient and effective well-trained security guards and stewards is of vital importance to the promoter, the artiste's management – and ultimately the audience. Not only do such employees manage the audience but they also protect the artistes, the equipment and those managing the event. The more highly trained the stewards the more likely they are to provide good security; however, the more highly trained they are the more expensive is the service that they provide. It is easy to cut corners, for example paying local rugby club members to stand on the door as stewards. However, untrained security staff lack direction, motivation and knowledge as well as insurance. Paying trained staff to work the door and provide security gives peace of mind to both the audience and those directly involved with the event. It is clear from this small example that the economic factors of concert management impinge on the health and safety of the audience. There are numerous examples of the economic impacts on health and safety elements of a live event and these will be referred to throughout the text.

As the macro environmental factors connected to the health and safety of events are discussed it will become clear that these factors do not work in isolation but form an underpinning structure of integrated elements. Although these connections are sometimes tenuous there are very few times when the macro factors will be used in isolation.

Geographical factors can affect the way in which access and egress from a site are controlled, as well as identifying whether a site is suitable to stage an event. If the venue has poor communications and is sited in the middle of a housing estate then not only will the event have to supply well trained stewards to ease the access of the audience through the community after the event but also supply monitoring equipment for sound. Such equipment will ensure that the venue does not cause nuisance to the surrounding area or endanger those attending the event. Such resources obviously incur costs but by ensuring that such elements are in place, the venue manager may continue to meet the licensing regulations and conditions and thus ensure further successful licence applications.

Politicolegal factors are inextricably linked to the health and safety within the venue. A rise in income tax or VAT increases the cost of services to the event management team, which in turn increases the ticket price. A change in Government may in turn change health and safety legislation which changes the priorities of those involved in the event industry. A change in legislation usually means an increased cost to those implementing the heath and safety procedures. Risk management and the development of robust all-encompassing risk assessment strategies can lead to a phenomenal increase in the cost of providing health and safety at concert venues. A change in licensing regulations and the institution of new conditions also has an effect on such costs. Local Councils may insist on the deployment of a barrier. Changes in the guidance regarding IEE regulations ensuring that Residual Current Devices are installed in all venues does not increase the cost of the promotion but increases capital outlay for venue managers, which in turn increases hire fees to cover the cost of the installation. However, human nature dictates that the more we increase these costs of an event or refurbishment the more likely corners will be cut in the search for profit.

Environmental factors are also an issue. Noise pollution has already been considered but there is also the problem of litter and exhaust fumes where large numbers of people congregate. The outside event has the added problem of light pollution and the monitoring of changes in wind speed, barometric pressure and rainfall, all of which influence the sound within an event. This can also have a direct or indirect effect on the safety of people at a concert, as environmental factors such as pollution and sound levels can cause harm to the individual. "Loud noise can cause irreversible hearing damage. It accelerates the normal hearing loss, which occurs as we grow older and it can cause other problems such as tinnitus and interference with communication. It can lead to the increase of other accidents and stress". (Hannam, C. 1997: 26). To arrest

Litter half way through Big Day Out 2001.

such harmful effects the planning and development of all aspects of the event have to be measured and monitored. The Environmental Health Officers have sophisticated measuring equipment to deal with these elements and this again costs money which does not increase the cost of the event to the organisers but increases the macro event costs as the equipment and staff time have to be attributed to a cost code in the local authority.

Technological factors such as new stage design, large screen playback, live relay and new sound and lighting systems all have their safety hazards and present an element of risk to those watching, managing and performing at an event. Safe structures are essential to ensure that those performing, managing and watching do so in the safest possible way. The development of new technology is expensive and brings with it its own problems of health and safety. New development means new directions and a new perspective on risk and safety management However, such developments do not increase health and safety risks per se.

Socio/psychological factors are also important as audiences, performers and managers need to feel safe in the concert environment. To enable this to happen all elements of the concert performance need to be safe. An audience entering

Feyenoord Stadium Holland-Stage set up

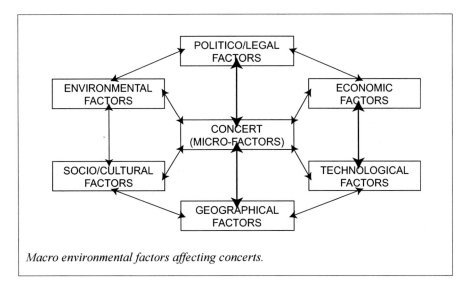

Macro environmental factors affecting concerts.

a venue will not consider the time it takes to set up the event or any of the problems that may have arisen during that set up. They are interested in seeing the performance and having a good experience. Their expectations are high and it is up to the managers of the event to ensure that they enjoy the performance in the safest possible environment.

To create such an atmosphere all the political and legal requirements in the licence need to be satisfied, which again costs money. To cut corners in such areas will cause the promoter immense problems as the show will not reach the requisite health and safety standards and thus as such will not be of a sufficient standard to proceed. Over the past five years a number of licences for shows have been revoked because of worries about the standard of heath and safety at the venue, and in the aftermath of Roskilde it has become increasingly important to monitor the safety of all sections of the crowd. This is no easy task as the crowd often act as a body, lose their individual identity, and move as a force as members of the crowd are carried along with the flow. This book looks at ways in which this type of behaviour can be avoided and the way in which concerts can be made safer for all those concerned.

The integration of macro factors is key to each individual event. No two events are the same and each licence shows this in differing conditions. These individual conditions are micro rather than macro factors and it is such micro factors that give each show its individuality. As each show differs at the micro

The new fence at Glastonbury 2002.

level it increasingly important for promoters to be aware of local conditions, ticket information policy and regulations in force at the venue which may be unique in the sector. Such factors include age limits, dress codes, curfew and alcohol regulations. The configuration of each venue differs in size, shape and capacity and therefore licence conditions are pertinent to each individual case. The licence for both indoor and outdoor events can be extremely complex, built structures for outdoor events and the myriad of shapes and sizes of indoor venues have to be taken into consideration during the application process. Those promoting large events also have traffic difficulties to contend with owing to the fact that large areas not usually used for car parking may be used, causing potential traffic congestion and delays. Other events have access and egress difficulties for emergency services because of the vast volume of traffic converging on the event. Traffic plans and travel plans have to be submitted to the police well in advance of the show to ensure that the trafficking of the event has been carefully considered. Some events have special ticket considerations and others have age problems because of under-age drinking. All these macro and micro factors have to be considered when putting together an event.

The Psychological Relationship Between the Audience and Health and Safety

The key to the success of any event is the way in which event safety is conveyed to those participating. In most cases the last thing on the mind of an audience member is how the safety has been organised and how safe the event is going to be. However if parents are taking children, or old people are involved, then this perception may change and the focus of the persons involved may be directed more on the way that safety has been organised.

The artiste, the audience and those working on the event expect a high level of health and safety to be in place whenever they attend or work in an event environment. The audience expects a total experience, which starts from the moment they see the event advertised and finishes sometime after they have told all their friends about the experience. If the experience is very good or very bad then it may figure in memories and conversations for years to come. The essence of the event is the adventure and the movement away from the normal. When visiting events many people find themselves lost in the world of the performer, and those about them become secondary to their enjoyment. For those surfing or stage diving the safety of others is a secondary consideration to the enjoyment of the event.

The way in which the safety of an event is configured is essential to the enjoyment of the event by the audience. If the audience or members of an audience do not feel safe before, after or during an event it will impact on many elements including repeat custom and trust of the promoter or the venue. The spin offs for an event that is perceived safe are manifold for those promoting them. These include confidence in the product, the promotion and the venue and may result in initial or further customer spend on this or future events.

The psychology of event health and safety works in a number of ways. Security personnel are viewed in two ways. Firstly there is the perception that the security guards are there to stop the enjoyment of the audience. Secondly there is the perception that the security guard is there to assist the audience with their enjoyment of the event. These two perceptions fluctuate. After carrying out research into these perceptions at my own venue I found that 60 percent of customers at rock, indie, thrash and metal gigs perceived that the security personnel were there to stop the enjoyment of the audience by regulating their behaviour. Subsequent research into folk, soul, MOR and progressive rock events revealed that 89 percent of the audience felt that the security personnel were there to assist the audience with their enjoyment of the event. The type of audience, their dynamic and their behaviour at the events governs these two viewpoints. Those in the first category are much more active in their pursuit of the total experience, which is shown through body surfing, moshing and stage diving. The latter audience

View from the Pyramid backstage area towards the main campsite, Glastonbury 2003.

group tends to be more passive and appreciates the musicianship and song craft rather than the enjoyment of the former.

It can be seen clearly from this that audiences behave in different ways and therefore different arrangements for different audiences must be employed. The positioning and behaviour of stewards should reinforce good health and safety practice with regular reviews of crowd behaviour and specific training of how to deal with new fads and crowd specific behaviour. People feel safe when they see well-drilled, well-organised staff carrying out essential duties. The way the crowd behaves can often be attributed to the way the audience interfaces with the performer. The HSE text 'Managing Crowds Safely' states:

"Performers can have a significant influence on crowd mood and behaviour, e.g. by jumping into the crowd or throwing items into it, or by calming the crowd, if pushing or surging starts to occur. Several acts/ performances at an event may attract different groups of people, resulting in considerable crowd movement. For example, where one particular performer has a large or enthusiastic following, the audience may suddenly surge forward and crushing could result." (HSE. 2000: 7).

A secondary reinforcement of good practice is the way in which the mechanics of the event are separated from the audience. There are many pop events today that attract a very young audience, which can cause major headaches for their promoters. By compartmentalising the hardware inherent in any performance and removing it from the audience domain the promoters are effectively reducing health safety and risk problems. People and machinery do not mix.

The manifestation of a well run and well timed event pays dividends as artistes feel that the event managers are in full control of the event and those watching feel that they are being rewarded by the total experience. An audience kept waiting without explanation is a dangerous audience. It is in the best interests of the promoter to keep to time as much as possible and to inform the audience immediately of any expected or unexpected delay. One key element to promotion is contingency – not just monetarily but also offering a number of alternatives for possible problems which may arise during an event.

The control of an audience and performers is vital. As far as an audience is concerned, control commences with their arrival at a communication point. This point may be a car park, the venue entrance, a bus or rail terminal or even an airport. Moving people in an ordered way to a venue or even just controlling the car park is vital to the development of audience health and safety. The efficient and effective movement of these people to reception areas to the venue results in a smooth passage into the venue. Large queues and crushing by the congregation of too many people converging at any one time on the entrance to a venue must be alleviated efficiently and effectively. Once in the event the semiotic evidence of where people can and cannot go is evident. This is taught to audiences at an early stage of their development and although many members of the audience try to access areas where passage is forbidden the majority play by the venue rules in such a matter. Although there are many dangers within the venue it is the access and egress which often cause problems owing to the large number of audience members wishing to enter or exit a venue at any one time. Slips, trips, falls and crushing are all elements that need to be alleviated. Obstruction of entrances or gated areas and walkways are a danger and the flooring in and around these areas must be kept clear.

Once entry has been made into the venue then there are primary, secondary and tertiary safety concerns that need to be addressed to ensure the safety of the audience and those working on the event as well as those performing.

Concerns include the way in which the audience or groups within the audience behave. Their interaction is a key element in the safety of others. The way in which the audience behaves has many factors, which are wrapped up in the crowd dynamic. The age, sex and ethnicity of the audience are all factors, which must be considered when identifying an audience type, as these demographics can often enable security to identify the type of behaviour expected. The genre of the music plays a key part, and also the way in which the artiste interacts with the audience often plays a part in whether an event is safe or not. If the gig is classical, jazz or blues the tendency is for the audience to attend to appreciate the musical dexterity or virtuoso capabilities of the performance itself. A thrash, nu metal, punk or indie gig attract an audience that like to stage dive, body surf and pogo which in turn cause difficulties for those in charge of the security and those taking part in the delivery of the concert. Pressure against the barrier, lateral movement of the audience, pressure from surfers and divers downward as well as medial pressure all exert an influence on the pit area. However, the danger here has to be tempered with the exhilaration felt by the fans themselves. Many attendees only go to concerts because they are able to express their feelings to the artistes through ritual and dancing. Take away such an integral part of the event interface and the event loses its impact.

The performers and workers on an event are managed in a different way.

The event arena is a hazardous place and such hazards cannot be overestimated. In the initial stages of a set up the crew has exclusive access to the arena area and the trucks so that the equipment can be unloaded and set up. It is essential that the area where the equipment is unloaded has easy access and is free from the risk of slips, trips and falls. When working in event arenas danger can be identified in three main ways. Firstly the danger, which is manifest in the equipment being unloaded, which consists of heavy and often sharp objects which can cut or crush those that are unloading or loading them. This risk is further exacerbated by the possibility of slipping, tripping or falling onto, over or on pieces of loaded or unloaded equipment. The second comprises electrical, gas and liquid materials, which can shock, burn, scald or sear. The third comprises the danger of falling from heights or being hit by falling objects. To alleviate the risks in this area is often difficult and therefore highly trained individuals are used to erect and dismantle the equipment. New crew should undergo rigorous training before they are allowed to assist in such work. The artistes have different expectations. They need to be protected from the audience and the equipment whilst on the premises.

The psychological development of health and safety can be split into three main areas of operation:

PHASE 1 The movement of the audience from home to the venue, their arrival and the communication of information before they enter the venue. The arrival and setting up of the equipment before the entry of the public to the venue. The arrival, sound checking and security of the artiste before the event.

PHASE 2 The entry or egress of the audience to and from the building at the beginning and end of an event. The entry and exit of the equipment before and after an event. The entry or egress of the artiste before and after an event.

PHASE 3 The behaviour of audience groups within the venue during the staging of an event. The interaction between the equipment and the audience during an event. The interaction between the audience, the artiste and the management during an event.

Behaviour is linked to genre in many cases and to enable the promoter to institute first class security operation the security firm or personnel must be familiar with the types of behaviour which are expressed by members of music genre groups. The orderly passage and frivolity of the fans of Rolf Harris at Glastonbury is totally different to the dissonance and fighting of the Meteors fans at the Garage.

It is these sorts of differences and the health and safety and risk elements which are connected to each aspect of a concert promotion that fundamentally change the way that the contractors and services providers view an event.

These people have to be aware of the dangers posed by their interaction and interface with the audience.

Food safety is also key in health and safety as well as cleanliness, correct toilet facilities and safely erected staging, lighting and sound structures. The special effects have to be managed correctly to avoid risk to health.

Health and safety factors and their relationship to the law in many areas are quite definite. Structures both permanent and temporary must abide by British and European standards when erected within a venue. Electrical appliances and wiring must abide by IEE regulations: "All electrical installations and equipment must comply with the general requirements of the Electricity at Work regulations 1989" (HSE 1999: 71). Food must be prepared to rigorous standards. All aspects of the event must comply with the licence for the venue, otherwise it contravenes the licensing act. However, alongside the law is a wide range of guidance, which is not in itself law but good practice identified to have been useful in the development of health and safety and risk prevention, across Europe and in some cases, the world. Although much of this guidance has been tested in a number of areas, often it is not universal in its application or has not been deemed sufficiently rigorous to form part of legislation. If after further testing and development it is thought that such guidance is essential to the practice and implementation of safety, it may be adopted as part of the regulations or conditions of the licence.

Owing to the nature of the live event this book is divided into three parts. Part one introduces and develops the theoretical concepts inherent within an event covering the management and planning, risk assessment and identification of hazards and legal aspects. Part two covers the application of the theory to the event focusing on the site and its management, stage design, regulations governing lifting operations, and toilets and waste facilities. Part three covers the human elements of event management including crowd planning, communications and welfare.

It must be stressed again that the Event Safety Guide is crucial to the planning and management of health and safety at live events and that this book has been written in an attempt to apply the guidance in these two publications to all aspects of the live event where appropriate.

REFERENCES

Frosdick, S and Walley, L (1999). **Sport & Safety Management**. Butterworth Heinemann

Hannam, C (1997)   **An Introduction to Health and Safety Management for the Live Music Industry**. Production Services Association

Huntington, J (2000). **Control Systems for Live Entertainment**. Focal Press

Menear, P and Hawkins T (1988) **Stage Management and Theatre Administration**. Phaidon, Oxford

Vasey, J (1999). **Concert Sound and Lighting Systems (3rd Ed)**. Focal Press

HSE (2000) **Managing Crowds Safely**. A guide for organisers at events and venues

HSE (1999) **The Event Safety Guide**. A guide to health, safety and welfare at music and similar events. HSE, London.

Chris Kemp

Chris Kemp has been active in the live music industry for the last two decades. He worked as a promoter and venue manager creating the Pitz Club and Clock Inn for Comedy in Milton Keynes where he promoted over 3000 acts including Iron Maiden, The Passadenas, Blur and the Stranglers, during a twelve year period. Chris is now a Professor and Dean of Faculty at Buckinghamshire Chilterns University College where he created the first ever undergraduate degree programme in music management in Europe. The programme goes from strength to strength with five strands of the programme now in operation and the further development of a research unit is one of the reasons for the publication of this book.

2 THE MANAGEMENT AND PLANNING OF HEALTH AND SAFETY AT LIVE EVENTS

Phil Winsor

Event Planning

Background

It is of paramount importance that this aspect of the live music event is fully explored and documented by those with individual key responsibilities. Failure to do so could have catastrophic outcomes, such as experienced at Roskilde Denmark in 2000, when concertgoers died. The consequences that emerge from such tragic circumstances could result in severe financial difficulties for the promoter / venue management as criminal, and civil litigation is likely to occur, with the potential for imprisonment, unlimited fines, and massive claims for damages against those adjudged to have been responsible, by possible neglect of their 'duty of care'. Even if precautionary insurance was in place, insurers may seek to refrain from meeting claims from individuals or businesses if 'due diligence' cannot be adequately demonstrated. Further, the insurance sector would certainly question whether or not to provide insurance for any future event. No insurance equates to a business venture failure.

The Key Players

One key problem with live music events is that there are many 'key players', and it can be unclear as to who is the person in overall control. e.g. venue manager, tour manager, or production manager. In reality they all have an important role to play, but there must be one person who has the ultimate responsibility, and be answerable to the Local Authority Licensing Officer or Senior Police Officer. On occasions, this individual may have multiple responsibilities, i.e. they may be the venue owner / proprietor, event promoter, Public Entertainment Licence holder, and be involved in production issues or management of the event. All these elements are too many for one person to deal with, no matter how experienced they may be. These overlaps can cause doubt as to who is doing what, where, and when. In these situations it is essential to clarify the decision-making process, and clearly set down the responsibilities in writing – otherwise errors or omissions will occur, confusion will reign, and the customer may have a bad experience, or a serious incident may occur.

An individual with overall responsibility can successfully manage this type of scenario by advanced detailed planning, ensuring that all the technical aspects, and the related safety issues are fully scoped, and competent contractors engaged to put in place the agreed arrangements.

Individual ' key players' will consider that their aspect of the live event is the most important. The answer to this potential problem is in getting those individuals to work together so that inter-personal relationships can be built upon rather than create possible conflict. A good camaraderie is essential on longer tours, but may have to be worked at. The live music entertainment industry is in part akin to a 'family' in that many promoters and suppliers know each other very well, and have frequently worked together over many years.

If there is not a clear demarcation of roles, and responsibilities, then a 'blame culture' may result, and this will undoubtedly cause difficulties for both individuals and the companies involved in the production. Those agencies on the periphery – the licensing authority or the emergency services, may get an impression, rightly or wrongly, that the event is totally disorganised. Procedures and protocols may not have been drafted or have not been followed. In order to ensure this does not occur requires the engagement of an experienced professional in live event management to co-ordinate production 'build up', monitor the event, and oversee a safe 'breakdown' and 'load out'.

As with any trade, an individual could be very experienced, and knowledgeable in a range of issues e.g. health and safety, stage construction, rigging, and site infrastructure, etc. Generally, this knowledge would have been accumulated over a considerable period of time though 'hands on' experience possibly augmented by attendance at specialist seminars, conferences or academic studies.

Alternatively, the individual may actually have very limited experience, but purports otherwise. This is a potentially dangerous situation and must be avoided by taking up references if the size of the event warrants it. Those providing services to the live music sector may not be able to demonstrate individual competencies by certification, although this situation is changing, as compliance with health and safety legislation is a major 'driver'.

As a consequence, a good production manager should be seen as a valued asset. They need to be skilful in ensuring that the relevant individuals are given reasonable preparation time, and are listened to. Contractors must be given flexibility in achieving outputs/outcomes, albeit within budgets. Pragmatism is an essential requirement to cope with all the conflicting demands. If all these 'skill sets' are in place, then they will gain the reputation of being a person who is easy to work with, and a true professional.

The Event Plan

The event plan can be in a number of forms/layouts. It could be encompassed in modern project management software programme using a laptop computer.

A 'milestone plan' would incorporate key dates for activities, contracting details, labour requirements, e.g. riggers, forklift truck drivers, minibus drivers, etc. An immense amount of detailed data can be put together, and using 'state of the art' technologies, transmitted globally. This is particularly relevant for international tours. Live entertainment is part of the 'global village' and all those involved, have to realise that this is the case.

The event plan may need to be developed in order to accede to the customer/client's format. There may be house-style considerations, and elements of it may be relatively brief or comprise detailed specifications that can then be forwarded to specialist sub-contractors, e.g. special effects, pyro-technician, or stage design team.

As there are so many different parameters, it is essential that the plan be documented. Creative thoughts must be transposed from the brain into a byte. There needs to be evidence as to what has been discussed, the decision making process, how the differing elements will fit together, who is going to do it, and who is going to pay for it – and when!

The whole process has to have continuity, and be capable of being audited to establish that 'due diligence' has been taken.

It has now become commonplace for an accountant(s) to be on tour with the' bottom line' figure being all-important. The live music industry has become far more sophisticated than in recent decades, and those that are in it, or aspire to be part of it, must be equally so.

Creating a Framework

An outline event plan will give a framework for the team to use. It will encompass a range of preliminary parameters, and some may be retained or rejected on the grounds of practicality or cost. It will need to cover all the main

components for the event:
- indoor or outdoor
- free or chargeable ticketing
- venue infrastructure
- event technical specifications
- event transport and parking arrangements
- relationships between relevant landowners and adjacent occupiers
- the venue management team
- the 'key players' - promoters, artiste tour management
- financial and security arrangements
- contact details for the venue locality - local authority and emergency services personnel
- contractors and subcontractors
- emergency contingency planning
- generic tour information and layouts
- local information - hotel accommodation, taxi firms, restaurants, etc
- post event - debriefing arrangements

Deregulation of Alcohol Licensing

The 24 x 7 economy is being encouraged by the UK Government through the deregulation of the alcohol licensing regime, and the provision of 'regulated entertainments'. The 'night time' (up to 11pm) and emerging 'late night' (up to 2am) economies in towns and cities in the UK are generally outstripping the resources available to the local authorities and emergency services to deal with the social and environmental impact of intoxicated human behaviour at the conclusion of live events taking place primarily in themed bars, and nightclubs – that impact on social and environmental situations.

There are many issues that need to be considered, and action plans formulated. 'Partnership' working by the authorities with the leisure sector is to be encouraged, where that may assist in dealing with such issues as:
- additional police patrols
- public transport - night buses
- an absence, or lack of taxis (hackney carriages) and private hire vehicles
- early morning refuse collection and street cleaning /washing down prior to the start of the next day's business

Training

Companies and individuals involved in making the arrangements for organised entertainment need to have some training and experience in doing so. Unfortunately, the current licensing arrangements in the UK for public and indoor and outdoor entertainments do not require a person to have experience in event management. They must only be a 'fit and proper' person by having passed the 'tests' applied through the Police National Computer records (PNC checks). However, organisers may be inviting hundreds or thousands of people to a live event. Venues have differing layouts from basic open plan designs of many thousands of square feet, to multi-floor, multi-compartmented, new or converted buildings that have an original, or 'created' ambience. The availability of many music genres in the same building at the same time is considered to be 'cutting edge', but the emergency evacuation routes in such structures may be complex, even with the latest photo-luminescent fire safety signage and advanced fire detection systems. These aspects will need to be considered within the event planning process.

Creating a Good Experience

A live music event should be an exhilarating 'experience' for the individual attending it, and as a consequence, it is a major 'driver' for the evolution of the industry. However, it can easily be a 'bad experience' unless the production team put in place adequate management systems that are reliant on trained, and competent personnel to undertake their specific tasks. New technologies will provide some 'added value' if used, e.g. closed circuit television (CCTV) and public address systems.

The management/production teams should ensure that unauthorised persons - 'blaggers' – do not get into the production areas, particularly where there are to be 'special effects' taking place It is vitally important that 'access all areas' passes, etc are strictly controlled, whatever the cost in PR terms.

Management teams must

Revellers at front of stage, Rolf Harris, Glastonbury 2002.

have a pride in their venue, and should strive to achieve and maintain a good reputation for delivering the right 'experience'. On occasions, a venue, possibly through no fault of its own, may get a reputation which it does not desire, which then proves very difficult to change.

Contractors' Responsibilities

Earlier in this chapter we discussed who the 'key players' are in event planning. In order to ensure that individuals, or companies, deliver what they are responsible for, commercial contracts should be used. Unfortunately, on occasion a contractor may not deliver what was ordered, and this can then create serious safety risks – e.g. insufficient freestanding safety barriers. It may have occurred through human error, cost cutting, or misunderstanding the specification. It is the responsibility of competent persons to ask questions of professional colleagues, advisers and contractors, so as to ensure that there is clarity in the process. As with any project, there will be instances when things do not go according to plan, and there is a need to solve the problem by creative thinking 'out of the box', and the carrying out of necessary works to ensure that the show goes on.

Locality

An aspect of the event management process that may not be given sufficient consideration is where the event takes place. Will a city, town, or village accept that it may be beneficial to them individually or collectively as a community? Residents may see the event as an absolute and total intrusion into their normal urban/rural lifestyle and be entirely adverse to it being staged. They may have seen an audience enjoying themselves via media coverage of an event, but to contemplate having them literally in their own backyard is likely to cause serious concerns and the lobbying of local politicians.

As a result of recent changes to local democratic arrangements, particularly in the larger urban areas, there has been resurgence in the powers of Parish Councils, which may also be termed Town or Neighbourhood Councils, and local government is being told by the central Government to listen to these bodies, and keep them informed, and encourage partnership working.

The live event industry is already a partnership of technical and creative individuals. Therefore there is a need to embrace those individuals whose local knowledge may be of assistance. If they are part of the team, they are less likely to be in a position to pour scorn or create disharmony in their community in respect of the event.

As a consequence, it is extremely important that the event plan, when it is at an early stage, is taken to the community representatives, explained to them, and they are engaged with. They may then accept that the event may not have the impact that they initially believed it would. For example the technical aspects of modern live event management can keep the sound levels extremely focused with directional short throw PA speaker systems. Financial penalties may be inserted into contracts. Traffic management consultants can devise creative routing solutions augmented with highly visible temporary signage.

Clear exit signs, Big Day Out, National Bowl, Milton Keynes.

This may seem an extremely parochial way of thinking, and potentially not a profitable use of the promoter's time. However, the input of time and energy can culminate in commercial spin-offs that assist that community, through short-term fiscal benefits, e.g. assisting in supplying goods and services, bed and breakfast accommodation, etc, and therefore a 'Win-Win' scenario can become a reality.

The Local Authority

It is extremely unlikely that the relevant officers of all the 460 plus local authorities in England, Scotland, Wales and Northern Ireland will all think, and operate in a similar manner in respect of live entertainments. However, there is a single document that will help immensely: *The Event Safety Guide - a Guide to Health, Safety and Welfare at Music Events* more commonly known as the 'Pop Code'.

The responsible officer at the relevant local authority could have a professional background in environmental health, building control, administration, law or licensing. It is entirely at the discretion of the local authority how they undertake what may be construed as purely an administrative exercise, when in reality it is not.

The local authority may deal with the matter with a rigid application of statute law and due regard to the Home Office Circulars and Health & Safety Executive guidance. The responsible officer may not have a particular interest in the live event industry, and does not carry out 'during performance' inspections in high risk venues - all night dance music events.

The technical expertise necessary in modern event planning and management has taken a quantum leap in the last decade, and it is incumbent on those promoting events to work on the basis that the local authority doing this as a purely administrative arrangement. They need to be supplied with the event plan, site/building plans, and supporting technical material that explains the issues, and the planned actions. The relevant local authority officers will then be able to scrutinise the documents, and request further information from the designers/suppliers. The aim of the process is to give a clear indication of how the event will take place so as to ensure the health, safety, and welfare of the performers, the supporting staff, and the audience, whilst minimising the impact that the event will have on the local community. It is important that written health and safety risk assessments are also made available for perusal.

Modern, purpose built arenas should be compliant with all the relevant design codes ensuring that there are sufficient fire exits, toilets, emergency lighting systems, etc.

Temporary structure design and construction has advanced at a phenomenal rate in recent years, using new materials and construction technologies; as a consequence the planning aspect is even more critical.

Construction of screens and barriers for Enimem, National Bowl, Milton Keynes 2003.

The underlying principle of working with a local authority so that the desired outcome is realised is the provision of good technical information and a willingness to take inexperienced personnel through the event management learning process without being, or appearing to be, condescending. In some circumstances the local authority may fully accept their naïvety in respect of the technical matters and engage event safety consultants. They will be able to undertake an assessment of the documents submitted in order that the local authority Licensing Committee can be properly advised on the application before them.

The local authority officers also may have

to consider the event in a wider context:

- impact on local tourism through the take up of bed spaces
- socio-economic impact, due to the provision of permanent or casual employment
- the local transportation system may need to be augmented with buses from outside the local area to provide a dedicated 'shuttle'
- the public transport terminuses may need to be given support in respect of policing and security
- policies on street trading may have to be reviewed due to the impact of fast food vendors
- waste management arrangements need to be reviewed, etc

These are issues that need to be researched, and possibly considered by the promoter in their preliminary costing. It may be prudent to offer some 'token' of goodwill by offering to provide, or at least make a financial contribution towards, these types of local issues.

Local authorities may have their own policies in place which may conflict with what the live event promoter is proposing, e.g. a circus troupe or act may be planned as part of the entertainment, but the local authority may have a policy against performing animals within their boundaries.

It is a major concern to many promoters that local authorities do not talk to each other when the same event is being taken to similar venues round the country. Promoters are asked to adapt the show to meet particular local requirements, very often without a sound technical or good legal reason for doing so. It is possible that the licensing officer does not have a full understanding of the issues, but does not wish to be exposed. However, professional colleagues are always willing to share 'best practice' advice and their practical experience. Public Entertainment Licence conditions that have been developed by experienced local authority officers at well known venues are commonly forwarded to other authorities if requested. This enables current 'best practice' to be used as a starting point and the document can then be amended accordingly. Further, professional intranet systems are being used allowing e-networking with both positive and negative information being communicated. This approach helps to prevent duplication of effort.

All local authority enforcement staff involved in the live entertainment industry have to start somewhere, and it can take decades of experience to be able to demonstrate clearly to those in the industry that their problems and concerns are fully understood.

If promoters perceive that they may encounter some difficulties with the local authority in respect of their arrangements, then it may be extremely beneficial to offer the relevant officers the opportunity to view the system, procedure, or act taking place, either in the UK or abroad e.g. viewing multiple safety barrier systems in use so that the 'pros and cons' of such arrangements can be scoped, and informed decisions made which could easily prevent serious injuries to concert-goers. Such arrangements would not be seen as a 'jolly' but a local authority acting in an extremely responsible manner, and being prepared to listen to those who may be better informed.

The UK's live music sector is probably one of the most creative and safety conscious in the world. The measures put in place by sector, and the enforcement agencies utilising the *Event Safety Guide*, referred to earlier, has no parallel anywhere else globally. However, complacency must be guarded against. All those involved, must continue to work together as new techniques/ technologies evolve.

Licensing Events

The legislation will set down the administrative process, but Licensing authorities must ensure that the rules of natural justice are applied at all times, when considering an application. Further, the personal views or prejudices of elected members of the Council determining the application must not be stated in public prior to the matter being heard as their forum acts in a 'quasi judicial' manner, i.e. like a court of law. All parties have to ensure that all the relevant facts and information are submitted in a way that is understood by those present, including members of the general public.

If the applicant can furnish adequate and detailed responses, then the matter will be proceeded with. If, however, issues arise whereby the applicant is unable to clearly demonstrate sufficient knowledge, then the matter could be deferred to a future date in order that a defence against the points raised is made. If the event has already been allocated a slot in the tour diary, and advance ticket sales have been made 'subject to licence', any delay may have severe financial implications.

If the local authority refuses to grant a Public Entertainment Licence then an appeal may be lodged, and the application heard afresh by the Magistrates Court – a 'de novo' hearing. The situation could arise whereby the Magistrates sitting on the licensing bench may have no knowledge of public entertainment licensing law and practice, and even less regarding the nature of the event that is being proposed and the potential impact that it may have on the locality.

Slightly bizarre situations can arise as a result of this scenario, with the licensing officer of the local authority and the applicant's licensing consultant being directed by the Magistrates to drafting a set of licence conditions on their behalf. And it could be to ensure the safety of 30,000 persons attending a weekend all-nighter (including camping)!

The underlying message is that licensing authorities' expertise is variable, and therefore their ability to be helpful or unhelpful will be similarly so. In order to ensure that a smooth process evolves, it is worth the applicant considering engaging experts in their field as part of the event planning team.

Local authorities have recently been recommended by the government - Department of Culture, Media and Sport (DCMS) – to use venue-specific licence conditions, with some standard conditions but augmented by additional conditions pertinent to the venue and the type of entertainment taking place. However, matters covered by other primary legislation must not be duplicated, e.g. health and safety, and fire safety. This approach will eradicate illogical anomalies that have caused concern to the leisure sector for many years. It is of paramount importance, therefore, that the current advice produced by the government, the voluntary sector, or trade associations is acknowledged, and used by local authorities as the foundation for specific licence conditions, covering such matters as on site paramedics, free water supplies, 'chill out areas', drug awareness/searching.

The types of premises used for public entertainments is vast, and local authorities have been directed by the Government to impose less onerous licensing conditions on low risk community facilities such as village halls. However, consideration still has to be given to the fact that these facilities may be utilised by novice bands for small gigs or practicing. If the electrical installation is unsafe, then a performer could be electrocuted. It is vitally important that there is an external 'driver' to ensure that basic safety checks occur or a life may be lost.

The government introduced a new Licensing Bill in 2003 dealing predominantly with the deregulation of the present alcohol licensing laws. It will also include 'regulated entertainments' encompassing public entertainments-music and dancing, theatrical performances, cinemas and late night refreshments. The new Act should be effective during the summer of 2004 depending on the transitional arrangements. The main change will be that the administrative functions will be transferred from the Magistrates Court to local authorities with enforcement primarily lying there, but with additional powers given to the police particularly to deal with urgent matters, e.g. public disorder, and noise.

A further issue that may prove to be a difficulty concerns the competency of personnel from abroad. For example, a local authority may be presented with a photocopy of a photo ID card or document issued by the Sheriff or Fire Marshall of a U.S. town or city regarding a pyrotechnician who is allegedly trained, and competent to USA standards. The pyrotechnician then goes on a world tour with a band arriving in the UK not aware of the accepted protocols, health and safety standards, working methods, and having a slightly different phraseology for commonly used pieces of pyrotechnic material. In order to overcome this type of problem the event production manager needs to be able to demonstrate that the individual's bona fides are satisfactory and the documentation is entirely satisfactory. Another example would be scaffolders /riggers or forklift truck drivers where the crews' competencies, including certification, should be demonstrable. They should be available for inspection in a file kept for inspection purposes by the tour manager.

With e-mails and faxes being a common way of communicating, providing a hard copy audit trail is not impossible, and would provide essential evidence if a serious incident were to occur.

The Safety Advisory Group

The Chief Executive of a local authority is required to ensure that public events taking place in their locality are considered in respect of public safety through the setting up of a Safety Advisory Group (SAG) whose membership will include some of the 'key players' involved in reviewing the event safety plan and detailed arrangements including local authority officers including the local Police, British Transport Police, Fire and Rescue Service, NHS Ambulance Trust, and Voluntary First Aid Sector. Experience indicates that if these individuals are kept well informed they can have an important input into the event planning arrangements.

It has taken the experienced practitioner years to assimilate all the vagaries of the live entertainment industry; it cannot be learned overnight. Those practitioners who do show an interest and endeavour to understand the issues normally find it extraordinarily rewarding to be part of a successful event planning team.

The Safety Advisory Group is not able to dictate actions – only to advise,

Bad practice – Throwing water into the crowd should be discouraged.

guide, and pass on 'best practice'. In some areas they will not give written advice due the possibility of litigation if a catastrophe were to occur.

The Police and Operational Planning

The role of the police in event planning is still evolving; so there is a need to fully understand their perceived role, their actual operational role, and the political interfaces which may not be entirely apparent but within which they have to work. Further, as in any business, there are financial pressures and budget constraints that senior managers have to factor in. The police have to ensure that they can resource the event coming to their locality without it having a detrimental impact on their normal policing arrangements. They solve this problem by purchasing additional resources – officers, specialist equipment, or support teams, e.g. a mounted section from other forces that have the spare capacity. Some of these additional resources that are considered necessary for the event to take place have to be paid for by the venue manager/promoter, who in turn is likely to pass the cost onto the ticket holder.

The policing costs for concerts can be substantial, but may be negotiable to some extent. The Home Office has provided the police with guidelines and a costs matrix. The requirement to adequately police the event can be made a licence condition by the local authority if requested by the Chief Police Officer.

As with local authorities, individual Police Area Commanders will have their own views on the live entertainment sector, and the impact that it may have on their officers, budgets and methods of policing.

Many different parameters will have to be scoped by them in undertaking a risk assessment of the event and the implications for their force:

- Is the event taking place indoors or outdoors?
- Does the venue have an annual public entertainments licence?
- Will there be sales of alcohol until 2.0am?
- Is it an occasional outdoor entertainment licence for a 'greenfield' site?
- Is the duration to cover a single day, a weekend or beyond?
- Will there be organised camping?
- Will the music genres have a substantial influence on the amount of security/ local policing required?
- What experience does the proposed security team have?

The operational teams will consider all these factors. The police have intelligence-gathering officers, and their own extensive networking arrangements locally, regionally and nationally. Once the artiste line up for a gig is known, they may come forward with reservations regarding an individual or individuals who may be appearing, e.g. crews who may have a previous track record of incitement or illegal acts of violence that could be detrimental to the safety of those present.

If artistes and crews with this type of reputation are coming to the UK then the police may insist on discussing their concerns face to face with the artiste and the tour manager with video evidence, so as to provide them with a 'due diligence' defence.

Crowd gathering in front of stage for Cypress Hill, National Bowl, Milton Keynes 2003.

The Taylor and Popplewell reports into the Hillsborough and Bradford disasters not only made a significant impact on stadium design in the UK, which are often used for music concerts; they also stated that the existing safety arrangements were less than satisfactory and that a thorough review was needed. The Government responded to these points with the Fire Safety and Safety of Places of Sport Act 1987.

The police now have to comply with the requirements of the Health & Safety at Work Act 1974, which requires their employers through the Chief Constable to undertake risk assessments. As a consequence, the police give more 'weight' to issues appertaining to the well being of officers when they are at work in these diverse environments. The risk assessment follows logical application processes involving hazard spotting, determining the risk factor(s), and the formulation of action plans. These in turn will result in additional training, the provision and use of specialist safety equipment, and reviewing the effectiveness of the arrangements.

An important aspect of policing events is that there has to be a judgement made between public order and public safety. On occasions, this can become a very fine line. If the senior police officer acting as the ground commander for the event (but who actually has little experience of gigs) observes what appears to be a dangerous situation unfolding in the audience near the front of stage barrier – moshing, body surfing or excessive crowd dynamic movement – he may quickly embark on a sequence of decisions and actions that may turn a cause for concern, into a potential disaster.

Witnessing individuals in a state of distress or undress being manhandled over the barrier by an experienced pit crew, who are trained to deal with such situations, can be a frightening experience. However, the majority of those individuals coming over the barrier are just trying to get close to their idol! They want to get into the 'pit' and to stay there as long as possible. Some do require medical treatment, and a very small number may require more specialist examination or treatment at a hospital.

However, if the inexperienced police ground commander took a view that this behaviour was entirely unacceptable, and public order was at risk or public safety was actually being compromised, may consider requiring the show to be stopped. This could lead to a very serious situation, that might well result in a greater number of potential casualties arising or even a riot taking place. In this type of circumstance, advice and guidance must be sought from the head of security or chief steward engaged by the venue or promoter.

This individual has accepted the responsibility for assessing the risk of the live entertainment, they will have had some dialogue with the production team and the tour manager, and no doubt the artiste's own close protection personnel. Together they will have worked out a strategy as to what can, and cannot take place, i.e. the artiste leaping from the stage and running along the front of stage barrier, leaning into the crowd, potentially causing hysteria, emotional distress and possibly violence in the audience.

If there is a very sound reason to stop the show, then a brief discussion can take place involving the police, venue manger, promoter, tour manager head of security as to the best way forward. It may be best dealt with by allowing the artiste to finish a particular number for a couple of minutes, then cutting the main power feed, with the secondary PA system being used by a member of the tour staff to announce that due to unforeseen circumstances the show is having to be terminated, followed by a request for everybody to carry out the instructions that are going to be given for an orderly evacuation. If a catastrophic event occurred then the head of security would get the show stopped immediately through pre-arranged signals to the on-stage sound engineers/ production team.

Police Intelligence Gathering

The police may seek to capture intelligence at a live event and their techniques in doing so may be overt rather than covert. The sight of police officers in black fatigues, boots, baseball caps, etc, armed with a massive telephoto lens or high-tech video cameras scanning the audience leaning up against the front

of stage barrier, is perhaps not a good idea when emotions are running high. Such an approach can actually have an adverse effect on the audience, and promote disquiet or anger. If the surveillance has to take place, then it should be undertaken with some element of common sense, using plain clothes personnel, perhaps even looking like press photographers. This would create a better atmosphere with the audience who may actually think they are going to appear in a national newspaper or glossy magazine rather than being viewed as a potential criminal.

Police photographers before filming Marilyn Manson, National Bowl, Milton Keynes 2001.

Policing and the Private Security Sector

In many areas, the police are now accepting that their role at events can be handed over to private security companies employing trained stewards. In the UK there are probably some of the most experienced heads of security, 'pit crews', supervisors, and concert paramedic support teams in the world. However, any team is only as good as its last event, and they need to work extremely hard at attaining standards of competency and maintaining it thereafter. One of the reasons for the change in emphasis in respect of this 'policing' role is one of cost and resources. The police will be at the event but with considerably less officers than used to be the case. The general public often feel safer if there is a presence of uniformed police officers even if they special constables.

The use of closed circuit television – CCTV – can highlight the face of the concertgoer moshing, body surfing or fighting, quite easily. A data logged 'freeze frame' still photograph can be reproduced for evidential purposes, and witnesses can view the whole incident in the emergency liaison control facility on site. Microwave telecommunication linkages can beam 'real time' pictures of traffic management systems in place around the venue, which can be utilised to advise police traffic officers or highway engineers that urgent amendments are needed to road closures, coning arrangements, etc.

In some constabularies they are reviewing the arrangements in respect of traffic management by putting a greater onus on the promoter to ensure the traffic management consultants are brought in to look at routes, signage, and car parking arrangements, all with an aim of ensuring not only the flow of traffic, but safe vehicle/pedestrian interfaces whilst minimising the number of police pointsmen that are required to direct traffic near the venue.

The police are refocusing on their primary objectives of maintaining law and order in the community that they serve, so event planners need to be aware of this shift in emphasis.

Emergency Planning

In event planning, the police, along with the other 'blue light' emergency services and the local authority will plan for the worst-case scenario – this is called emergency planning. Local authorities have specialist emergency planning officers (often ex-military personnel), but they can come from a variety of professional backgrounds. The emergency planning team will require that the venue have a major incident plan in place. This will be applicable not only to events taking place either indoors or outdoors at large capacity venues but also those with a low capacity, 3,000 if the intrinsic risks are high, such as at all-night 'dance music' events.

The key to good emergency planning is to consider everything that could possibly go wrong, and then to test the arrangements that are in place to deal with such situations. This will involve not only the emergency services but also personnel from the production team, the venue, the voluntary first aid sector, and local authority officers who will provide immediate responses involving highways, victim support, health, safety and welfare, etc.

In order to understand the rationale of emergency planning, the conceptual aspects need to be clarified.

Command and control systems are used by all the emergency services that can declare a' Major Incident' independently of each other:

'Gold'   - Strategic
'Silver'   - Operational
'Bronze' - On site information gathering (forward control point).

In the event of any major incident, the senior police officer will always assume overall control of the situation as they can request additional governmental support – military and/or specialist scientists, for instance.

'Gold' is most likely to be at the force headquarters. In some instances 'Bronze' and 'Silver' may actually be on the same site, but more likely 'Silver' will be at the nearest operational location/station where there are existing infrastructure/communications in place. 'Bronze' could be the scene of the incident, or the emergency liaison office/control room at the venue.

In some situations a major incident may not be declared, but the problem on site may be such that the 'Silver' directs the' Bronze' personnel and other related services, including the on-site security teams, to take certain courses of action to effect a solution. In addition, at the end of an entertainment, relevant staff may be required not to leave the venue until Police 'Silver' is satisfied that all is well the crowds have dispersed and, the 'Bronze' teams from each agency can be stood down.

In order that these arrangements actually function properly, the Major Incident Plan previously referred to, is normally written by a trained police officer. The venue management team will have involvement, as will the security and other emergency services, along with the local authority. The police can only write part of the document, and all the other individuals and teams must have an input so that they have some 'ownership' of the document. Also, taking this approach will help ensure that it is relevant, up to date, and operational issues can be scoped, and put into the document. When the document has been finalised, copies must be circulated. It should contain site plans, including one with an overlaid alpha-numeric grid in order that specific locations can be identified by emergency services personnel directed to the site of an incident that has occurred.

The plan needs to be tested, and this is effected by undertaking a 'desktop' exercise where a scenario will unfold, and the responses of all the key individuals, and teams will be tested by introducing a range of scenarios, mis-information, and unusual circumstances to ensure that the theoretical problem solving solutions will work.

Fire extinguishers backstage, GWR Roadshow, 2002.

Fire Safety

In recent years, there has been a move away from the use of prescriptive standards to the concept of a fire safety risk assessment - Fire Precautions (Workplace) Regulations 1997. Historically fire safety was a formal certification process, looking at the structural elements rather than the type of activity taking place within the venue, be it a permanent structure, or a temporary plasticised textile marquee. Mainstream items such as escape route travel distances, fire exit widths, fire fighting equipment have not been forgotten but staff training, reviews of systems and procedures, and scoping unusual hazards that require careful control, such as real flames produced by sophisticated liquefied petroleum gas equipment, have to be analysed.

The premises may be multi-compartmented, with different occupiers or it may be under the direct control of a single management team. As a consequence, the fire safety arrangements may have to be 'fire engineered'. This is a complex solution but sometimes necessary, and will involve multi-stage fire detection systems, automated communication systems between parts of the building, and a water sprinkler installation.

The audience age and profile needs factoring, as do the implications for disabled persons, or wheelchair users, who in the event of an emergency may have difficulties in moving unaided to a place of safety. In certain buildings they may have to remain, either alone or with an escort in a 'refuge' – an area designed to withstand heat and smoke for at least 30 minutes whilst rescue is made.

The fire safety risk assessment may be undertaken by a professional person who is trained in fire safety/fire engineering, or it could be somebody with relatively little experience and knowledge who has undertaken a course of instruction and is using detailed checklists to ensure that all the issues are scoped, and the necessary actions put in place, to ensure that the premises comply with the legislation. The venue's insurer will then be satisfied that the 'best practicable means' have been taken in order to exercise 'due diligence' so that any subsequent claims can be carefully considered. It is also possible that this approach will result in lower insurance premiums. If the fire safety risk assessment is undertaken on a do-it-yourself basis, then the local fire safety officer may review it, and provide further guidance upon request.

In the UK we have experienced serious fires involving multiple fatalities e.g. The Starburst Club (Isle of Man) and at Valley Parade (Bradford Football Club). In more recent times fire safety incidents at live entertainments in the UK are thankfully a rare event, but they still occur abroad. In Chicago USA. in 2003 a pyrotechnic real flame special effect caused polyurethane foam insulation on the walls of a nightclub to ignite resulting in 97 deaths.

Pyrotechnics

Another source of both fire and flame in a relatively controlled manner are pyrotechnics. Dependent on the nature and size of the display, pyrotechnics

Pyrotechnics on forklift, Big Day Out, National Bowl, Milton Keynes 2001.

may be handmade to create a particular effect or be purchased from abroad and used by trained personnel. There are instances when a shell launched to 1500 feet does not explode, and comes back down to earth with a bump! If an individual is standing in the way they will sustain a serious injury such as a compound fracture of the upper arm – or be lucky and just have a glancing blow to the side of the head. These are true scenarios and therefore pyrotechnics have to be given due respect. The fall-out area has to be carefully considered and made secure. The majority of the audience at a show thoroughly enjoy the spectacle of pyrotechnic displays, and manufacturers are making them bigger, brighter and louder. Rock musicians have taken it to another limit by actually placing a 'bomb tank' (a lidded steel drum that contains exploding fragments of pyrotechnic material) under the drum riser. The effect on stage is dramatic!

During Performance Inspections

An operational crew from the local Fire Station will often visit the venue when the entertainment is occurring in order to ensure that the Fire Safety Certificate and/or Licence conditions are being complied with. It is important, that they can actually get their fire appliance close enough to the building / temporary structure in order that they could fight a fire, or evacuate casualties if necessary. The operational Fire Officers will access areas of the structure, checking the fire fighting equipment, escape routes, fire exit doors, documentation and the accessibility of hydrants, dry riser inlets, etc. If deficiencies, or contraventions are found, then a report is made for action under Fire Safety legislation or if appropriate forwarded to the licensing authority.

Fire safety is given an extremely high ranking by elected members of local authorities responsible for Public Entertainment Licensing. They have absolute discretion on many issues, but one area where they will probably never depart from is professional fire safety advice. It is essential that any personnel working in the live entertainment sector understands and appreciates this situation as a departure from the advice provided could easily result in a fatality, and a subsequent appearance at a Coroner's Inquest.

At outdoor events, promoters may engage the services of professional Fire Officers and their equipment to create, in effect, a private fire service. If these arrangements are to be put into place, it is preferable to ensure that the local Fire and Rescue service are aware of this intention in order that on the day of the event no tensions are created.

Merchandising and Concessions

To put on a live event, wherever its location, costs money, and a way of balancing the budget is to ensure that merchandising arrangements are maximised through letting concessions to companies or individuals to provide services that the audience, etc. will expect in one form or another. Generally these fall into three main areas:
- tour merchandising,
- food and beverage,
- 'branding' - banners, posters, etc

Tour Merchandising

The artiste or promoter will engage a specialist company to arrange for the manufacture, storage, distribution, and sale of tour merchandising: the ubiquitous t-shirt, sweat shirt, beanie hat, through to an expensive looking football shirt with a No 8 on the back (circa £60).

Programme sellers will find many places to sell their wares, which can include blocking fire exits, and pedestrian/vehicular access routes in and out of the premises. They often operate on a commission basis so there is a good reason to place themselves in locations where there is a high density of the audience. As a consequence, this issue needs firm management. Poster sellers find similar locations, although they prefer an area to lay the merchandise out for viewing.

Due to copyright laws, official tour merchandising is often the subject of counterfeiting, and this can have a major impact on the profitability of the tour. In many instances the company designated to provide the official merchandise will liaise with the Trading Standards Officers of the local authority in whose area the event is taking place, along with police officers, so that covert surveillance can take place on known outlets, storage facilities or 'handover' points for the counterfeit or 'bootleg' merchandise, as it is known. A co-ordinated raid may then take place, so that the individuals involved can be arrested, the suspect counterfeit goods seized, and checked by 'copyright agents' acting on behalf of the bona fide manufacturer/artiste with those involved being dealt with by the judicial processes if necessary. Unfortunately, the fines imposed at a court may not equate to anywhere near the financial benefits to the bootlegger, and the loss of revenue to the brand.

Food and Beverage

Food at live events is normally associated with traditional take-a-way foods such as burgers and chips, chicken and chips, etc. but in increasingly more locations exotic ethnic fast food is available on offer, including Chinese, Indian, Italian and Thai. High flavour natural foods include freshly made lemonade, and organic foods.

The hygiene standards of kiosks, vehicles, and trailers in use today are generally good although some rudimentary tented structures have been erected – and then closed down by local authority Environmental Health Officers working in partnership with management team. It is likely that they will have had pre-meetings with the food and beverage concession holder, and obtained lists of the vendors details so that checks can be made with regard to their suitability to trade. At some venues, traders' vehicles are checked before entry into the venue is permitted and 'failures' have to remain outside until the key issues are rectified to a satisfactory standard. During the event inspections may be carried out under the Food Safety (General) Regulations 1990.

Consession van, GWR Roadshow, 2002.

The more enlightened concessionaire will insist that the traders wear suitable clean and washable over clothing, often with a brand name, corporate logos, corporate colours, etc. so that the correct image is portrayed. The trailers may also have plastic 'skirts' round them so they also look attractive.

Alcohol sales are very lucrative. At large outdoor shows the volume of beer drunk per day could easily equates to approximately a pint per person in attendance, hence the need for road tankers of draught beer, or 40 tonne HGV's loaded with plastic bottles of wine, beer or cocktails. Draught sales will require 'high tech' fill machines, and rapid chillers requiring a considerable amount of electricity to be arranged via the on-site electrician. In most instances plastic containers will be used for dispensing drinks, but modern innovation has created plastic 'crown top' bottles that look identical to the those normally manufactured from glass. These can be recycled, but this is an aspect of the leisure sector that is still in its infancy. Some enlightened local authorities are working in partnership with venues and promoters on this issue as the landfill tax on waste increases yearly.

Branding

These are opportunities to attract additional income by selling advertising space in many different ways such as inflatable beer or soft drink containers, banners and vehicles and tethered 'inflatables'. These marketing opportunities do not normally cause a problem, but they can restrict 'sight lines' for the audience if care is not taken, or require the input from structural engineers so that a temporary structure does not topple over in high wind speed conditions due to the loadings of an inflated balloon.

Phil Winsor

Phil Winsor is the Chief Environmental Health Officer for Milton Keynes Council. He has the responsibility for a diverse range of functions including health and safety, food safety, noise control, and entertainment / alcohol licensing. He is working with the Security Industry Authority regarding the changes to Door Supervisor training and licensing.

A native of Milton Keynes, Phil has contributed to its development since its inception as a New Town in the 1970's through spending his entire professional career there. As a consequence, he has seen the evolution of the Milton Keynes Bowl ('The National Bowl'), dealing with the event planning, and licensing arrangements for such global artistes as David Bowie, U2, Michael Jackson, REM, Eminem and Robbie Williams.

Phil has been involved in the use of The Sanctuary Music Arena, Milton Keynes that has a national reputation for 'cutting edge' all-night dance music events – formally the 'Rave' scene. The venue's detailed licensing conditions were standard setting prior to the "Safer Clubbing" initiatives developed by the Home Office.

In recent years, he has lectured at Buckinghamshire Chilterns University College, the Emergency Planning College, to Essex Constabulary, and also presented papers at various professional seminars. In 2003 he became an external examiner at the Buckinghamshire Chilterns University College.

A milestone in his career was being a Member of the Working Groups who wrote both editions of the Event Safety Guide – 'The Pop Code'.

3 RISK ASSESSMENT AND THE IDENTIFICATION OF HAZARDS AT LIVE MUSIC EVENTS

Philip Winsor

Introduction

The Health and Safety at Work Act 1974 set down the statutory responsibilities for employers, employees, and the self-employed, so as to ensure the health, safety and welfare of persons at work, and also those persons on site, who were not employees, e.g. members of the public. This last point was a major shift in emphasis away from previous decades of workplace legislation that was firmly entrenched in a factory working environment.

The general public were now afforded legal protection if injured as a result of a work activity by a third party. The impact of this far-reaching approach has been to raise standards of health and safety in many environments, although a minority of individuals seem to have let these developments pass them by.

In the UK, the Health and Safety Commission (HSC), an executive body set up by the Government, with an operational arm called the Health and Safety Executive (HSE), work with many partners and stakeholders to draft newly amended legislation for the government, and to advise, educate, inform, and enforce the UK's health and safety legislation.

In 1992, the whole concept of health and safety in a working environment moved on dramatically. For many decades prescriptive standards set down in legislation were removed at a stroke. They had become outdated; many were not coherent with modern manufacturing, let alone the live entertainment sector. They were replaced by The Health and Safety Executive with new Regulations, Approved Codes of Practice and Guidance on the following subjects:

- Management of health and safety at work
- Provision and Use of equipment at work
- Workplace health, safety, and welfare
- Visual Display Units, (now called Display Screen equipment)
- Personal Protective Equipment
- Manual Handling

The key factor in all of these new documents was the innovative concept of undertaking a process called a "risk assessment", the aim of which was to 'flag up' the hazards, and the extent of the control measures necessary to control the risks in a working environment.

The risk assessment process has to be undertaken by a competent person, but that does not mean that they require a formal academic, or vocational qualification. In many instances a skilled operative with good experience of the tasks involved would suffice, as they would be aware of the intrinsic dangers or hazards present in their particular working environment.

The Concept of Risk Assessment

Risk assessments have to be carried out when new working arrangements, equipment, etc are introduced. Existing documents need to be reviewed on a regular basis so that they are 'living documents'. They can be kept and stored electronically, thus making communication with other interested parties easier.

As is often the case with the introduction of new legislation, certain individuals quickly consider themselves to be consultants or experts in this new area of work. Generic risk assessments may be produced that are often inadequate in content, and possibly irrelevant, and as a consequence do not meet the legal requirements for that particular type of working practice because not all the relevant issues have been adequately addressed.

All companies, contractors, and sub-contractors have to undertake this approach to their work planning; but if less than five persons are employed, then the risk assessment details do not have to be recorded – but a record should be kept to show that the exercise has been undertaken.

The entertainment sector was fortunate that in 1993, the *Guide to Health, Safety and Welfare at Pop concerts and Similar Events* - 'The Pop Code' was published. The code was then augmented, and updated in 1999 as the *Event Safety Guide – A Guide to Health and Safety and Welfare at Music and Similar Events*. These documents were produced under the auspices of the Health and Safety Commission and the Home Office; therefore they carried a considerable amount of 'weight' and would be accepted as 'best practice' by a court of law. Fortunately for those tasked with writing risk assessments, they had a vast array of potential hazards in the live music sector set out before them to consider in relation to their own venue, and helpful information on the control measures that could be introduced.

It is perhaps worth reflecting why these two documents were produced in the first instance. Two young men went out for the day to enjoy themselves along with thousands of others at the Monsters of Rock Festival at Donington Park and died as a result of unforeseen circumstances. When the US rock band 'Guns n Roses' took to the stage, there was a sudden crowd surge in the arena, and a section of the densely packed crowd collapsed. Although the security stewards acted swiftly, and efficiently, to extract as many people as they could from the affected area, those two young men could not be saved.

The promoters of this event lobbied the Government for new national guidance on event safety through the MP for that area – North West Leicestershire. Other promoters, through their professional body, the Concert Promoters Association, realised that such an incident could have easily occurred at one of their gigs. As a consequence there was a considerable impetus for change. A vast amount of technical information and industry 'best practice' was brought together culminating in the first edition of the 'Pop Code' being published five years later. This was a defining moment in respect of looking afresh at how concerts and other public entertainments were planned, and produced with safety at the forefront of the entire process.

The' Pop Code' soon became dated, as new genres of music were created, illegal 'acid house' became legal 'raves', and hardcore 'dance music' became mainstream. The second edition of the 'Pop Code' had an entire chapter devoted to this development. At the same time, the London Dance Forum produced their own document, *Dance Till Dawn Safely*, addressing the clubbing scene in London, which was quickly being replicated in other towns and cities throughout the UK. Once again, all those involved in the 'cutting edge' of music scene developments had to take notice of the advice that was being put forward so that lives could be saved by tackling the problems of illegal substance use and dehydration.

The Definition of Risk Assessment

In essence, Risk Assessment is a matter of starting with a blank piece of paper and scoping all the issues concerning the event, i.e. the event planning arrangements: technical details, specifications, etc. and highlighting all those where there may be a hazard involved.

However, it is of paramount importance to understand the difference between the two main terms used –'hazard' and 'risk' as they are often confused.

Hazard

A 'hazard' has a number of definitions and may include, 'anything which has the potential to cause harm to people', 'a situation that may give rise to personal injury', 'the result of a departure from the normal situation which has the potential to cause injury, damage, or loss'. At a live event it could be a dangerous structure, premises, a substance, a situation or an action. It is therefore entirely inclusive, and many situations that may not in the first instance be considered to be a hazard are in fact so. Further, less obvious hazards may be missed, or not recognised, and therefore ignored.

Hazards themselves will vary in severity, as set down below:

Major   **Death, major injury, or an illness causing long term disability.**

Serious   Injuries or illness causing short term disability.

Slight   All other injuries or illness.

Risk

Risk is defined as 'a chance of loss or injury', 'an exposure to a hazard', 'the probability of a hazard leading to personal injury and the severity of that injury', 'the probability of harm, damage, or injury'. The term implies an element of uncertainty.

Actual harm to the individual may not arise in every case. It may be mitigated by effective controls in the working environment. Those measures will need to be ascertained by the competent 'key' individuals engaged by the promoter. Latent effects need to be considered such as the accumulative impact of high noise levels over many years of exposure at gigs.

It is worth remembering that risks do not become an issue until people come to the venue!

The likelihood of harm may be considered as follows:

High   A certainty or near certainty that harm will occur

Medium   **Harm will often occur**

Low   Harm will seldom occur

Some assessment models will give a rating figure against each category, so that when multiplied the end result is an actual figure that may assist in determining a risk rating for particular aspect of the entertainment along with overall risk categorisation.

RISK = LIKELIHOOD x SEVERITY

Severity

2 – Minor Injuries   4 – 3 day injury   6 – Major injury

8 – Single death   **10** – Multiple Deaths

Likelihood
1 – Very unlikely   **2** – Unlikely   **4** - Possible   **6** - Probable
8 - Very Likely   **10** - Certain
Using the above model the highest rating would be **100** and the lowest **2**
100- 48   Unacceptable
40 – 32   Risk reduction necessary
24 - 16   Control measures essential
12 – 2   Monitor
It therefore follows that many potential hazards and risks need to be prevented, avoided, or minimised so far as is reasonably practicable using the best practicable means available at the venue, and to do so on each and every occasion when people are at work or the public have been admitted to the entertainment.

Danger
Implies 'a thing that causes peril', 'liability of exposure to harm'.

A Practical Perspective
In order to adequately scope the situation, the first thing to do is to detail the apparent potential hazards whilst walking around the venue, both internally and externally, and viewing from ground level, or below to the top of any structure (temporary or permanent). Photographs can be useful evidence, or an aide memoir.

A 'desktop' survey could be undertaken, but this may omit important facts unless augmented by information provided by a knowledgeable third party.

Examples of common hazards:
- Objects falling from heights
- Overcrowding
- Public disorder
- Special Effects
- Collapse of a temporary structure(s)
- Excessive crowd movement within a confined area
- Vehicle: Pedestrian interfaces
- Site characteristics e.g. watercourses, bridges, access/egress points
- Camping

The following is an emergency planning scenario that brings together a number of these issues.

A temporary scaffold structure comprising the front of the house mixer and lighting tower is built 8m high 6m wide and 6m deep. It collapses onto the crowd due to incorrect wind loading calculations when the structure is fully sheeted during unexpected storm force winds.

The identifiable hazards are:
- 'Quick fit' Metal scaffold tube structure
- Live electric power supplies
- Ladder access only to two upper bays
- Key structural members (diagonal braces) of the scaffolding structure had been removed in order to facilitate loading in of additional equipment without supervision.
- Ground movement due to very heavy rain over the preceding two weeks causing reduced load bearing capability of the ground; resulting in structural movement as additional loads are applied – e.g. Lighting / PA rigs, video screen.
- Plastic sheeting fixed with one-way ties on all sides, designed without any 'blow-out' panels or quick release connections.
- Loadings exceeded the structural engineer's calculations.
- Unauthorised persons on structure who had' blagged' their way on to the site through lax security.

The risk category in this scenario would be **high** as such a catastrophic collapse could occur if all the hazards were collectively in place in such weather conditions.

A collapsed structure would result in the highest category of severity, i.e. serious injuries being sustained and probably fatalities occurring to members of the audience adjacent to the structure, and the working crew who were on it.

Risk Prevention

The next part of the exercise is to decide what could have been done to prevent such an incident occurring.

Such decisions could comprise:
- Ensuring that an assessment is made of the ground conditions. If the indications are that the ground conditions are soft, problems are likely to ensue. In this situation the imposed loads will have to be spread over a

larger area using bigger spreader plates, or bearers. Any increased costs will have to come out of the contingencies budget.

- Ascertaining what the local weather has been like in recent weeks. Seek out good local knowledge, e.g. a groundsman or site caretaker. Obtain accurate weather forecasts, and base decisions around this information, including contingency plans.
- Ensuring that the temporary structure is designed by a structural engineer who fully understands the guidance on this topic produced by the Institution of Structural Engineers.
- Although temporary structures may not require Building Regulation approval if they are erected for only a limited duration, it is most likely that the Local Authority Licensing Officer will ask a Building Surveyor or Chartered Structural Engineer to look at the plans and calculations for the structures. Site visits are likely during the 'build up' phase; therefore it is essential to advise them of the commencement date in order that they can be satisfied with the arrangements. It would be a folly to build the structure and then have to demolish it, and start again!
- Modern 'quick-fit' scaffolding systems have the advantage over 'tube and coupler' systems in respect of the speed of erection and dismantling, However, a drawback is that diagonal braces that are essential for structural integrity can very easily be removed with a small hammer.

  Therefore the structure must be checked by a competent person at the end of each lifting operation.
- Ensuring that covers or sheeting on the structure are preferably made-to-measure. The front of house mixer will have been designed in advance for either a single show or a tour. As the structures are modular the sheeting can be designed to fit, with 'blow out' panels or quick release panels using 'Velcro' strip fasteners so that if the wind loading becomes critical, they can be removed in order to allow the wind through the structure rather than imposing loads against the sheeting, which could cause it to fail.
- Ensuring that when loading equipment onto upper bays of the scaffold structure that a competent person undertakes the work. Heavy equipment such as 'followspots' are lifted up with a forklift or reach truck. The driver must hold a certificate of competency for that type of truck. If they do not, they must not undertake the operation at all.
- The Production Manager must ensure that all staff competencies are

checked, and copies of individual certificated competencies held on the production file so that they are available upon request.

- Ensuring that there is a suitable security barrier around the tower. These are normally the steel freestanding design.
- The security stewards at the structure should be fully aware of the types of wrist bands or passes in use on the day of the event as they can be changed at short notice. Only those persons in possession of the correct credentials should be permitted access.
- Ensuring that the power supply to the front of house mixer can be isolated, so that rescuers can deal with the casualties rather than having to worry regarding whether or not there is going to be an electrical discharge.
- When scoping the hazards of an event, regard needs to be given to its size, permitted capacity, audience age and profile, and if there has been any history regarding actions of the audience or the artiste. Generally, the promoter will be able to provide this information, which can then be crosschecked with Local Authority Licensing Officers so that an accurate picture can be built up.
- As can be seen, the process is not overly complicated, and action plans/ safe systems of work can be easily developed.

Evaluating Risks - a stage further

- At live gigs there will be other issues that will need to be taken into consideration.
- If the event has a licensed bar, individuals may drink to excess and become a security problem, or sleep it off in potentially dangerous locations.
- Concertgoers may have taken illegal substances en route to the event, or have hidden them on their person so that they can take them whilst they are at the event. This type of behaviour, along with a natural adrenaline 'rush' through excitement is likely to result in the first-aiders being required to give assistance.
- At Heavy Metal/Punk concerts it is commonplace for 'moshing', 'stage diving', and 'body surfing' to take place. This behaviour can lead to extremely dangerous situations occurring. Unfortunately, those individuals participating believe that it is their 'right' to do so regardless of what danger they expose others to, let alone themselves. An emerging way of dealing with this hazard is to have a policy of robustly dealing with those

involved using the security stewards and CCTV systems on site. The concertgoers will be given information through announcements, and/or highly visible warning signs clearly stating that this type of behaviour is unacceptable and those participating in it will be removed from the event. In practical terms the security 'pit team' will decide that if an individual comes over the front of stage barrier once through this type of behaviour they will have their hand stamped with ink. If they come over again and are identified by this mark, then they will be ejected from the event. This again is an example of a hazard being identified, a control measure put in place, and action plan being 'rolled out' so as to minimise the likelihood of serious injuries occurring. Historical data on rock concerts proves that to be the case, but a strong will is required to effect change. Some concertgoers would argue that taking risks is part of adolescence, and 'growing up', or a contravention of their human rights to prevent them from doing so!

Duty of Care

Although it is a legal requirement to undertake a risk assessment, and to document the outcome in certain circumstances, the promoter and the venue management also have a common law 'duty of care' to the clients. If a fatality occurred the H.M. Coroner's inquest would explore whether or not a risk assessment had been undertaken. If it had, and the actions that should have followed were not put in place, then the verdict of the inquest could attach some element of neglect to a party involved, which would be given 'due weight' by an insurance company, and a criminal court. The verdict of an inquest may also influence the outcome of civil proceedings for damages.

Litigation

Unfortunately, the UK seems to be following the 'model' of the USA, in respect of litigation against any party considered to be responsible or 'to blame' for an incident that has had some material effect on the individual, either physically, or mentally so that claims for compensation can be made. There are legal practices known as 'Ambulance Chasers' who offer a no-win, no-fee package to the person seeking damages through the courts, although in practice, after the professional fees are taken away from any award, the individual who commenced the action may not actually find that there is a great deal left for themselves.

After the Event: Reviewing Actions

If it is considered necessary to make any changes to arrangements, then these should be documented so that there is a full audit trail for the enforcement officer to follow.

An existing venue should have its own safety policy statement, and systematic procedures, and protocols that need to be followed. These can be cross-referenced to the event risk assessment. For a one-off event on a 'greenfield' site, new documents would be required – although it may be possible to 'cut and paste' many elements from other documents if they already exist. However, if it were not the case then it would be a matter of scoping all the issues and bringing them together e.g. the event plan, detailed plans, etc,

Contingency plans need to be considered and drafted, in conjunction with the emergency services and local authority. The Police may lead on the issue as the Senior Police Officer at an event when a serious incident occurs takes control and has overall responsibility. The document is normally known as the Major Incident Plan for the event. It is in effect a 'method statement' as to how each agency will respond, and interact when a major incident has been declared.

Ensuring that there is a good 'safety culture' at an event rather than a 'blame culture' is important. When problems occur, which in reality they always do even with good planning, then there should be open and honest dialogue between professionals so that solutions can be worked up, evaluated and amended plans/actions put in place without delay. An example of this would be that if the weather conditions became severe, and there was a risk of pyrotechnic debris falling into the crowd rather than into the designated 'fall out' area, then the pyrotechnics show would be curtailed. To many this would be a common sense approach, and it is, and that is why this concept of risk assessment is not rocket science; it is a matter of making considered judgements in a rational manner.

Live events involving crowds can only be managed to a certain extent in advance. However, by having a professional and highly trained 'pit team' those members of the audience who are at the highest risk due to dynamic crowd movement near the stage can have the incidence of serious injury dramatically reduced by the use of good quality free-standing barrier systems with top edge protection so that the thoracic area of the human body is not put under undue stress. The design incorporates a tread plate so that the weight of the individuals standing on it will not allow it to tip over.

Where there are very hazardous situations, such as the use of real flame, pyrotechnics or liquefied petroleum gas (LPG) effects, then these need to be carefully installed and have 'fail to safe' control measures designed into them if at all possible. All variants of this type of equipment /effect must be thoroughly tested for efficacy of operation. Even with all this pre-planning, malfunctions, or human error can occur. In most instances, the effects can be quickly curtailed by a competent operator, although once ignited, pyrotechnics have to burn for their pre-determined period.

Stewarding

Properly trained stewards at a live event are of paramount importance, and their duties would normally include the stewarding of the following areas:
- Gates/entrance/exit points
- Back stage area
- 'Pit' area possibly including a paramedic team
- Hospitality
- Artistes change / tune up rooms, and the 'Green Room'
- Pyrotechnic / LPG gas effect storage, and display locations
- Emergency Liaison Centre (office)
- Security team, communication base control
- Shuttle Bus embarkation point at the end of the show

Detailed methods of working will be required, and a clear hierarchy of responsibility decided upon involving the tour management, production, security office, artiste's personal protection team, and the Police 'Bronze' commander on site.

Transport Arrangements

Transport arrangements will need to include issues covering car, coach and motorcycle parking arrangements, and their interface with the public, working personnel, and the venue's emergency procedures.

A 'shuttle' bus operation

Lane security, Big Day Out, 2002.

will require detailed planning with the local transport operator, so as to ensure that the disembarkation / embarkation point(s) is properly stewarded or policed. The facility must be properly signed from the venue, and there must be managed loading arrangements so that there is not a crush. Pedestrian barrier 'filter' systems will need to be put in place in order to reduce the number of people being able to board busses at the same time.

If 'satellite' car parks are being utilised then there may be the necessity to have marshals at strategic points along the pedestrian route so that people do not get lost; these points will also need to be lit. An alternative to marshals is to mark the route with temporary 'high vis' highway line paint that washes off during rain fall over a 12 week period.

Camping

Camping arrangements will need careful consideration as the local authority may have model standards regarding the physical layout of the site, and the facilities that must be provided so as to ensure safety, and reasonable standards of hygiene.

Glastonbury camping 2003.

The First Aid Plan

This will contain detailed procedures, and site arrangements so that the voluntary first aid teams on site in ambulances and at temporary medical centres, triage areas, etc, can ensure that all casualties are dealt with in a prompt, effective manner with priority being given to those patients in greatest need following an initial assessment There will be a need for close collaboration with the local Ambulance NHS Trust who have a statutory role in dealing with responses to emergency situations and liaising with the local NHS hospital trust, particularly the Accident and Emergency Department consultant.

A Safety Culture

The live music sector has come a long way in a fairly short time in ensuring safety is properly considered, and the cost implications managed as effectively as possible. The event organiser cannot afford to disregard safety as to do so would be to put their business in jeopardy.

In the UK there has been consolidation in the number of main promoters participating in the sector. These are the key individuals who have been driving safety standards onwards and upwards. They have participated in the drafting of both editions of the Pop Codes, and are anxious to ensure that those going to live events have a 'good experience'.

Innovation and creativity are the key words in the industry, as each artiste wants to be different and even more stunning on stage, but pushing the boundaries back even further must be done safely. The hazards may not be completely removed because artistes want an 'edge' to their performance, but the risk both to themselves, their support teams, and the general public can be minimized to a large extent because a thorough risk assessment of the whole

St John Ambulance unit treating minor injuries at National Bowl, Milton Keynes.

performance has been undertaken. It is not just a matter of complying with the legislation; it is actually simple common sense.

REFERENCES

HSE (1999) **The Event Safety Guide**. A guide to health, safety and welfare at music and similar events.

4 LEGAL ASPECTS OF HEALTH AND SAFETY AT LIVE EVENTS

Ben Challis

Introduction

This chapter is designed to introduce the relevant laws which govern event safety. It examines an event organiser's legal responsibilities and how the law determines who has the legal responsibility and liability for health, safety and welfare at live events. The chapter has been developed in the hope that it will give practical advice rather than detailed legal analysis. It is a disclosure about the law, but not an attempt to provide a text book review of the law itself.

The Sources of Law in the United Kingdom

The main sources of law are *legislation* and *common law*. Legislation is the law contained in statutes. These are Acts of Parliament such as the **Health and Safety At Work Act 1974**. The Common law is case law, dealing with the decisions of the courts in the United Kingdom. There is a third and growing source of law in the United Kingdom, *European Law*, resulting from the United Kingdom's membership of the European Community.

The Concept of Reasonableness

Whilst laws are drafted to be as clear as possible, the provisions of statutes can never cover every scenario. This is why the courts are asked to decide how, when and to whom the law applies. The law does not always (because it cannot always) give a definitive answer to every situation. The law often uses the concept of 'reasonableness': the **Occupiers Liability Act 1957** provides that an occupier must do *all things reasonable in the circumstances* to ensure that a visitor is reasonably safe. **The Health and Safety at Work Act 1974** places a duty on employers to do all things *reasonably practicable* to ensure the health and safety of the employer's workforce. The question often asked is 'what is reasonable?' This is not always easy to answer. It will depend on the circumstances of the case, current industry and social practices, current industry standards, observance of relevant regulations and the role of the parties involved. Activities which might be reasonable in a small club (and therefore discharge an event organiser's obligations) might be wholly unreasonable if utilised for a major arena show. Hopefully some of the examples given in this chapter will illustrate this.

Responsibilities and Liabilities

Anyone involved with the staging and presentation of live events will have some responsibility for their own actions and may possibly have responsibility for others' actions. Responsibilities and liabilities are primarily laid down in statutes such as the **Health and Safety at Work Act 1974** and the **Occupiers Liability Act 1957**. However certain basic principles (such as negligence) are enshrined in common law.

Employers and independent contractors are responsible for ensuring the safety of their own work force and the safety of those affected by their activities. The self-employed also have certain responsibilities. Wherever possible this chapter suggests which party would have primary responsibilities, although other parties might also have some joint responsibility, and therefore joint liability to the public and others.

Criminal and Civil Law

In the United Kingdom (and in most other jurisdictions) there are two separate systems of law – the civil law and the criminal law. The civil law governs relationships and transactions between people. Examples of civil law are contract law, family law, torts and property law. The civil law provides remedies to those who have suffered (normally called the *plaintiff* or the *claimant*) through the activities, omissions or breaches of those who have caused the injury or damage (called the *defendant*). The criminal law is a body of rules implemented by the state which prohibit and prescribes certain forms of behaviour. The state enforces sanctions and penalties when the rules of the criminal code are broken. This chapter is primarily concerned with civil law responsibilities but event organisers should be aware that criminal sanctions can also apply to event safety issues.

The Law of Negligence : Primary Responsibilities in Event Safety

The law of Tort

'Tort' is the French word for a wrong. Torts are civil wrongs. Civil wrongs can be contrasted to criminal acts although one action might result in a potential liability for two claims, one civil and one criminal. If D assaults P, D is liable to be prosecuted for assault and criminal sanctions such as fines, community penalties or imprisonment might be applied by the criminal courts. But P can also sue D in the civil courts for trespass to the person and claim damages for the injury and loss he/she has suffered. Negligence is a tort.

Negligence

The case of *Donoghue -v- Stephenson (1932)* set out the basic principles of negligence in English law. The case concerned food poisoning suffered by Mrs Donoghue whose bottled ginger beer was contaminated with the remains of a decomposed snail. As Mrs Donoghue didn't buy the ginger beer (her friend did) she had no action in contract law. The case decided that:

"In English Law there must be and is a general conception of relations giving rise to a duty of care. The liability for negligence is based upon a general public sentiment of wrongdoing for which the offender pays."

The case created the concept of negligence as an action in civil law allowing injured parties to sue wrongdoers for their loss and damage.

The Duty of Care

The case decided that in certain circumstances individuals and/or organisations will owe a duty to others. This duty of care was defined in the following way:

"You must take reasonable care to avoid acts and omissions which you can reasonably foresee would be likely injure your neighbour."

So an event organisers will owe a duty of care to 'neighbours'. This duty is to avoid acts and omissions which the event organiser could realistically foresee might cause harm to others

Who is the Duty Owed to?

The duty of care does not extend to everyone but it does extend to those who are classified as a 'neighbour'. The judge in *Donoghue -v- Stephenson*, Lord Atkin, defined who that neighbour was:

"Persons who are so closely and directly affected by my act that I ought reasonably to have had them in my contemplation as being affected when I am directing my mind to the act or omission in question."

As a bare minimum, event organisers will owe a duty of care to members of the public attending events and to their employees as clearly these people will be affected by the actions of an event organiser. Event organisers may also owe a duty of care to others, including sub-contractors, self-employed workers and suppliers. But the duty may extend to those on neighbouring land, trespassers and members of the emergency services.

Liability for Negligence

To find a defendant liable for negligence any claimant will have to satisfy the court of the following:

- That the defendant must have owed the claimant a duty of care
- That the defendant through an act or omission *breached that duty*
- This breach *caused* loss to the defendant
- The loss is not too 'remote'.
- That the defendant has no relevant defence

From what has been outlined above, the event organiser owes a duty of care to avoid acts or omissions which they might reasonably foresee could injure their neighbour. For an injured party to bring an action for negligence against a defendant they must show that the defendant breached that duty of care. The test of whether or not the duty of care is breached is an objective test – what level of care and skill was required by the activity carried out and has the defendant measured up to that level? It is important to realise that where there is an increased probability of harm from activities carried out by the defendant then there will be an increased burden on the defendant to discharge those activities safely and competently. There will be negligence when the defendant falls below the standard of care required in the circumstances to protect others from the unreasonable risk of harm. Common professional or industry practices and codes of conduct will often be used as a benchmark against which behaviour is tested – but they are not in themselves the final determinant of negligence or a breach of the duty of care.

In practical terms the event organiser needs to ensure that he/she does all things practical and reasonable to ensure that those working at events and attending events are safe. Implementing and conforming to industry guidelines, industry good practice and conforming to relevant legislation and regulations will go a long way to discharge this duty of care and facilitate a safe event.

If a duty of care is owed to the claimant and there has been a breach of that duty of care the claimant must show that on the balance of probabilities his or her loss was *caused* by the negligence and not by some other intervening act or natural cause.

In the event of a breach of the duty of care a plaintiff must establish that he/she can claim damages. To recover damages in respect of injury caused by the defendant's actions or omissions the claimant must establish that the injury was of a foreseeable consequence of that negligence. The loss must not be too remote. The case of *Overseas Tankship (UK) Ltd -v- Morts Dock & Engineering Co Ltd The Wagon Mound (1961)*, a case usually referred to as *The Wagon Mound*, sets out this general principle. Oil from the defendant's ship was carelessly spilt onto a wharf. This oil then caught fire and damaged the wharf. The court held that whilst it was foreseeable that the spilt oil might damage the wharf it was not foreseeable that a fire might start so the claim for damage caused by the fire was disallowed. The reason behind this rule is to prevent a defendant being unjustly punished for his or her negligent acts or omissions.

Defences to Negligence Actions

There are a number of defences which a defendant may raise against a claim of negligence. One established defence is that the claimant voluntarily assumed a risk of injury – she or he knew of the risk and accepted it in his or her free will. Another is that the plaintiff is partially to blame. Another is that the claimant was involved in some criminal activity at the time.

Businesses often seek to limit liability by way of contract terms or by waivers or notices of exclusion of liability. The **Unfair Contract Terms Act 1977** restricts a defendant's reliance on this defence by preventing exclusion by way of contract terms any limitation of liability for negligently causing death or personal injury and limits other exclusions or limitations of liability by making them subject to a test of reasonableness.

The **Consumer Protection Act 1987** prohibits reliance on any provision which purports to exclude liability in respect of damage caused by defective products.

A court can also reduce an award for damages if the court finds that the claimant has some responsibility for the injury and damage she or he has suffered and the defendant raises the issue of contributory negligence. **The Law Reform (Contributory Negligence) Act 1945** provides that the courts can now reduce awards:

"to the extent that the court thinks just and equitable having regard to the claimant's share in responsibility for the damage."

Finally the issue of *illegality* might be raised by the defendant - where the claimant was involved in some illegal activity which was material to the claim being brought against the defendant. However, illegality will not always defeat the claim in negligence. You will see in the next section of this chapter that the act of trespass will not necessarily defeat a claim by the trespasser against the owner and/or occupier of premises where the trespasser is injured.

Occupiers' Liability

The Occupiers Liability Act 1957

Occupiers' liability refers to the liability that the owner or other occupier of premises has to visitors. The liability will arise if visitors injure themselves in some way due to the state of the premises or because of things being done on the premises. Clearly this Act has great relevance to event organisers and activities at venues and premises.

Liability for defective premises rests upon the *occupier* and the occupier's liability is primarily defined in the **Occupiers' Liabilities Acts 1957**. The occupier of premises owes a common duty of care to all of his/her visitors. The Occupiers Liability Act 1957 Section 2(2) provides that an occupier must

"take such care as in all the circumstances of the case is reasonable to see that the visitor will be reasonably safe using the premises for the purposes for which she/he is invited or permitted by the occupier to be there."

If the occupier is in breach of this duty of care then the injured party will have the right to bring a legal action in the courts against the occupier. To see where responsibilities for safety and liabilities for injury lie it is necessary to ask a number of questions:

- Who is the *occupier*?
- What are *premises*?
- Who is a *visitor*?
- What about uninvited visitors - *trespassers*?
- What is the *duty of care*?

Who is the Occupier?

Responsibility and liability for premises extends to two types of occupier. Firstly the occupier can be the person (which includes a company) actually occupying the premises. Secondly, liability can be imposed on some other person who is responsible for defects or dangers at the premises, such as a landlord. The leading case defining the 'occupier' is the House of Lords decision in *Wheat -v- Lacon (1966)*.

The defendants owned a public house of which R was the manager. R and Mrs R occupied an upstairs flat. This had a separate entrance to the pub. Mrs R ran her own small business taking in paying guests. One of the guests fatally injured themselves on the staircase. The question arose as who was liable as *Occupier* for the guest's injury. The case established that there could be more than one occupier, in this case three defendants, the owners of the pub, R, the manager, and Mrs R. The test of who is the occupier is one of **control**. Does the potential defendant have some degree of control over the premises.

Clearly venue, premises and site owners are occupiers for the purposes of the Occupiers Liability Acts 1957 (and for the 1984 Act). By applying the above case we can also see that an event organiser could simultaneously be an occupier alongside the venue owner – both have a degree of control over the premises. The 'occupier' of a temporary block of seating at a venue for the purposes of the Occupiers Liability Act might include any or ALL of the following: the site owner, the promoter, supervising security and the provider of the seating.

Premises

In simple terms premises obviously include pubs, clubs, theatres, arenas and stadiums. The definition of premises is wide and will include outdoor sites and could include moving vehicles. The definition will also include temporary and moveable items such as scaffolding, staging, portacabins, ramps and lighting rigs.

Lawful Visitors

The 1957 Act provides for a duty of care to lawful visitors. Visitors are those invited to the premises by the occupier or those licensed to enter or use the premises by the occupier. Even so, the definition of a visitor is not always clear and the law sometimes finds that someone who you might otherwise think was a trespasser is actually a visitor. This is particularly the case with children. There might be a danger on premises which is alluring to children. Here the occupier must do all reasonable things to protect that child because the law may find that the child is a visitor not a trespasser and/or that a higher standard or duty of care is owed.

Trespassers

Liability to trespassers is regulated by the **Occupiers Liability Act 1984**.

The Act provides that there is a duty owed by occupiers to uninvited visitors in respect of danger due to the state of the premises where three conditions are met:

1. The occupier must be aware of the dangerous state of the premises or have reasonable grounds to believe that the premises might be dangerous, and
2. The occupier must know or have reasonable grounds to believe that uninvited visitors might enter the premises and might come into the vicinity of the danger, and
3. The risk of injury to the uninvited visitor is one in which all the circumstances the occupier should have taken some precautions to guard the uninvited visitor against.

So if you are a event organiser and you are aware or might have reasonable grounds to believe that your paying customers, band guests or even trespassers might try to gain access to a secure area where they might be at risk (and there are many backstage at a concert) then the event organiser must do everything practicable in the circumstances to protect visitors – invited or uninvited – against that risk or danger. Section 1(4) of the 1984 Act provides:

"Where an occupier of premises owes a duty to another in respect of such risk, the duty is to take such care as is reasonable in all the circumstances of the case to see that he [the uninvited entrant] does not suffer injury on the premises by reason of the danger concerned."

A simple warning or notice will not always discharge the liability of the occupier to a visitor. However section 1(4) of the 1984 Act provides that with a trespasser the duty of care can:

"In an appropriate case, be discharged by taking such steps as are reasonable in all the circumstances of the case to give warning of the danger concerned or to discourage the person from taking the risk."

The Duty of Care

The **Occupiers Liability Act 1957** regulates the duty of the occupier in relation to structural defects and other dangers due to the state of the premises. The Act also extends to dangerous 'things' on the premises and dangerous conditions which might be caused by the acts or omissions of the occupier.

Section 2(2) defines the duty of care owed to a visitor to premises:

"The common duty of care is a duty to take such care as in all the circumstances of the case is reasonable to see that the visitor will be reasonably safe in using the premises for the purposes for which he is invited or permitted by the occupier to be there."

Whether the standard required by the common duty of care has been met is a question of fact. Section 2(3) of the Act provides that

"The circumstances relevant for the present purpose include the degree of care, and the want of care, which would ordinarily be looked for in such a visitor so that (for example) in proper cases:

(a) occupier must be prepared for children to be less careful than adults; and

(b) occupier may expect a person, in the exercise of his calling, will appreciate and guard against any special risks ordinarily incident to it. So far as the occupier leaves him free to do so."

This means that an occupier must take special care with children. Clearly something which might not be a risk to a normal adult might well be a risk to a child. Conversely, an occupier can expect that a professional is carrying out a specialised task to guard against the normal risks inherent to that profession. If there is faulty wiring on premises then this is a risk to visitors. If the occupier asks an electrician to repair faulty wiring then the occupier can expect the electrician to take precautions against the normal risks in electrical repairs.

In summary, the event organiser or responsible party must do all things reasonably practicable to ensure that any visitor is reasonably safe. As with negligence, ignoring or flouting normal industry good-practice, relevant regulations and guidelines, the conditions of a public entertainment licence or the instructions of the emergency services will almost certainly mean that a person injured at an event will have a strong legal claim against the relevant party or parties who are occupiers of the premises.

Warnings

A warning will not always absolve the occupier of liability. Section 2(4)(a) of the Act provides that

"where damage is caused to a visitor by a danger of which he had been warned by the occupier, the warning is not to be treated ... as absolving the occupier from liability, unless in all the circumstaces it was enough to enable the visitor to be reasonably safe"

Where a promoter invites a band onto a stage whilst knowing there are problems with the lighting rig, the promoter will not absolve himself of liability by posting a sign saying 'warning, overhead lights may drop'.

Assumption of Risk

In certain circumstances the visitor can assume the risk – by agreeing to take the risk after being warned – and in these cases no duty of care will be owed to the visitor. But simply knowing of a risk (as opposed to the visitor assuming the risk) does not necessarily discharge the occupiers' liability. The concept of contributory negligence also applies to occupiers' liability and a visitor can be found partially responsible for his/her injury or damage.

The Unfair Contract Terms Act 1977
As we saw with the law of negligence, The Unfair Contract Terms Act 1977 invalidates any contract term or notice or warning which purports to exclude or restrict liability for death or personal injury resulting from any breach of the duty of care under the 1957 Act where the premises are occupied for the business purposes of the occupier.

The Health and Safety at Work Act 1974
Outline
Section 1 of the Act (the HSW Act) sets out the preliminary purposes of the act. These are for
> (I) securing the health, safety and welfare of persons at work and
> (II) protecting others against risks to health and safety in connection with the activities of persons at work

and
> (III) for controlling and managing the use of dangerous substances and
> (IV) for controlling certain emissions into the atmosphere.

The organisation and control of an event may involve a number of different people and different organisations. It is important that event organisers, promoters, production companies, self-employed individuals and contractors are fully aware of their own respective legal responsibilities under the HSW Act.

Contractors and subcontractors have legal responsibilities under the HSW Act of ensuring, as far as is reasonably practicable, the health, safety and welfare of their own employees and of those affected by their work and activities. The self-employed also need to be aware of their responsibilities under the HSW Act to ensure their own heath and safety and the safety of anyone affected by their work.

Duties of Employers to their Employees
Section 2 of the HSW Act sets out the duties of employers to their employees.

Section 2(1) provides that:

It shall be the duty of every employer to ensure, as far as is reasonably practicable the health, safety and welfare at work of all his.employees.

Section 2(2) provides that this duty extends in particular to:

(A)   "the provisions and maintenance of plant and systems of work that are, so far as is reasonably practicable, safe and without risks to health;

(B)   arrangements for ensuring, as far as is reasonably practicable, safety and absence of risks to health in connection with the use, handling, storage and transport of articles and substances;

(C)   the provision of such information, instruction, training and supervision as is necessary to ensure as far as is reasonably practicable, the health and safety at work of his employees;

(D)   as far as is reasonably practicable as regards any place of work under the employers control, the maintenance of it and the provision and maintenance of means and access to and egress from it are safe and without such risks

(E)   the provision and maintenance of a working environment for his employers that is, as far as is reasonably practicable, safe, without risks to health and adequate as regards facilities and arrangements for their welfare at work."

Duties to other people

Section 3 of the HSW Act places a duty on employers (event organisers, contractors, sub-contractors) and the self-employed to safeguard those not in their employment, for example the public.

3.1 "It shall be the duty of every employer to conduct his undertakings in such a way as to ensure, as far as is reasonably practicable, that persons not in his employment who may be affected thereby are not exposed to risks to their health or safety.

3.2 It shall be the duty of every self-employed person to conduct his undertakings in such a way as to ensure, as far as is reasonably practicable, that he and other persons (not being his employees) who may be affected thereby are not thereby exposed to risks to their health or safety."

The duty is to do everything reasonable to protect the public and others who are not employees. This might include informing and warning those affected by their work of matters which might be relevant to the public's health, safety and welfare which might include the movement of plant, emergency and evacuation procedures, noise levels or curfew arrangements.

A recent example of the application of the HSW Act was the prosecution of

Monmouthshire Council for breaches committed during the foot and mouth crisis. The Council employed a slaughterman to cull animals with a rifle. The slaughterman then took 'pot shots' at unrestrained sheep during a kill. The field where he did this was surrounded by public roads and close to a trading estate. The criminal prosecution against the slaughterman failed but the HSW Act prosecution against the Council succeeded and they were fined £100,000 plus costs for these breaches. The breaches were the risks to the health and safety of council workers, the police, the slaughterman himself and members of the public.

Premises

Section 4 of the HSW Act places a duty on those who have any extent of control over non-domestic premises (and access to and exits from premises) to ensure that as far as is reasonably practical the premises are safe and without risks to health. As we saw with occupiers liability, there may be any number of people and organisations who might have some degree of control over premises and it is important that all interested parties do everything reasonably practical to identify responsibilities and take appropriate measures to ensure the premises are safe for those who work there.

Other duties

Section 5.1 of the HSW Act provides that there is a general duty on persons in control of premises to use the best practicable means to prevent the escape of noxious or offensive substances into the atmosphere. Section 6.1 provides that persons who design, manufacture, import or supply any article (or substance) to be used at work must ensure that such articles or substances are tested and safe for work and that relevant instructions and information are available about such articles or substances.

General duties of employees at work

Section 7 places a duty on employees. This is a duty while at work to
(A)   "Ensure the health and safety of those who may be affected by his acts or omissions at work; and
(B)   as regards any duty or requirement imposed on his employer .... [to] take reasonable care for the health and safety of himself and others and to co-operate with him so far as is necessary to enable that duty or requirement to be performed or complied with."

The Management of Health and Safety at Work Regulations 1992

These Regulations are primarily concerned with the assessment of risk in the workplace and the identification of precautions, which might be necessary to protect both workers and members of the public. This applies to employers and the self-employed. Were there are five or more employees in a business or organisation the assessment must be recorded and detail what measures have been taken to address concerns. The regulations also provide that employers must have systems in place to deal with emergencies and serious danger. A good example of this would be evacuation procedures and the duty is placed on the employer to have proper procedures and trained staff to deal with an emergency evacuation.

The Reporting of Injuries, Diseases and Dangerous Occurrences Regulations 1995 (RIDDOR)

RIDDOR provides that certain work related accidents and other dangerous occurrences must be reported to the relevant enforcing authority for health and safety matters. In particular a report must be made if an employee is killed or suffers serious injury and where a member of the public is killed or is taken to hospital. Other serious occurrences such as the collapse of scaffolding or failure of lifting equipment must be reported.

Employers Liability

A common law action

In the previous section we have seen that a duty of care is owed by employers to employees under the HSW Act. Alongside this statutory duty (and other statutory provisions including provisions for levels of compensation for industrial accidents and for compulsory employers' insurance) the common law provides an effective remedy in law for injured employees because of the high level of damages which can be awarded.

In simple terms employers owe their employees a duty of care at common law. This was defined in the case of *Wilsons and Clyde Coal Co Ltd -v- English (1938):*

> "A duty which rests on the employer and which is personal to the employer, to take reasonable care for the safety of his workmen, whether the employer be an individual, firm, or a company, and whether or not the employer takes any share in the conduct of operations."

This duty is personal and is a non-delegable duty and The duty extends to three main areas of responsibility
- The provision of competent staff
- The provision of adequate premises and plant
- The provision of a proper and safe system of working

A breach of this duty by the employer leaves the employee with the right of an action against the employer for damages.

Employer's Liability for the Acts and Omissions of Employees

In certain circumstances an employer will be *vicariously* liable for the acts and omissions of those working for him/her. This means that the employer will be liable in place of the employee. However it is important to distinguish the liability of an employer from the position where the act or omission is that of an *independent contractor*. In general terms an employer will be liable for the acts or omissions of an employee but not for the acts or omissions of an independent contractor. Every act done by an employee in the course of their employment is treated as being an act done on the orders of the employer and therefore the employer will be responsible for those actions. Conversely an employer is not responsible for the actions of his independent contractors.

At common law the test is whether or not a contract of *service* (an employer/employee or master/servant relationship) exists or whether a contract for the *provision of services* exists (an independent contractor). The test is primarily one of control. What level of control did the employer have over the actions of the person who committed the tort? A person is an employee where the employer retains control over the actual performance of the work.

The classification of who is an employee and who is an independent contractor is not always easy. The standard statement on employees and the self-employed people for the **Health & Safety at Work Act 1974** is:

> "If people working under the control and direction of others are treated as self-employed for tax and national insurance purposes they may nevertheless be treated as employees for health and safety purposes. It may therefore be necessary to take appropriate action to protect them. If any doubt exists about who is responsible for the health and safety of a worker this could be clarified and included in the terms of a contract. However, remember a legal duty under section 3 of the HSW Act cannot be passed on by means of a contract and there will still be duties towards others under section 3 of the HSW Act. If such

workers are employed on the basis that they are responsible for their own health and safety, legal advice should be sought before doing so."
(*The Event Safety Guide* p186)

Even where the person who has committed the tort has been identified as an independent contractor, the employer may still be liable for the independent contractor's actions where:

- the employer has authorised the independent contractor to commit the tort
- where the employer is jointly negligent
- where a duty is non-delegable

The Extent of Employer's Liability

Once the employer-employee responsibility is established the courts will look to see if the employee has committed the tort in *the course of his employment*.

If the act was committed in the course of employment the employer will be vicariously liable for the employee. The definition of those employee acts are included within the 'course of employment' is wide. It will include many unauthorised acts and prohibited acts unless these are clearly unrelated to the employee's work.

There would be a presumption that the employer of a security guard who deliberately assaulted a member of the public attending a event would be responsible for the security guard's actions unless it was clear that the guard's actions were wholly unrelated to his activities as a security guard – for example if the guard knew the person assaulted and the act was a personal vendetta against that person.

In **Mattis -v- Pollock (t/a) Flamingos Nightclub** (The Times Law Report 16 July 2003) the Court of Appeal held that a club doorman who stabbed a person in the vicinity of the club in revenge for an earlier violent attack on him in the club was acting in the course of his employment and so the club owner was vicariously liable for the doorman's actions.

The doorman was involved in a fight inside the club. The knifing happened after the doorman had gone home to get a knife and then attacked the victim some 100 metres away from the club. The victim was seriously injured. The doorman was convicted in a criminal court for grievous bodily harm (GBH) and sentenced to 8 years in prison. This civil action found that the club owner was liable for the actions of the doorman and so the victim could claim damages against the club. The doorman was not registered and was expected to maintain order and discipline and to perform his duties in an aggressive and intimidating manner. This meant that the doorman was violent both on the premises and off them and thus the stabbing was directly linked to earlier activities inside the club when the doorman was on duty. Even though the doorman's actions were motivated by revenge the club owner's were liable in law for his actions.

This case follows on from a recent case where the police were held liable for an assault by an off-duty policeman on a third party even though at the time of the assault the police officer had borrowed a police van to move his girlfriend's house in when he wasn't working.

Earlier cases such as **Daniels -v- Whetstone Entertainments (1962)** established that employers had a liability for door staff's actions whilst they were in the course of their employment.

Product Liability
The Common Law Duty of Care
The case of *Donoghue -v- Stephenson* (the 'snail in the ginger beer bottle') sets out a basic action for a consumer to sue the manufacturer of a defective product. Mrs Donoghue brought the action in negligence against the manufacturer as she had no right of action in contract law as it was her friend who had purchased the drinks. The case decided that manufacturers owe a common law duty of care to consumers and consumers have a right of action against manufacturers in negligence for defective products. However, the common law has now been substantially revised by statutory provisions.

The Consumer Protection Act 1987
This Act implements the 1985 European Community Directive on product liability providing a new system of remedies for consumers against manufacturers. The Act also provides that the supplier of defective goods may also be liable in certain circumstances as will the retailer of branded products even if the retailer did not manufacture those goods. The definition of 'goods' is of fairly wide definition by the Act but includes, in effect, any manufactured goods **(by** any process) and electricity. **The Consumer Protection Act 1987** is often used alongside the **Sale of Goods Act 1979** which provides remedies for consumers against retailers for goods sold which are not of fit and proper quality. The liability under the Consumer Protection Act is for defective products. The test of defectiveness is whether or not the product is as safe as people would be generally entitled to expect. Anyone who suffers injury (or property damage in certain circumstances) caused by a defective product can recover their loss under the provisions of the Act.

Product Liability and Event Safety
It may seem at first look that product liability has little relevance to the organisation of safe events. However the law is relevant in certain circumstances where members of the public are inured or suffer loss from defective products. This could include food poisoning from contaminated beef burgers or injury caused by defective pyrotechnics.

Nuisance and the Use of Land
Private Nuisance
The basic definition of the tort of private nuisance is the *unreasonable*

interference with the use or enjoyment of land. At common law a landowner has a freedom to use and enjoy his or her land as she or he pleases. Obviously this right has been limited by statutory provisions (planning requirements, restrictions on the use of land) but private nuisance provides an action when the enjoyment or use of land is unreasonably interfered with.

A nuisance may be suffered when one property suffers from activities on another's land or where that activity spreads onto their own land. Water, fire, smoke, noise, fumes, toxic gases and heat could all be a nuisance. Many examples of private nuisance are now controlled by statutory provisions. For example the **Environment Act 1990** gives local authorities the power to deal with noise nuisance.

At common law the remedy of an injunction to prohibit future repeats of the nuisance lies alongside a remedy for damages to compensate the injured party for the nuisance itself.

Public Nuisance

Public nuisance is a nuisance which interferes with the rights of public at large. It is a crime and covers acts ranging from obstructing the highway to selling impure food. A public nuisance may also be a private nuisance directly affecting both the public and private land users. As with private nuisance many acts which constitute public nuisance are now regulated by statute. However at common law the action will lie. The classic definition of public nuisance is found in *A-G -v- PYA Quarries Ltd (1957):*

> "A public nuisance is a nuisance which is so widespread in its range or so indiscriminate in its effects that it would not be reasonable to expect one person to take proceedings on his own responsibility to put a stop to it, but that it should be taken on the responsibility of the community at large."

Event organisers should be aware that acts such as causing crowds or vehicles to block the highway and conducting operations off the highway which menace the safety of those on it have both been held to be nuisances.

Rylands –v- Fletcher

The case of *Rylands -v- Fletcher (1866)* adds a further right of action against a person who being a 'non natural user of land' allows anything to accumulate on that land which is likely to do harm if that thing escapes. What this means is that if D brings onto and keeps anything on land which is not naturally there, and this escapes, then D will be liable for the damage caused as a result of that thing escaping even if he did not cause the escape.

The facts of *Rylands -v- Fletcher* are that the defendant had a reservoir built on his land. Through the negligence of an independent contractor who failed to block up underground shafts, water flooded the plaintiff's mine on neighbouring land when the reservoir was filled with water. The escape of water stored on the defendant's land which wasn't normally there on the land caused damage to the plaintiff and for this the defendant was liable.

Other 'things' which have fallen within this rule when 'brought on to land' include explosives, sewage, water and petrol and event organisers could face possible actions where they fall under the provisions of the rule in *Rylands -v- Fletcher.*

The Criminal Justice and Public Order Act 1994 (CJPOA)

The CJPOA was passed in response to concerns about the activities of New Age Travellers, aggravated trespasses by groups such as animal rights activists and environmental protesters and the growing numbers of illegal raves on farmland, public spaces and in disused property. The CJPOA has no direct relevance to legal and licensed entertainment events but may have some impact on event organisers who suffer unlicensed events peripheral to their own licensed events.

The CJPOA substantially increased the powers of police and local authorities to move on unauthorised groups of travellers and the police are able to stop illegal raves before they start.

Section 63 of the CJPOA gives the police powers to
- direct people to leave land if two or more are preparing for a gathering or if ten or more are waiting to attend a gathering. It is a criminal offence not to comply.
- seize vehicles and sound equipment in the possession of those who refuse to leave.
- stop people within a five mile radius if they believe they will attempt to attend a rave and direct those people not to proceed. It is a criminal offence not to comply.

The Act also covers trespass: The CJPOA made section 39 of the Public Order Act 1986 more effective by giving the police powers to direct trespassers illegally residing on land to leave the site. Section 61 of the CJPOA
- extended the 1984 Act to cover all trespassers on land (even if previously invited)
- extended the Public Order Act to minor highways

- reduced the number of vehicles that need to be involved to six
- provided the police with powers to remove vehicles (section 62)

Section 77 of the CJPOA gave similar powers to local authorities. Section 78 provides that removal orders (from the Magistrates Court) can be obtained to enforce directions.

Insurance

The Insurance Policy

The first part of this chapter sets out the basic responsibilities and liabilities which effect event organisers. Any prudent event organiser will take out and maintain a comprehensive insurance policy covering, at least, the event organisers' liabilities as an employer, and to the public and for products. These are known as employer's liability, public liability and products liability insurance. The **Employer's Liability (Compulsory Insurance) Act 1969** requires that employers insure against liability for bodily injury or disease sustained by employees or apprentices in the course of their employment.

The indemnity

An insurer will indemnify the insured against a set of defined 'occurrences' to a pre-agreed financial limit. For small companies a typical policy would provide £10,000,000 of cover against employer's liabilities and £1,000,000 against public and product liability.

Organisers of large events will often take out a specific public liability insurance policy, perhaps to an indemnity limit of £20,000,000 at major stadia to provide indemnity in the event of multiple claims from persons injured or killed at an event. The basic cover for public liability is an indemnity against any claim for bodily injury or illness or disease caused to any person (except an employee) and against loss and damage to physical property of third parties. A typical policy will also cover a loss arising from trespass, nuisance or interference with any easement of air, light, water or way.

A policy may also indemnify the insured against legal costs and expenses arising from any prosecution under the **Health and Safety at Work Act 1974** or the **Consumer Protection Act 1987**. However, a typical policy would not cover any fines or other penalties imposed.

Contractual Liability

Many contracts between event organisers and third parties will have detailed provisions governing the allocation of liability in certain circumstances and the assumption or waiver of liability. In particular, venue hire agreements often have specific provisions governing risk and insurance. It is not necessarily the case that an insurance policy will cover those risks adopted by an event organiser under the terms of an agreement with a third party.

In particular a typical policy may not indemnify the policy holder against liability adopted by an agreement which would not have attached to the policy holder in the absence of such an agreement. It is therefore vitally important to fully inform insurers of all relevant risks and the terms of relevant third party agreements.

Licensing

Legislation

Licensing is regulated by a number of statutes in the United Kingdom, applying variously to London, the rest of England and Wales and Scotland. More recent legislation such as the **Public Entertainment Licence (Misuse of Drugs Act) 1997** and the **Fire Safety and Safety of Places of Sport Act 1987** apply to the whole of the United Kingdom. The Event Safety Guide (HMSO 1999) is a very useful reference for this area of law.

Enforcement

The enforcement of licensing is the responsibility of the relevant local authority (as detailed below). The local authority has a statutory duty to consult with the police and fire services.

The enforcement of health and safety legislation in the leisure and entertainment industries is the responsibility of the relevant local authority except where the local authority is organising the event when responsibility passes to the Health & Safety Executive.

England and Wales

The Local Government (Miscellaneous Provisions) Act 1982 (Schedule 1) and the **London Government Act 1963** (Schedule 12) provide that responsibility for controlling places of public entertainment (music, dancing, etc) rests with the district council or in London with the relevant London Borough. Where there is no district council the responsibility rests with the county council. In Wales responsibility rests with the county council or a county borough council. It would normally be an offence to organise public entertainment without a licence or to be in breach of any terms or conditions of a licence granted.

The licensing of public entertainment applies to:

- all indoor events (except bar events with two or less performers)
- outdoor events in Greater London
- outdoor events for the public on private land outside of Greater London
  If the local authority has adopted the 1982 Act.

For these events a local authority will have a very wide discretion with the terms and conditions of the licence. If the event does not fall under the above headings then the local authority may only (Schedule 1 4(4)) impose certain terms and conditions for particular purposes:

- secure the safety of performers and others present
- ensure there is adequate access for emergency vehicles and provide toilets and sanitation.
- prevent unreasonable noise and disturbance to the neighbourhood

But clearly terms and conditions imposed for these purposes and the terms and conditions imposed under the wider discretionary powers should and can be used by a local authority to ensure that the event is safe for all, has adequate hygiene facilities, proper access and causes the minimum disruption possible.

In addition, a local authority will have the power to require the licensing of private events where such are promoted for private gain under the provisions of the **Private Places of Entertainment (Licensing) Act 1967.**

Scotland

The **Civic Government (Scotland) Act 1982** provides that the local government area council may licence public entertainment in its area provided it has decided to do this. However this only applies when an admission charge is paid. It is an offence to promote an event without a licence. When granting a licence the council can impose terms and conditions regulating matters such as start and finish time, audience capacity and noise levels.

The **Licensing (Scotland) Act 1976** provides that entertainment events may take place on premises where licensed under the Act. Premises include clubs, cinemas, theatres and dance halls and the licence will permit the sale of alcohol where an entertainment event is taking place.

Misuse of Drugs

The **Public Entertainment Licence (Drugs Misuse) Act 1997** was enacted to allow local authorities to revoke licences (or not to renew licences) where there was as serious problem with the supply of controlled drugs on premises. The concern will be raised by the police and the local authority may deal with the problem by imposing terms and conditions on a licence.

Summary

Event organisers and those involved with health, safety and welfare at events need to be clearly aware of their responsibilities in law. These responsibilities and liabilities arise from:

- the law of *negligence.*
- duties owed to employees and the public under the **Health and Safety at Work Act 1974** and to employees and for their employee's actions at common law.
- responsibilities and the duty of care owed to both lawful visitors and trespassers under the **Occupiers Liability Act of 1957 and 1984**
- the law of *nuisance* and statutory provisions governing nuisances
- product liability under the Consumer Protection Act 1987
- relevant event licensing provisions.

REFERENCES

Mullis, A & Oliphant, K (1997) **Torts** Macmillan Press, London

Brazier, M (1993) **Street on Torts** Butterworth Heinnemann London

Health & Safety Executive (1999) **The Event Safety Guide** HMSO

Trespass and Protest: Policing under the Criminal Justice and Public Order Act 1994 Home Office Research Study 190 1998.

Cases
A-G -v- PYA Quarries Ltd (1957) 2QB 169

Donoghue -v- Stephenson (1932) AC 562

Mattis -v- Pollock (T/a Flamingos Nightclub) (2003) Times Law Reports

Overseas Tankship (UK) Limited -v- Morts Dock & Engineering Co The Wagon Mound (1961) AC 388

Rylands -v- Fletcher (1868) LR 3 HL 330

Wheat -v- Lacon (1966) AC 552

Wilsons and Clyde Coal Co Ltd -v- English (1938) AC 57

Ben Challis

Ben Challis read law at Kings College London and the City University and became a barrister in 1985. He has a wide experience in the entertainment and music industries and has, since 1993, worked with the Glastonbury Festival as the Festival's Executive Producer for television. Ben's other clients have included BT, Pioneer and the Prince's Trust. He also sits as a magistrate in Hertfordshire and lectures in law at Buckinghamshire Chilterns University College. He edits the Law Updates page for www.musicjournal.org.

HEALTH AND SAFETY ASPECTS IN THE LIVE MUSIC INDUSTRY

PART 2
THE APPLICATION:
THE APPLICATION OF THEORY IN PRACTISE

5 MANAGING THE SITE FOR AN EVENT
Richard Selley

Introduction

One area which needs to be considered in any enquiry into Health and Safety at events, is the suitability and upkeep of sites for large outdoor events. The sites for these large outdoor events vary enormously from fields such as those used for the Glastonbury Festival, parks or stately homes such as Knebworth or Woburn Abbey, football stadiums such as Wembley and purpose built venues such as the National Bowl, Milton Keynes.

The Role of the Site Manager

At any venue, whatever its outdoor location, the site manager must be fully conversant with all the elements which comprise the totality of the site. The site manager must aim to present the area in the best possible condition for the activity in prospect. This must include safe and environmentally friendly processes and practices. The site manager can also contribute to the general atmosphere of the promotion by the encouragement of a friendly, helpful and supportive attitude to all those involved in the event. The site manager must also recognise that many of his responsibilities, such as the security and safety of the site, may be delegated to others for the duration of the event. It is therefore crucial that the site manager starts dialogue at a very early stage of the event planning and does not employ an arms length policy with those staging the event.

Landscape maintenance must be completed prior to the arrival of the event organisers. Grass and hedges must be cut and the detritus cleared away and there should be no litter of any description on the site. All services must be fully maintained and function effectively and efficiently and the security of the site must be in order and thus the site manager can hand over responsibility at a moment's notice. It is common courtesy for the site manager to be provided with a detailed schedule of operations to be carried out for the duration of the event, comprising times of arrival of the various contractors, set up and show day details, as well as breakdown, loadout, collections of refuse, etc, and a time for inspection of the site and final departure. A layout plan should accompany this schedule.

In many cases, where one-off events are not the only activities taking place during the programmed event time, it is often possible for the site manager to maintain a programme of on-site activities which do not clash with the one-off event. For example, at the National Bowl, Milton Keynes, evening cycle racing and daytime motorcycle training take place around the perimeter roads. As this does not affect the get-in of a show, these activities continue during the event set up.

There is a shared responsibility between the venue management and the promoter to ensure that the site is a safe working environment for personnel and this is reiterated through on-site practices where all personnel also have a safety responsibility, not only to themselves but also to others. This safety responsibility is crucial to the smooth operation of an event and many statutory and non-statutory elements must be abided by to ensure the smooth running of an event. Statutory notices must be displayed and protective clothing, such as hard hats, must be available and used where overhead work and dangerous practices are taking place. Where heavy gear is being moved, unloaded or constructed and the described action includes a mechanical linking device, LOLER regulations apply. It is also important that ear protection, safety foortwear, gloves and goggles, as well as protective clothing, are available for the use of those working on site when necessary.

Certification of fork life drivers, and whether climbers and riggers are competent to work at height must also be checked and recorded.

The National Bowl, Milton Keynes: A Case Study

Crowd gathering, front of stage, Enimem 2003.

As site manager of the National Bowl at Milton Keynes, this venue will be used as a case study for this chapter. The National Bowl as a venue has been used for live events since the early 1980s. It is not only used for live music events, but for sports events, children's' events, garden shows and community activities. The venue has hosted a plethora of large concerts, including Police, Queen, Metallica, Guns and Roses, Robbie Williams, Michael Jackson, Erasure and Eminem. The venue also features community events, including corporate entertainment bookings, cycle racing in the summer and year-round motorcycle training, including the CBT Certification. The backstage area and ground under the stage itself has recently been upgraded from grass to hard standing and this area must be clear and sterile before an event takes place; all services must be maintained and manholes checked and unlocked and checked. Before any event takes place, the safety system in the roof of the stage structure should be checked and passed as serviceable and the green side screens fitted.

When the National Bowl is hired out as a venue, all services and the stage framework are included. However, all other services, such as toilets and back-up generators have to be brought in.

Site Preparation

Prior to a concert, a number of jobs have to be carried out to ensure a safe and pleasant experience for both the internal and external customers. These jobs include jetting the foul water system to ensure that it is clean and free flowing; this is usually carried out once per season. The water system is complex, with 43 outlet points, which often play host to the local rabbit population who regard the pipes as custom built burrows

Forklift taking barrier to front of stage, Enimem 2003.

to the main pipes linking to the trunk foul sewer. At one concert, a blockage backed up to a main manhole cover on the perimeter road which blew off with disastrous (brown coloured) results. Jetting the foul water system is not only important to ensure clean free-flowing water, but also to ensure that bacteria, animal excrement and the possibility of dead or dying animals passing on diseases are alleviated.

Toilets

Recycling toilet units are used in the arena where there are no outlets. These are especially useful on the disabled platform and at the First Aid points. However, these need to be carefully stewarded as lazy and selfish people ignore the notices on the doors and use the toilets that are meant for others, often causing distress and danger. The provision of polyjohns outside the gates for the queuing fans to use prior to entry are vital, not only to enable fans who sometimes queue for over 24 hours, to use the toilets, but also to alleviate queue pressure and agitated fans. If not enough polyjohns are provided, this will cause anger and possible danger within the queue. Toilets are an important element of the entertainment licence. The number of units for the size of audience and the ratio of male units to female will be specified in the licence document and this must be adhered to in order to ensure that the show goes ahead. Plumbing needs to be carried out carefully and efficiently with all pipework situated to the rear of the units, well away from the feet of the members of the audience as it constitutes a trip hazard, and also away from those who may have mischievous intent which could cause serious consequences at the concert.

Steps and handrails to the toilet units must be checked for stability and effectiveness as a loose handrail or a missing step could cause an incident which could end in a concertgoer suing a promoter for negligence.

Water pressure is important, as people tend to use the toilets en masse during the intervals between artistes on stage. There is a pattern to the way in which toilets are used and thus the timing of the artistes at the event will determine the water pressure. At these peak times, it is possible that every cistern is filling up at the same time and during these periods problems can occur. This issue is addressed at the National Bowl by the use of fire hydrants as supply to the toilet facilities. However, this is only on the understanding that a plumber will always be available to disconnect the hydrant supply if the fire service has to access it out of need or emergency. It is clear that if there is a fire, the toilets must wait.

Another key aspect of toilets that are being used throughout an event or festival is the lighting which is necessary to avert danger in the darkened cubicles. This lighting for toilet facilities is normally powered by generators which must be carefully fenced off from the audience to avert tampering

Toilets, Glastonbury 2002.

and danger. A service team is constantly working to replace toilet rolls, clean up the toilets, and to check the efficiency of the units. As in all health and safety elements, this service team must be monitored to ensure that they are providing a quality service and keeping up with demand. The site plumber, mentioned above, will also be available on site throughout the event in case of any water problems, including leaks and malfunctions. Clarity of signage is imperative and should inform members of the audience of the availability of alternative toilets in nearby areas. This is essential as it prevents large queues building up at the most obvious toilets nearest to the exit. Stewards and security staff should also be briefed to give advice on the nearest toilets and alternative ones.

The Perimeter Road
On the perimeter road, a public information tent is sited, staffed by local people. The tent houses a chemist outlet for sunscreen and other essentials. This information tent is essential as many concertgoers find themselves without a number of elements which they need to survive the event. These can be purchased or information can be given on where to purchase these essentials. Within the tent, location maps are prominently displayed and a meeting point is clearly marked for those who become separated. Within the site a number of first aid points are strategically placed, both on the perimeter road and on the arena itself, and all have direct contact with the main St John Ambulance marquee where the doctors are based. There has traditionally been a pay phone facility, but with the advent of the mobile phone, this service may no longer be necessary, although, with 65,000 people at an event, all trying to phone out to friends at the same time, it is often difficult to get a signal and therefore a landline is important.

The remainder of the perimeter road, with the exception of the emergency access route, is taken up with food units. These units are spaced 5 meters apart, due to fire regulations, and a similar distance is marked off and vacant next to the steps and exits to facilitate emergency access and egress if necessary.

Percussion taps for drinking water are

Washing facilities, Glastonbury 2002.

available both on the perimeter road and along the front of the stage area. The number available is governed by the size of the audience. Tents occupied by the Samaritans and welfare groups often appear and are welcome owing to the number of physical and psychological problems which can occur at concerts.

Before a concert takes place, an arena check will be made to ensure that no debris has been dropped which could be used as missiles. A search is also made for holes or ruts that have been left which could cause tripping. If such elements are found, they are filled with sharp sand, as grass will grow into such a medium very easily so ensure a supply is available on site. If the area in front of the stage looks unsightly, due to bad weather conditions and vehicle movements causing rutting, which often fills up with water and then makes it impossible for people to sit down in the arena, the area is often filled with sand to level the ground, especially if large areas of the arena have turned to mud. It has been known for the whole area from the front of the stage to the mixer tower to be covered with Tildernet fabric as a cosmetic operation to give a flat surface for the use of those attending the concert. All structures, including the main sound and lighting tower and the delay towers must be barriered and stewarded and any scaffolding, which may be a danger to the audience, must be padded to minimise its hazard potential. By barriering and stewarding these points, a double health and safety measure has been put into operation as the audience can clearly see that the area inside the barrier is out of bounds and is stewarded to stop those from entering who wish to cause either nuisance or to get a better view.

Opening the Gates

Prior to the opening of the gates, a last site meeting of all management personnel takes place. This is usually in front of the stage and if everyone is satisfied with the state of the site, the gates are opened. The rule in opening the gates is that it is better to open early rather than late, as the audience will become agitated. The security team is

Gate lanes ready to open, Enimem 2003.

very aware that the opening of the gates is a potentially dangerous moment as the hyped up fans race into the arena for the best possible positions at the barrier. Crowd management strategies are used to slow the crowd down as far as possible. Crowd monitoring by CCTV is transmitted to the emergency liaison office and also to the police control rooms, where images from the roads, the car parks and the arena are constantly viewed so that response teams can be activated if and when problems occur. Bottles and cans will have been taken from audience members as they enter the gates. Experience has shown that these items can be used as missiles, either thrown towards the stage or across the audience. However the activity of taking these bottles and cans from people at the gates is quite futile in reality as plastic bottles or beer, wines and spirits can be bought inside the arena and these can be used as missiles.

From the moment the fans enter the venue, the question of health and safety becomes much more complex. There are a group of people who are working on the event with the added problem of another large group of people who are intent on enjoying themselves often testing arrangements to the limit.

A safety plan, drawn up by the emergency services and all parties involved in an event, gives guidelines for dealing with the many and varied scenarios which may occur. For a capacity audience of 65,000 in the National Bowl, the security team would be in excess of 150 personnel with police presence also available if needed. On the first day of the Eminem concert, at the National Bowl in June 2003, 310 security personnel were on duty. The number was then increased on subsequent days as several unsavoury incidents took place during the three-day event.

The organisers plus the police, fire, ambulance and environmental health service staff the backstage emergency liaison office, and it is from this office that the whole event is monitored and key decisions on strategy are made. However, on a micro scale, the security team have the power to act quickly and efficiently to prevent small problems escalating. The front of stage security team are well practiced and on a hot day with a good show they are kept very busy dealing with the most tightly packed section of the audience. Fainting, asthma attacks, heat stroke, crowd surfing and lack of water are all reasons that concert goers come over the barrier for onward transmission to the first aid team, feeding fans back into the audience or ejection from the venue, dependent on the reason for them ending up over the barrier. From the First Aid tent the aim is to return the audience members to the main audience if possible after treatment and rest. In some cases fans need to be transported by ambulance to the doctors at the St John main base and, on rare occasions, to Milton Keynes Hospital.

The Role of the Site Manager During the Show

During a concert, the role of the site manager is to move around the site finding and addressing problems and responding to reports and requests. Typically these centre on water leaks, litter, holes in the fence and bushes, extra crowd control barriers being needed, stones being present on the arena floor, and a host of smaller items. Owing to the nature of the site manager's role, contingency planning is key. Stock equipment has to be assembled, tested, and placed ready for actions. Such items include water sprayers for small camp fires which although not permitted are abundant across the arena, and are quickly doused by security personnel. Loud hailers are another piece of equipment which security use for crowd control at access and egress points and a myriad of special signs are created which may be needed at short notice.

Monitoring of the car park situation is also an important part of the site manager's role. At the National Bowl this is particularly important, as there are more remote car parking sites at a distance from the arena. This job has been carried out by helicopter but is usually carried out on foot or bicycle to ensure that the car parking is organised correctly and that vehicles are safe.

The shuttle bus operation from Milton Keynes Station to the venue drops the concertgoers 300 metres from the arena. Thus, arrangements at the boarding and dismounting areas need to be in place at specific times before and after the event to ensure efficient and effective access and egress to and from the Station. Liaison with the police on matters of timing is therefore most important.

A site manager with local experience is invaluable to the promoter and venue owner, as he/she acts as the eyes and ears of those in charge of the event whose ultimate responsibility is to ensure that an event is safe and successful. Without a site manager to maintain the site, a great deal of time and money would be spent on readying a site prior to the show. Site managers must be practical, able to act on their own initiative and capable and willing to turn their hand to anything necessary to solve problems and facilitate a conducive environment for contractors and promoters to work within. The role of the local site manager is not only to deal with problems that arise, but also to bring in local expertise such as welders or specialist plant when needed.

The End of the Show: Egress

The end of a concert is another high-risk period, not only because this is the time when people will be leaving the venue, but also because a popular way of signing off an event is with pyrotechnics. Pyrotechnics and their management is a highly specialised operation where wind direction and fall out areas are planned well in advance. However, there have been occasional incidents where people have broken bones after being hit by falling debris from fireworks. At the Big Day Out at Milton Keynes Bowl in 2002, the pyrotechnic base was a forklift truck, which was an incredibly safe way of keeping the fireworks away from any prying hands. At most concerts there are instructions from the stage about how to leave the arena, but the security team execute a well-practiced routine to avoid problems. The crowd is usually happy and willing to co-operate as they have had a good time at the event.

Two major problems, however, can occur outside the venue. These are the possibility of failing lighting and also poor signage, which can cause havoc for both pedestrians and motorists. An incredible amount of rubbish on the ground is revealed by the exiting crowd, which may cause a hazard if set alight by groups who wish to stay longer than the mass audience. Therefore, this will need urgent action. With multiple exits at Milton Keynes Bowl there is a possibility of friends who travelled to an event together, or met up there, becoming separated. This is often caused because people arrive in daylight and leave in darkness. There are mobile lighting columns in the car parks but despite this and the issue of car park tickets with information on them, people still manage to either get disorientated or lost. The major problem with this is that many people do not ask for assistance and try to find their way back into the event or to another gate and become upset, agitated and often panic-stricken. As the stewards are not local, although they are given a briefing and site map in advance of the show, they often struggle to be of any help at all because they have a lack of local knowledge. At the end of the event there are always a number of "waifs and strays" that have to be looked after by local staff or those in welfare who eventually work out where their vehicle or partner is.

The exit of the performers causes another problem for security, as often a large number of fans cluster around the backstage gates in hopes of a glimpse of their idols. The main problem with such clustering is that the artistes and their entourage, as well as pantechnicons and crew buses, will all exit at the same point. It is a well-known fact that vehicles and people do not mix and if security is not tight, people can stray in front of oncoming vehicles, causing injury or even death. Therefore, a contingency plan must always be prepared for such eventualities.

After the Show: Restoring the Environment

As soon as the show finishes, the de-rig commences. Everyone in the team knows exactly what his or her job is and the turn around can be extremely quick, particularly if the next night's gig is at the other end of the country or abroad. On leapfrog tours, where at any one time two productions are on the road, the quick de-rig is not as crucial.

Rubbish is generated on a massive scale at Milton Keynes Bowl but the contractors who clear the site are extremely efficient and use locally recruited labour. They are well equipped, well supervised and enjoy the work in hand, and it is often the case that cash and other valuable items are recovered as they clear up. The cleaners and litter pickers work from the outer limits of the territory inwards. In this way it means that roads, verges, local shops and parks are cleaned first so that the neighbouring housing estates and industry are kept happy and thus complain little and are unlikely to oppose the licence at the bowl on future occasions. It is clear that the team working at the Bowl need the support and goodwill from local parish and neighbourhood councils to work effectively and efficiently.

Within the venue each contractor has to clear their own equipment, but inevitably bits and pieces of timber, scaffolding, pallets, containers, binding and other assorted items are left behind even by the cleaning teams. People have even been known to leave expensive cars in the car parks, probably with good reason, to collect them next day, not realising the possibility of theft and damage.

A generous supply of large rubbish skips is always necessary, with the crusher type particularly useful but they do need an electrical supply. Good use of them is made whilst they are on site and it is ensured that the cleaners visit every nook and cranny of the perimeter and the event site.

Environmental considerations include noise before, during and after the event, which is monitored by the local council Environmental Health Department. Traffic disruption is kept to a minimum by a well-tested operational set up, initially by the Police and Highways Department, but often handed over to a private concern. The closing of roads in the vicinity of the venue at strategic times is a very effective and efficient tool.

In the early days of the National Bowl, car parking was free. This is no longer the case and with the reduction of adjacent land available for parking, remote car parks and even separate shuttle bus systems will have to be considered. If neighbouring parks and industrial estates are used for cars and a vigilant eye has to be kept on the effects of such use, particularly in inclement weather any damage must be dealt with immediately to ensure continuing good relations with our neighbours. Any complaints, such as the use of shrub beds as toilets, must be addressed as soon as the team are made aware of the problem. Gates and footpath bollards must be repositioned as soon as possible after the event to avoid such complications as gypsy invasion.

Trackway aluminium sheeting gives excellent ground protection by spreading the load across a wide area. However, such sheeting is extremely expensive and there is never enough to service an event. Although the reinstatement of small grass areas is most easily achieved with sharp sand, larger areas will need rotavating, levelling and seeding which these days can be facilitated by one operation by one machine and this is part of the 'making good' process of the site.

At the end of the season it is amazing how quickly the site comes back to normal, a few heavy downpours of rain to wash away the last traces of dirt and mess, and to encourage the grass to grow will help nature to revitalise the venue. The winter season usually revitalises the Site Manager as well when a quieter programme reduces the number of site visits for him. To conclude, he or she should always stay open-minded and flexible to the ever-changing scenario of venue management. The terms of the entertainment licence may change, land use of adjacent areas may alter, police requirements develop in response to problems and different acts and promoters are always bringing in new ideas and systems.

Richard Selley

Richard Selley has been the local site agent for The National Bowl at Milton Keynes since the mid 1980's serving successive managing agents since Milton Keynes Development Corporation built the venue in the 1970's. These managing agents include Sony/Pace, Harvey Goldsmith and currently Gaming International.

As site agent Richard looks after the venue as a key holder and shows prospective customers around the site. He supervises any contractors working on the site and advises the management of any work required.

Richard also co-ordinates the multiple uses of the venue including concerts, garden shows, car boot sales, cycle racing and motorcycle training.

6 SAFE STAGE DESIGN
Roger Barrett

Introduction

Stages come in many different shapes, sizes and designs, but inevitably it is the large structures, used for major events such as Party in the Park, and world tours by the leading rock groups, which get all the attention in guidance documents and at seminars.

However there are numerous smaller outdoor events that use a stage of some sort. Most are annual events and for many of the organisers it is the only event they promote each year. As a result, such organisers tend to live in a vacuum where event safety is concerned and being budget led it is hard to persuade them to pay for a 'proper job'. This places a considerable burden on enforcement officers, many of whom will have little more contact with temporary stages than does the event organiser.

At first sight there are many ways of building a stage, especially for outdoor use. Closer examination shows that virtually all stages use one (or a mixture) of four basic construction methods. These are described later.

Although there are significant differences between stages used outdoors and those designed for indoor use, they share two common requirements. They must resist forces applied to the stage surface and they must have proper calculations applied.

Most stages are 'demountable' (i.e. they are made up of many smaller parts which can be dismantled and re-used over and over again). Parts, especially small important ones such as bolts and securing pins, can get lost and damaged and the contractor must have a management system in place to ensure that each structure is actually complete.

Responsibilities

It is a considered view that the contractor (and the contractor's engineers) should take *total* responsibility for any failures in a temporary structure. The local authority is generally required to ensure the safety of performers and the public. This can be achieved in one of two ways, the choice depending on the authority's assessment of the contractor:

a) Examine and approve the calculations and the structure if the authority is in any doubt as to the ability or willingness of the contractor.
b) Check that the management and quality control systems of the contractor and their engineers are adequate to deal with the structure in question.

With the more complex structures it should not be the role of the local authority to 'approve' the structure itself as it is not their area of expertise and they cannot be aware of all the factors affecting the structure. A third party approvals route for repetitive structures is available through LANTAC (Local Authorities National Type Approval Confederation.

General elements applicable to all stages

This chapter is written for people who have to hire stages and for those people who have to inspect or approve them. It is not a design guide for staging suppliers who should know where to find the required information.

Calculations

Without exception all stages should have adequate calculations and these should be in a form that is understandable. This may sound obvious but if they are computer generated and you don't know which software package was used, or worse still they aren't even in English, you have no chance of assessing them.

Large complex stages may have a computer printout running to thousands of pages and there is little to be gained from looking at all of them. A suitable compromise is to accept a series of conclusions drawn up by a structural engineer based on the data provided by the computer analysis. The usefulness of these is enhanced if the contractor supplies a list of critical points to be checked on site, especially if these are cross-referenced to the conclusions provided by the structural engineer.

A stage that does not have calculations should not be built. (If a stage has not been created by using specifically designated calculations then there is no way to check if the stage is safe or unsafe and therefore should under no circumstances be built.)

Floor Loadings

There is a long-standing British Standard floor loading requirement for permanent stages. However, several stages built to the standard collapsed during the 'Punk Rock' craze in the 1970's due to stage invasions by the audience, encouraged by the performers. It was very difficult to measure the dynamic forces created by large numbers of pogoing punk rockers, so the BSI uprated the static floor load requirement. (from $5kN/m^2$ to $7.5kN/m^2$) in BS6399 pt1. *(Note that the 1996 revision of BS6399pt1 has introduced an alternative stage loading of $5kN/m^2$ for stages not in 'public assembly areas' [Table 1, C4])*

Although measured in kiloNewtons, which baffle most people, the 7.5kN/m^2 requirement correlates to parking cars five high all over the stage surface. This is a considerable load to withstand, and generally requires specially built floor units.

It is notable that if the platform is being built to accommodate members of the public the lower static loading of $5kN/m^2$ applies. Recent guidance also points to the requirement for a stage or platform to be able to resist a horizontal load applied at the surface level. Temporary demountable structures (TDS) suggests that stages should be designed for a static vertical load of $5kN/m^2$ and a simultaneous horizontal force of 5% of the vertical force applied in any one direction.

It is extremely difficult to comply with these standards when using conventional scaffolding, and regular scaffold boards, even when they are covered in plywood. If you really have no alternative, the plywood, or similar covering is essential to prevent cables, feet or fingers being trapped between individual boards.

Indoor Stages

Many stages are built indoors or in a tent and therefore need no roof. Consequently they do not need to resist any wind load (unless the tent collapses!) which is the constant problem with all outdoor stages. Indoor stages are likely to be built either of system scaffolding or one of the many purpose manufactured systems. A lack of handrails and poor stairs seem to be the biggest causes of stage related accidents indoors. There should be a handrail on all sides except the front edge of any stage over 600mm high and at every staircase, regardless of height.

Outdoor stages tend to be very temporary and when it gets dark it does so gradually. These two factors tend to make people very careful and their eyes have time to adjust to changing light levels. Indoor stages are often built in the same place repeatedly and at the start of an event the light level can change abruptly from full on to total blackout almost instantly. A combination of familiarity and temporary blindness has caused many accidents.

Stages with a narrow gap to an adjacent wall have been responsible for some very nasty accidents where people have stepped into the gap and become wedged in. The front edge of the stage, physical obstructions and stair edges should all be marked with white or luminous tape. White tape should be a minimum 25mm wide to be visible and for high stages 50mm is preferable.

Purpose Built Modular Systems

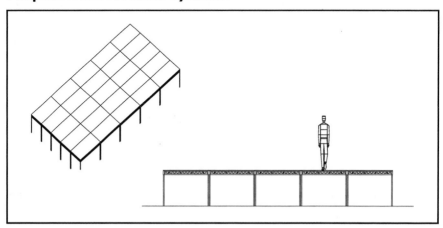

Purpose built stage systems always have a method of linking the sections together. Under no circumstances should sections be joined together with a 'bodge' such as gaffa tape or plastic cable ties around the legs. If a stage is made up of modular units from different manufacturers, particular attention should be paid to the joins between dissimilar sections. Many current designs use short lengths of scaffold tube as legs. If made of aluminium these should be no more than 0.5m long and if made of steel should be no more than 1.2m long. Longer legs need to have diagonal bracing fitted to maintain structural integrity. Every day in this country there are many such stages being built and used, often in local authority venues. All proper stage systems have calculations, and the more they are asked for the more quickly the situation will improve.

Barriers

Many designs of free-standing crush barriers can slide on the hall floor if subjected to a combination of a slippery surface (or a sprung floor) and sufficient crowd pressure, a problem often dealt with by using the stage as an anchor. *never* permit this unless a competent person can produce calculations to show that it is safe. It is bad enough if a barrier moves under crowd pressure. It is infinitely worse if the stage collapses at the same time. It should be noted that the design and safe use of barriers is another separate subject.

Outdoor Stages

Outdoor stages should always have a roof and side walls to provide weather protection, unless used for something such as a dance group with acoustic music. Such a structure is immediately at risk from wind loads, which are almost always higher than you think. Many structural failures involving outdoor stages are due to the wind, often on part-built structures.

Before considering types of stages it is worth pointing out that any concert or event site is likely to have other structures, including towers to support loudspeakers and lights, supports for advertising banners, and supports for large scale props and other scenic elements.

All these are likely to be built of scaffolding, and their stability is directly affected by the ratio of their height to the smallest base dimension and their weight. Again calculations are required, but a good 'rule of thumb' is that if the tower is clad on the sides, it is likely to require additional anchorage if the height to base ratio is greater than 1:1.

Even completely unclad, no tower should exceed a height to base ratio of 3:1 without additional support or anchorage.

Wind Loads

For many years wind load calculations have been based on BS CP3, which did not consider the situation of partially enclosed structures such as stages and made no allowances for seasonal factors, proximity to the coast, etc.

This has changed recently, with the publication of BS6399 pt2. However this was written specifically for permanent structures and it is widely acknowledged that there is insufficient advice available to designers of temporary structures.

TDS offers a chapter on potential techniques for dealing with wind loads on temporary structures, although at the time of writing this is under review.

A description of the basic construction techniques for outdoor stages follows, and it is important to realise that each contractor will have their own way of utilising these, and dealing with the associated problems.

Types of Stages

Type 1: Structures where the floor base and the roof supports are designed as one integral whole. This could be described as the 'classic' construction method.

Type One stages are capable of dealing with large loads and poor ground surfaces as they spread the loads efficiently. Careful design and meticulous attention to detail provide a good degree of redundancy (.i.e failure of one part transfers loads to those surrounding it).

Larger numbers of semi-skilled labour are required to assemble the multitude of small parts. Skilled supervision is therefore essential as missing parts could negate the redundancy inherent in the design, leading to possible catastrophic failure. They are generally expensive to build, as they do not lend themselves to pre-fabrication.

The roof is usually a custom made fabrication that hangs from the structure, which in turn is usually made of system scaffold. Predominant systems are those from SGB (Cuplok), GKN (Kwikstage) and Layker (all round).

The weight of all the components (and equipment) helps to resist the wind loads, frequently to the extent of no additional anchorage being required.

If correctly built, they are very stable, safe structures.

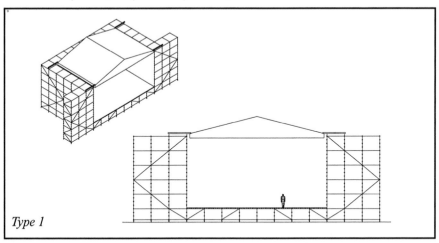

Type 1

Type 2: Structures where the roof supports straddle the floor structure.

This type offers advantages in erection speed, as the roof supports usually take the form of pre-made masts or towers. This technique is becoming very popular, being used for stages of all sizes. The potential cost savings of less labour and far fewer parts appeal to many, but the problems have to be clearly understood:

- High point loads on the ground.
- Little self weight to assist in resisting wind loads, and due to the slender structures that are possible, resolving the wind load problem becomes crucial.
- Many designs tie the bottoms of the masts into the stage base. For this to be acceptable as a method of resisting wind forces the base has to be constructed as a unified whole, and not as a collection of individual units.
- The roof has to be very strong. Any deflection tends to buckle the masts.

Larger stages that use this technique invariably use components specifically designed for the purpose, whilst many smaller structures use masts or tower hoists designed for the very different purpose of lifting goods in industrial or construction environments. Almost without exception, these components have little resistance to horizontal forces (wind loads, etc.) and are therefore responsible for many structural failures. To overcome this problem you will often see guy-ropes being used. Apart from the potential hazard caused by the guys themselves, a large part of any windload is then transmitted vertically

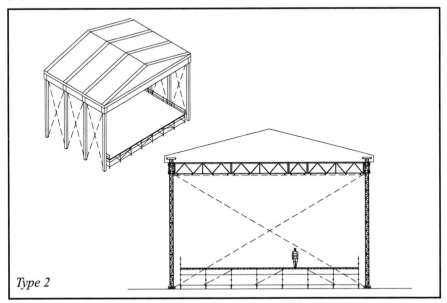

Type 2

down the mast, and in combination with the weight of the roof may over-load the mast.

Type 3: Structures where the roof and its integral supports sit on the floor structure.

This category usually consists of a purpose-built roof structure, such as a dome type or part of a marquee roof. Very few marquees have been designed to be safe with one end missing, and again calculations should be available.

As the floor decking rarely provides much resistance to uplift, any roof structure in this format suffers from the difficulty of anchoring it to the floor structure to resist the wind load.

By way of example, one such marquee-based roof blew off a stage in 1992 whilst a 60-piece orchestra was rehearsing beneath it. The roof landed behind them in a tangle of aluminium and fabric. Fortunately no-one was injured, and the concert went ahead without a roof. There were calculations in existence to show that the roof structure had adequate strength, but based on the (incorrect) assumption that it was properly anchored down.

Stages to this design at the bottom end of the market often use an inflatable roof, which is based on 'bouncy castle' technology. These often rely on being fixed to the stage decks to resist uplift. Where the stage floor is made of Steeldeck or any other similar brands, such structures do not meet UK wind load requirements as the decks are not heavy enough to hold themselves down in strong winds, let alone the roof.

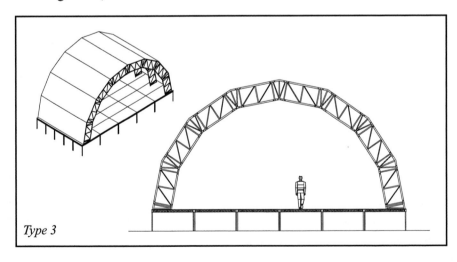

Type 3

Type 4: Structures which are completely integral.

Fully integral designs are much less common. The single biggest problem is size limitation due to what can legally be carried on the road.

Initial manufacturing costs are usually very high. Most stages of this type are vehicle mounted and so access to some sites can be a major problem.

There are however significant benefits:

- Erecting procedures can be mechanically assisted, by the use of hydraulics or winches, etc.
- Speed of erection and safety are improved as there are very few loose parts to miss out.
- Very few crew are required so skill levels can be higher.
- There are drastic reductions in manual handling, which is a general problem in the industry.

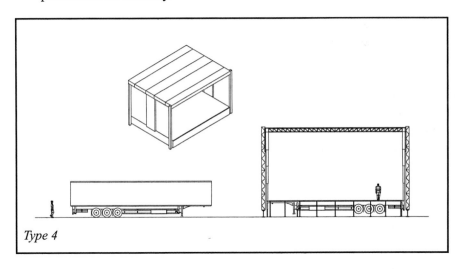

Type 4

Stage Check-List

Drawings and Calculations

Have you got the drawings and calculations? Do you have someone who can check that what is built matches the drawing? If not, get a signed statement from the contractor saying that it does match the drawing, and listing any deviations, along with the name of the person authorising the deviations. It is no use relying on the Event Safety Co-ordinator for this checking function unless they have specific skills in this area.

If heavy roof loads are expected, is there a system for verifying what these actually are to ensure that the structure is not overloaded?

Construction Checking

If scaffolding is used in the construction, is there a system **in use** for checking all the connections are made correctly? Modern system scaffolds can usually be checked visually, but traditional tube and clip cannot. Each coupling must be individually checked.

By law all lifting and rigging equipment should be identifiable, tested and certificated. Is it?

Foundations

Are the foundations OK? Depending on the leg loads and the ground conditions a 12" square of plywood may be quite adequate. On the other hand a roof mast may need a four ton block of concrete or a steel spreader plate on top of a mat of railway sleepers. If you don't know what is required, ask the contractor to provide details. If they can't, won't or just don't, should they be building it at all?

Handrails

Are there adequate handrails? Note that a stage is a place of work, for which the handrail specification is much lower than for a public place.

Ramps

If the stage is big enough to have a loading ramp, it will inevitably have cases on wheels pushed up it. What happens at the top? Can the smaller ones roll under the handrail and fall on someone working or passing below? What happens at the bottom? Can a runaway case roll into a public place; across a road; into the catering tent, or over **your** foot? These problems are easy to overcome, so insist on them being sorted out.

Is the ramp made of bare plywood? It **will** be slippery if it gets wet or muddy. Some coated plywoods are even slippery when quite dry. Ask for a non slip surface to be laid.

Stairs

Are the stairs safe? Try running up and down them as if you were in a panic. Do they still feel safe? If not, they probably aren't safe. Ask for them to be improved.

Forklift Trucks

Does the construction involve forklift trucks (or worse still telehandlers)? The drivers obviously have certificates of competence, don't they? It is no use asking on site, because they almost certainly won't be carrying them, so ask the stage builder at a planning meeting to arrange for copies to be forwarded.

If the construction involves work on the public highway they need third party insurance and possibly a normal driving licence as well. Have they got them?

Health & Safety

Is there adequate supervision of the construction, and is the work-force trained? Un-trained workers need enormous amounts of supervision. Again, ask for details at the planning stage.

Does the contractor have a policy on the number of hours worked each day? Tired crew make very un-safe crew.

Ask for copies of risk assessments, safety policies, employment and supervision policies, method statements and of course public liability insurance.

Are there satisfactory arrangements to keep members of the public away from the work area?

Are there first aid facilities for the workers before and after the event?

Fire Safety

Is all the fabric used for the roof and walls flame retardant? Is there a certificate to prove it? Are the correct fire extinguishers available? In spite of the erroneous advice in the 'Yellow Guide' and the 'Event Safety Guide' there should be **NO** water extinguishers or hose reels on outdoor concert stages.

Concert stages invariably have extensive electrical supplies and in any case there should be nothing on stage that needs water to extinguish it.

Electrical Safety

Although not a structural item, virtually all stages use copious amounts of conductive metals in their construction, and current Electricity regulations require this to be bonded to Earth.

Scaffolding with a painted finish may require extensive treatment to provide acceptable earth bonding. Aluminium, galvanised scaffolding and welded metals (as in fully integral designs) are excellent conductors and so much easier to bond satisfactorily.

Viewing Facilities for Wheelchair Users at Outdoor Entertainment Events

Most event organisers now routinely expect to supply special facilities for people with disabilities. This will become mandatory when the Disability Discrimination Act becomes law in 2004. The most obvious of these facilities is the provision of raised platforms for wheelchair users attending events with a standing audience. This guidance is offered to assist in specifying and designing such platforms.

Local Authorities may require the provision of platform(s) as a condition of an entertainment licence and will be responsible for the enforcement of Health & Safety regulations in relation to the structure (except at Local Authority organised events).

The existing published guidance on the subject of facilities for wheelchair users is applicable to permanent facilities such as theatres, conference venues and sports stadia.

Following requests from a number of event organisers and local authorities for guidance on how to interpret these requirements for a temporary facility, the following information has been prepared by Star Events Group Ltd. It has been submitted to the Advisory Group On Temporary Structures (AGOTS) for consideration for potential publication.

Star Events Group Ltd. has taken existing guidance published for permanent facilities and made the minimum number of deviations required to meet the specific case of events on temporary 'green-field' locations.

Consideration has been given to the types of structural systems commonly in use in the events industry. As many of these are still based on deck units of imperial dimensions (Typically the 8' x 4' Steeldeck units) the nearest equivalent imperial units are given to allow the specified minimum dimensions to be met when using these systems.

Existing Guidance

Guidance specific to permanent facilities can be found in:

BS 8300 Disability Access (British Standards Institute)

The Draft Revision of Part M of The Building Regulations 2000 – Access to and use of buildings (Office of the Deputy Prime Minister)

Guide to safety at sports grounds (Department of Culture, Media & Sport and The Scottish Office)

Designing for spectators with disabilities (Football Stadia Advisory Design Council)

General Principles

The design has to start with the location. It is essential that a platform and its occupants do not block the sight lines of other attendees. Failure to address this may result in crushing around the platform. Whilst wheelchair users will appreciate the provision of the facility, no-one likes being 'on display' and this also dictates both the location and the height.

As with all event goers, wheelchair users need access to facilities such as toilets and concessions, which again can affect the choice of location.

Many wheelchair users need to have an able bodied assistant or simply wish to share the occasion with a friend, who may or may not be a wheelchair user. Where able bodied assistants/friends are accommodated on the platform, it is essential that there is a management plan to ensure they remain seated if this would interfere with the view of people standing behind the platform.

The orientation should also be considered. Where possible the platform should face squarely to the entertainment. Oblique angles are both uncomfortable for the wheelchair users and may reduce the platform capacity due to having to partially turn each wheelchair.

The access ramp has a critical safety function in the event of an evacuation. The ramp and the area it leads to should be completely free of any potential source of fire such as non flame retardant plastic toilet cubicles, burger vans, etc.

Consideration should be given to providing a staircase access located away from the access ramp. This enables able bodied users of the platform to access and exit the platform without waiting for wheelchair users on the ramp. In the event of an emergency evacuation a staircase provides access for emergency personnel whilst the ramp is being used to evacuate wheelchair users.

Platform Specifications

Platform height

The essential requirement is to enable wheelchair users to see whilst not raising them to the point of feeling they are 'on show'. At most typical events, where a standing audience is

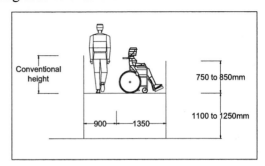

watching entertainment on a stage of at least 1.5m (5') high, the wheelchair users platform height is likely to be between 1.1m and 1.25m. (Stages with a platform height of less than 1.5m are usually unsuitable for a standing audience on a level site.)

Surface

The surface of the platform must be level and free of bumps and gaps. Under no circumstances are scaffold boards or battens a suitable surface, unless overlayed with 18mm plywood, firmly screwed into place.

Edge protection

Given the number of able bodied people that may be on the platform, handrails should be fitted to all sides except the front. These should be to the normal standards for a public venue.

Consideration should be given to keeping the front handrail at a height of between 0.75m and 0.85m to avoid the eyeline height of most wheelchair users.

The front edge of the platform should have a toe-board or upstand to prevent the front wheels of wheelchairs from dropping off the edge.

Infill

Apart from the usual requirement to position a skirt around the platform to hide the sub-structure, consideration should be given to extending this up to the handrail. This provides a useful 'modesty' screen and provides some degree of shelter from the wind. The resultant loads from the wind must be dealt with in the structural design.

Signage

The access points to the platform should be clearly signed to indicate the platform is for the use of wheelchair users.

Loadings

It is entirely possible that in the event of a stewarding failure, large numbers of people could gain unauthorised access to the platform. Platform surfaces should therefore be designed to the accepted standards for public assembly spaces (See BS6399 Pt 1) that requires a capacity of $5kN/m^2$. This concurs with the requirement in Temporary Demountable Structures.

This design loading should also apply to the access ramp.

Access ramps

The failure to supply a suitable ramp access is one of the most common problems with platforms currently available. Key requirements include the correct angle. An absolute maximum angle is 1:12. but an angle of 1:15 is strongly recommended.

On a platform of typical height of around 1.1m, this implies a ramp of around 16m to 17m long. This can cause a number of problems and the usual convention is to build the ramp along one long side of the platform although in many cases a change of direction will be required. The ramp can then gain stability from the main platform structure and is less likely to create an obstruction for other users of the venue.

There should be intermediate level landing areas to avoid over-exertion. It is recommended that the longest travel distance between landings should not exceed 8.0m. Very often such landings can also be used at changes of direction (see below).

Suitable Size

A ramp should be between 1.0m and 1.3m (4') wide, measured at the narrowest point (i.e. between handrails, etc). It is not recommended to be any narrower as there is a distinct risk of wheelchair users catching themselves, or part of their chair on the handrail system. It is also not recommended to be any wider as this could allow a wheelchair to turn sideways across the ramp, with a higher risk of overturning.

Changes of Direction

Given that some wheelchairs will be pushed up the ramp by an able-bodied assistant, or may be of greater than usual length, any change of direction should have greater dimensions than the width of the ramp.

A change of direction must only be accomplished with a level landing. Each leg of the ramp should have a minimum landing length of 2.0m (8') when measured in the direction of travel from/to that leg.

Non-slip Surface

Normal plywood is extremely slippery when wet and conventional paints do little to improve this. Given that wheelchair users will be relying on friction between the ramp surface and their wheels, and some users may be assisted with able bodied people pushing or holding, then the non-slip surface is critical to maintain safety.

Various options are available to create a non-slip surface. These include:
- Proprietary non-slip paints (often sold for use on boat decks)
- Home-made mixtures of gloss paint and sharp sand
- Roofing 'felt' firmly tacked or glued to the surface (very short lifespan with constant use)

In any event the ramp should be free of gaps and uneven surfaces, ridges, etc.

Edge Protection
The ramp should have normal handrails for the use of able bodied people and should have suitable edge protection to prevent wheels slipping off the edge. An upstand of around 75mm in height has been found sufficient for this.

Visual Identification
The ramp edges should be painted in a contrasting colour to the ramp surface for the benefit of people with impaired vision. The two best contrasting colour combinations for people with one or other form of 'colour-blindness' are Black/White and Blue/Yellow. The use of greens and reds is not recommended.

Seating Arrangements and Capacities
The optimum seating arrangement is to have a quantity of fold-flat or similar chairs available and allocate these as each user arrives. Wheelchairs can be positioned side by side, with a chair behind, or chairs can be interspersed with the wheelchairs, according to the requirements of the users. Where gangways are limited it is essential they are not blocked by seats for able-bodied assistants.

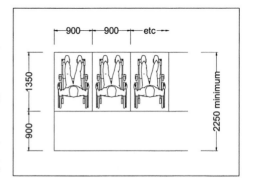

Platforms for a Single Row of Wheelchairs
Each wheelchair should be allowed an area 0.90m wide and 1.35m deep. Assuming that one row of

wheelchairs is at the front of a platform, there should be a gangway behind this first row of at least 0.9m wide.

This dictates that the minimum platform depth for a single row of wheelchairs is 2.25m (8'). This is conveniently just under the standard 2.4m or 2.5m staging units used by many suppliers.

Multiple Row Specifications and Capacities and Platforms for a double row of wheelchairs

A platform with two rows of wheelchairs can still operate satisfactorily with a single gangway between the two rows, giving a minimum platform depth of 3.6m (12').

Platforms for a triple row of wheelchairs

Where three rows of wheelchairs are to be accommodated, then two gangways are required (behind the first row and in front of the third row). This requires a platform depth of a minimum 5.85m (20').

From these dimensions, it can be seen that the 'traditional' platform of 4.8m or 5.0m (16') in depth is not an economic size, although it does provide for two rows of wheelchairs with more space between the rows.

Capacities

When working out the number of wheelchairs and chairs within a row, allow 0.9m per wheelchair and 0.5m per folding chair.

Platform dimensions based on the above criteria have the following capacities

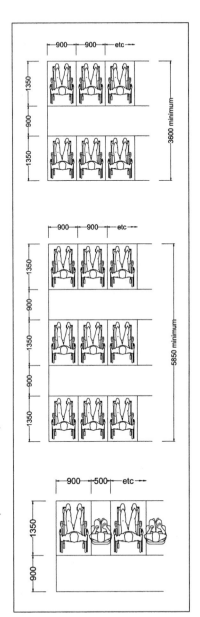

(assuming an equal number of wheelchairs and folding chairs) as shown in the following table.

These capacities assume that the access ramp allows direct access to each gangway. If it does not, then the capacity should be reduced by the relevant area needed to gain access to the gangway(s).

Platform width	X	2.5m deep (minimum)	3.6m deep (minimum)	2.85m deep (minimum)
5.0m		3	6	9
10.0m		7	14	21
15.0m		10	20	30
20.0m		14	28	42
25.0m		17	34	51
30.0m		21	42	63
40.0m		28	56	84
50.0m		35	70	105
60.0m		42	84	126

REFERENCES

HSE (1999) **The Event Safety Guide**. A guide to health, safety and welfare at music and similar events. HSE, London.

Institution of Structural Engineers (1999) **Temporary Demountable Structures**. Guidance on Design, Procurement and Use. ISE, London.

HSE (1999) **Safe Use of Lifting Equipment**. HSE, London.

Roger Barrett

Roger Barrett has specialised in outdoor events for over 30 years. He has just celebrated the 27th anniversary of Star Hire (Event Services) Ltd, which he founded in 1976. The company supplied stages and related structures to events of all sizes and in the last decade their stages have been used in 30 different countries.

Roger was the technical director of Star Hire and its sister company Star Rigging. Both companies, which are now divisions of the recently formed Star Events Group, of which Roger is Director – Group Development, are active across the whole range of music, corporate and sporting events and are approved or exclusive suppliers to many major promoters, venues and broadcasters.

Roger has had a long involvement with industry trade associations that are committed to improving standards. He is the chairman of the UK's Advisory Group On Temporary Structures and represents the UK production industry with the Health & Safety Executive.

He is also a member of the International Live Music Conference Safety Focus Group (ILMC-SFG) which was set up in 2001 in the wake of the nine deaths at the Roskilde pop festival to review all aspects of concert safety.

He had major input into the two main UK event guidance documents, the 'Event Safety Guide' and 'Temporary Demountable Structures'. He has made regular presentations since 1994 at the Emergency Planning College regarding the safety of temporary structures.

Roger holds the only European Patent for mobile trailer stage design and has also published a handbook for event organisers.

7 LOLER REGULATIONS
Roger Barrett

Introduction

If you work in the events industry, the *Lifting Operations & Lifting Equipment Regulations 1998 (LOLER)* probably affect you in some way. You may never leave your office, but you could be liable for the actions of freelancers who are employed by someone who works for you. The information in this section is offered to assist you in checking whether you have any responsibilities under the LOLER regulations

On 5th December 1998, a major change in the law governing Lifting Operations in the UK was introduced. Virtually all the previous legislation was repealed on this date and the new regulations have a significant mandatory impact on the events industry. LOLER applies to ALL Lifting Equipment, whether existing, new, second-hand or leased, etc. and to ALL Lifting Operations without exception.

The law is called *The Lifting Operations and Lifting Equipment Regulations 1998*. In addition to this, the HSE has published an Approved Code of Practice (an ACOP) which gives further guidance on how to comply with the new law. In effect, complying with the ACOP should protect you from legal action.

The HSE is intending to publish further guidance for specific industry sectors such as Agriculture and Construction but it is notable that the events industry is not mentioned so far. The purpose of this section is to set out the basic responsibilities and duties of various persons in the events industry.

Definition and Scope of Lifting Equipment

The definition of lifting equipment is extremely wide. It includes such items as pre-fixed rigging points in the roof of a venue, chain hoists, steel wire ropes, round-slings ('spansets'), shackles, eyebolts, trusses, the bar of a six lamp bar, hook clamps, PA cabinet suspension chains, stage roofs, etc. Other devices frequently used at events such as scissor lifts, counterweight flying systems, etc are also included.

Of particular note, all ropes, harnesses, caribiners, strops and other equipment used for work positioning by riggers is also included.

Even companies who do not use conventional lifting equipment are involved if they operate vehicles with tail-lifts, forklifts trucks, etc.

Lifting Equipment

The person or organisation responsible for a piece of lifting equipment has to appoint a 'competent' person to carry out an assessment of the use of that piece of equipment. This competent person has to decide on a suitable interval at which each piece of equipment must be thoroughly examined and/or inspected. The requirements for this examination/inspection and the results of each examination/inspection have to be recorded. This information can be recorded in any way that can be accessed by the person responsible for the equipment. Every piece of lifting equipment must be identifiable and marked with its Safe Working Load (SWL) or Working Load Limit (WLL). Any equipment not so marked must not be used for lifting.

Lifting Operations

Separate to the equipment inspections above, a risk assessment must be carried out by a competent person to assess the Lifting Operation being planned. This assessment should cover the type of load being lifted, the risk of the load falling or striking a person, the risk of the lifting equipment itself falling or striking a person. This Risk Assessment must also be recorded.

The competent person who carries out the assessment of the Lifting Operation will not necessarily be the same person who carries out the inspection of the Lifting Equipment.

Repetitive operations only have to be assessed once although periodic reviews should be undertaken to ensure that the Lifting Operation assessed has not changed in any way.

It should be noted that the requirement to carry out this risk assessment comes from the HSW Management Regulations and not specifically from the LOLER regulations.

Responsibility and Liability

The employer of any person carrying out Lifting Operations is ultimately responsible for compliance with the LOLER regulations. Therefore a Production Manager who hires a rigger will take on the liability. The precise employment method (PAYE, contract, free-lance, self-employed etc) makes no difference. Similarly the employer retains responsibility for any Lifting Equipment used in any Lifting Operations.

This employer responsibility cannot be delegated. Consequently, everyone in a chain of employer/employee relationships (no matter how long) could be held liable in the event of enforcement action. Therefore a Band (or Management Company) that employs a Production Manager who in turn employs a rigger could be liable for compliance with the LOLER regulations. Also the responsibility cannot be avoided by employing persons with their own lifting equipment.

It appears that the only way to avoid the liability is to make another organisation responsible for all aspects of lifting. If a Band or Production Manager employs a Service Company that supplies the Lifting Equipment, the personnel, and manages all Lifting Operations, then the responsibility for complying with the LOLER regulations would appear to remain with that Service Company.

It is an untested legal point as to whether a Production Manager would still be held liable if they were to instruct the Service Company how to carry out a particular lifting operation.

It is also the responsibility of the employer to ensure that any person tasked to carry out any Lifting Operation is suitable competent.

Whoever is responsible, they have to ensure (and be able to demonstrate) that every Lifting Operation is:

a) properly planned by a competent person

b) appropriately supervised

c) carried out in a safe manner

The Documentation Trail

The new regulations are quite clear on this point.

1) 'Documentation' means any retrievable recording system.

2) No documentation needs to be given to a third party if a Lifting Operation is entirely 'in-house'. This means that one company must own the Lifting Equipment, employ the staff and control the Lifting Operation. It does not matter where this operation takes place. In this specific case the 'documentation' only needs to be available for inspection on 'reasonable notice' from the enforcing authorities. (The HSE advises that they consider three working days to be reasonable for the production of documentation).

3) Documentation must accompany any use of Lifting Equipment that is not

in-house. Any person who hires (or borrows) lifting equipment from someone else has a statutory duty to ensure that the LOLER regulations are being complied with and so must be in possession of the relevant documentary proof of inspection and examination. Similarly, anyone that hires out Lifting Equipment must supply documentation to prove that it has been examined and/or inspected. This documentation must accompany the equipment at all times that it is being used by a third party.

4) The LOLER regulations cross-refer to The Management of Health and Safety at Work Regulations 1992. These require a risk assessment to be carried out to identify the nature and level of risks associated with a Lifting Operation. Every individual, partnership or corporate body that is responsible for Lifting Operations (or has employees that carry them out) is responsible for ensuring that this Risk Assessment is carried out and is available for inspection.

Special cases

Forklift Trucks

If fitted with pneumatic tyres, a method of checking that the tyres are inflated to the correct pressure must be provided. This is because the machine will not be stable with one or more soft tyres.

PA Cabinets and Video Screen Modules

Any device permanently fitted to a cabinet or module to assist in lifting it is considered to be part of the load and so outside the requirements of the LOLER regulations. However, the owner of the equipment still has a general responsibility under HSW Acts to ensure that any such lifting point is properly designed and of adequate strength. Note that any external fitting that locates into the fixed pick-up points does come under LOLER regulations.

Definitions

Competent Person: (To assess Lifting Operations) "Someone with adequate practical and theoretical knowledge and experience of the planned lifting operations."

Lifting Accessory: Individual items such as shackles, slings, eyebolts, truss sections, hook clamps, etc.

Lifting Assembly: A collection of Lifting Accessories used to join a load (or combination of loads) to a Lifting Machine or to support the Lifting Machine itself. Assembled trusses, fly bars, ground supports and stage roofs all come into this category.

Lifting Equipment: The generic terms for all items found in the workplace that can be used to lift a load. Note that winches for pulling loads along the ground do not count (although other legislation applies) and activities such as carrying a parcel are also excluded as no mechanical assistance is in use.

Lifting Machine: A device, power driven or manual, which is used to raise and lower a load. Examples of power driven machines include chain climbing hoists ('motors'), forklift trucks, tail-lifts, cranes, etc. Examples of manual machines range from a crowbar to a Tirfor winch.

Specific Regulations

A number of changes to existing practice in the events industry are required by the LOLER regulations.

Regulation 6(1) requires that measures are taken to minimise the risk of a load falling in the event of an equipment failure. In practice this could mean the use of multiple hoists of adequate capacity so that the load will not fall if one hoist fails. This may have a particular impact on trusses that are traditionally lifted on two hoists. Obviously, failure of either hoist will cause the truss to fall and it appears that one answer could be a minimum of three hoists per truss (or inertia reel devices). A similar problem occurs with single hoist PA clusters.

Regulation 7(a) requires all Lifting Equipment to be clearly marked with its Safe Working Load (SWL).

Regulation 7(b) requires that those items whose SWL varies according to how they are assembled (truss sections for example) must be accompanied by sufficient information for the user to assemble and use them correctly. This will almost certainly require that the person responsible for the assembly of such parts is 'competent'.

ACOP 7 requires that where the weight of a Lifting Accessory is significant in relation to the Safe Working load of the Lifting Machine with which it is used, the accessory should be marked with its self weight. Again this applies to trusses, PA fly beams etc. which can be a significant proportion of the capacity of the hoists used to lift them. An individual shackle is not a significant proportion of the capacity of such hoists and so would not need to be marked with its self weight.

Note that a hoist could also be a Lifting Accessory if it is in use to hang one truss from another, for example.

Regulation 8(1) requires that loads should not be moved by the use of Lifting Equipment when there are people underneath unless adequate measures are taken to protect them. This requires a stage or similar area to be cleared whilst trusses and other production equipment are being raised and lowered during a load-in or load-out, but would not preclude the use of moving trusses during shows where adequate fail-safe systems are in place.

The Quick Guide to Responsibilities

Bands and Management Companies

If you employ riggers (freelance or otherwise) to rig equipment for your shows, or hire in rigging equipment or stage roofs, you should assume that you have the same responsibilities as Production Managers.

Production (and Stage) Managers

1) Ensure that all persons you employ to carry out Lifting Operations are suitably competent.
2) Ensure that all Lifting Equipment (including stage roofs) that you hire in is accompanied by adequate LOLER documentation. Keep this with the hired in equipment.
3) Ensure that a Risk Assessment is carried out for all Lifting Operations and is available for inspection.
4) Ensure that safe systems of work are in place (i.e. Don't let riggers lift loads when persons are underneath).

Promoters and Event Organisers

You should ensure that any contractors you use are complying with the LOLER regulations. If you hire riggers directly you will have similar liabilities as Production Managers (above).

If you hire a stage with a roof that will be used to support Lifting Equipment, check that all the structural sections of the stage roof and its supports are LOLER compliant. You may be liable for any Lifting Equipment used by a touring show you promote. This may have a significant impact on foreign productions, especially those from outside the EU where no equivalent to the LOLER regulations exist.

Riggers (Self-employed)

You have the same obligations as any other user of Lifting Equipment. As a competent person you should ensure that any employer is complying with the

LOLER regulations. In particular:

1) Check that all Lifting Equipment you are asked to rig has documentary evidence that it has been inspected.

2) Make sure that all your own equipment that you use for work positioning (harness, caribiners, slings and strops, ropes etc) is all identified and inspected in accordance with the manufacturers recommendations. You can do this yourself if you are competent to inspect Lifting Equipment. Have a simple document available that details your equipment, when it was last inspected and by whom.

Service Companies Owning Lifting Equipment

1) Appoint a 'competent' person to review the use of the equipment and determine a frequency and method for inspections and thorough examinations.

2) Have the inspections and examinations carried out, and the results recorded.

3) Supply proof of the above to any third party using the equipment.

4) Ensure you get LOLER documentation from the owner of any Lifting Equipment you hire in.

5) Appoint a competent person(s) to assess, plan and supervise each Lifting Operation.

Venues

If you supply purpose designed lifting points ('house points') in the roof of your venue, or any kind of structural lifting grid, these have to be inspected and examined under the LOLER regulations. Copies of the inspection and examination reports should be made available to all venue users who use the house points so that the venue users can themselves comply with the LOLER regulations.

Finally

If after reading this section you think you have any responsibilities at all under the LOLER regulations, we strongly suggest that you buy a copy of *Safe use of lifting equipment* which contains the full LOLER regulations, the HSE Approved Code of Practice (ACOP) and additional guidance.

The ISBN number is 0-7176-1628-2 and it is obtainable for £8 from HSE books: Tel: 01787 87765, Fax: 01787 313995.

8 TOILETS AND WASTE FACILITIES
Philip Winsor

Introduction

If there is one topic that causes concertgoers to feel let down, particularly at a large outdoor event, it is the standard and condition of the 'loos' as they are generally termed in this new Millennium. It is probably because everybody needs to use them at sometime during the gig, due to our basic human functions and therefore everyone has an opinion or view to share with their fellow beings.

The promoter has little control over the artiste's performance on the day, but they do have a vast amount of control over the standard of the portable toilet accommodation and washing facilities that are brought onto site for the event, or the state of the permanent facilities.

Over the last decade, as with many other aspects of the live event sector, technology and standards have moved on apace. Although, if the loo queues are too long, and with human nature being what it is, the gender sign on the door will either be misread, or ignored. Those who cannot wait at an outdoor show will head off in to the bushes! And experience indicates that this is not just a male trait.

Background to the Legislation

Since 1982 premises holding Public Entertainment Licences issued by the Local Authority for music, dancing, and indoor sports require suitable and sufficient sanitary accommodation and washing facilities on site. In permanent venues, the British Standard 6465, Part One, 1994, sets down the number of toilets, urinals, and wash-hand basins required, dependent on the total number of persons at the venue and the ratio of males to females likely to attend. As a consequence, there is an element of flexibility for architects, etc to work within.

For outdoor events with an Occasional Public Outdoor Entertainment Licence in place, the second edition of the Event Safety Guide is used as the point of reference. This will again refer to the number of people attending, the duration of the event, and the male to female ratio so that the number of facilities required can be calculated.

For local community events with music as an ancillary element, and with a gate opening time of six hours or more:

Female   - one toilet per 100 females;

Male   - one toilet per 500 males plus one urinal per 150 males.

If the gate opening time is less than six hours:

Female   - one toilet per 120 females;

Male   - one toilet per 600 males plus one urinal per 175 males.

These are general guidelines but these figures may be too high for short-duration or events without peak periods, such as country fairs and garden parties, or be too low where there are licensed bars or where camping is being permitted.

At licensable outdoor entertainments, the licensing authority can stipulate not only the amount of sanitary accommodation and washing facilities required, as a licence condition; they can also stipulate the type of facility, e.g. single free-standing units with their own integral facilities, flushing systems, lighting and sanitising fluid, or the traditional trailer which can be of a basic design, and construction through to something with high-class fittings and interior design.

The type of facility provided will be dependent on the numbers attending, the audience profile, available space and on-site services-water supply, foul drainage (sewerage), and electricity. Each location will be different and on occasions the plumbers have to be creative, and quite ingenious to ensure that all the fitments function as intended.

The second edition of the Event Safety Guide increased the standard markedly in respect of female toilet provision and as a consequence this necessitated more units having to be accommodated in the same space that was satisfactory under the old standard - first edition of the Event Safety Guide. After space constraints, water supply and foul drainage are the other two most important factors.

Supply

A major problem in the UK during the summer months can be the supply of this type of equipment. There is normally a finite amount available for hire so if there are a plethora of outdoor events then shortages will occur. In this scenario, lower grade units may have to be obtained from the construction sector. In other instances, units will be moved from one event to another without returning to the depot for proper cleansing and maintenance.

By ensuring that the planning element takes place in good time, such potential problems should, and can be avoided. In all circumstances, the production manager must ensure that the contractors fulfil their contractual obligations in respect of the specification of the equipment that was ordered.

Access

It should be remembered that a wide variety of individuals will use the facilities, and they may not all be ambulant. As a

Portable toilets at GWR Roadshow, National Bowl, Milton Keynes.

consequence there will need to be specific facilities for disabled people, e.g. a 'disabled pod'. This unit will come complete with a ramp and be fitted out with suitable handrails, taps, and flushing controls etc, in order that a disabled person can utilise the facility independently. They will generally be sited adjacent to specific viewing locations for disabled persons and have stewards nearby to ensure that this facility is not overtaken by able-bodied persons.

Single freestanding units do not have access problems for most concertgoers; but the trailer units may do so as their step access/handrail arrangements can be extremely variable, with design, construction, or maintenance faults whereby in muddy, or wet conditions a person can easily slip, and injure themselves on a metal tread, or the entrance door. Such deficiencies can cause accidents to occur, and may result in litigation at a future date. All these matters are fairly easily dealt with by a little forethought, and ensuring that quality standards are insisted upon when the order is placed, through to supply, installation, and commissioning.

Plumbing Arrangements

If foul sewerage is available on site, then it should be checked prior to having temporary facilities connected as if it is only used intermittently, vandalism might have occurred in the interim.

Plumbing specialists can ensure that the gradient/flow is adequate and there are no obstructions.

In the event of some concern, then CCTV cameras can be inserted into the pipe to check quickly if there are any obstructions or damage, e.g. broken pipes, bad joints, ingress of roots, etc, so that the remedial works can be effected prior to the sanitary accommodation arriving on site.

Water Supply

If trailer units are going to be provided, then it is of paramount importance that there is a sufficiency of supply. The venue may have a water ring main system that is supplying not only the sanitary accommodation but also backstage catering and the drinking water for the audience. If the concertgoers abuse the drinking water taps on a hot day, then there may be a loss of water pressure to the flushing cisterns in the trailer units, resulting in a toilet that cannot be flushed. Sewage will quickly accumulate in the toilet pan and cause a blockage which will then put the individual toilets or trailers out of service.

Where a water supply problem is identified, plumbers can install temporary storage facilities with pumps, by creating a very large cistern or mini 'reservoir' so that loss of pressure does not occur.

Vandalism

Although the facilities are provided by the venue/promoter for use by the general public, it is the latter who, for some obscure reason, take great delight in vandalising the equipment, either by placing toilet rolls down the toilet pan bend, or by jumping on the foul water connections on the outside, thus allowing raw sewage to flow through the venue, contaminating people's skin and clothing and causing absolute havoc to the food vendors along the way. The supplier can reduced the likelihood of this occurring by careful placement of the units, and some basic screening of the susceptible pipe work, etc.

Maintenance

It is absolutely imperative that an on-site maintenance crew is available to both clean and re-stock toilet paper in the toilets, to check them for vandalism damage or ill-treatment in any form and where problems are occurring to bring the on-site plumber to effect repairs. In order to do this, the cleaning crew will require to be in radio contact with the production team and the on-site plumbers who are normally based in a 4 x 4 vehicle along with their tools, spares, repair kit, etc.

Washing Facilities

This is a real problem area at large concerts. In those areas where there is restricted access, e.g. backstage, VIP, hospitality, crew catering, etc, then hot and cold water supplies with soap and towels are not a problem. However, as far as the general public are concerned, any measures put in place to provide running hot water would be abused from the outset. As a consequence, normally only cold water is available or an alcohol based disinfectant 'rub' which is rather unkind to broken skin!

Waste Receptacles

It will be necessary to provide bins, sack holders, or similar, for nappies, feminine hygiene products, etc, so that they are not placed in the toilet pan, and cause subsequent blockages.

Sewage Disposal

The vehicles used will generally range from small lorries to large road tankers; therefore the imposed weight may be a problem, particularly at 'greenfield' sites. It may be necessary to install temporary roadways that will take the loading particularly in soft ground conditions. Alternatively, the sewage may have to be pumped some distance in order that it can be retained in a cesspool, which will then be emptied by a vacuum tanker. All waste will have to be transported by a licensed waste carrier to a licensed waste disposal point.

Staff Facilities

Generally these are of a reasonable standard, but on occasions there may be problems in respect of the facilities used by the food handlers employed in the catering concessions. The disinfectant 'rub' would be acceptable for personal hand washing after using the loo, but may need to be augmented by thorough hand washing on returning to the unit, as it will have a hot and cold water supply available.

Information

Anyone who appears to a concertgoer to resemble event working crew or 'officialdom' will be frequently asked where the toilets are. This is because the signs indicating the location of the toilets and washing facilities for the respective genders are frequently not conspicuous enough. Large, high level signs need to be provided to direct people in the general direction of the toilet accommodation, and as they get closer to it more specific eye-level signage will be needed to direct them to the most suitable facility. In addition, any information leaflets handed out by hospitality staff, the information point, etc, should indicate where the toilets are. Alternatively, the information could be printed on the reverse side of the retained part of the ticket.

Important Issues

- A queue is considered to be a maximum of ten persons at peak times.
- The mean service time is 64 seconds for a male, 75 seconds for a female
- Unit internal/external specification
- Single or mixed gender trailers
- Articulated trailers with ad-hoc fittings with high level access providing low level of privacy
- Freestanding type units - translucent roof/artificial lighting, flushing / recycle, disinfectant 'rub' dispensers
- Latrines – shallow/deep, plastic lined or unlined
- Urinals – 4" half round plastic eaves gutter, canvas back cloth, galvanised steel sections
- Sewage – sewage collection/tank systems
- Sewerage-Mains drainage connections, temporary cesspools, pits
- Layout arrangements to reduce security risks, illegal substance use, ensure privacy
- Temporary or permanent power required for any pumps, artificial lighting in hours of darkness, supply requirements to event promoter
- Janitorial supplies, alcohol based cleaners, soaps (bar, gel, liquid), paper towels (disposal arrangements)
- Supply of feminine hygiene products
- Locations-Queuing areas, parking areas, venue, campsites
- Potential problem regarding insurance cover
- Security – hirer's problem

HEALTH AND SAFETY ASPECTS IN THE LIVE MUSIC INDUSTRY

PART 3
THE HUMAN ELEMENT:
DEALING WITH THE INTERNAL AND
EXTERNAL CUSTOMER

9 CROWD SAFETY PLANNING FOR MAJOR CONCERT EVENTS
Mick Upton

The Background Legislation

The presentation of large-scale open-air concert and festival events is certainly not a new concept, neither is the controversy that appears to surround them. As early as 1972 the 'New Society' publication observed that:

> "Open air pop festivals are inclined to be lumped together in the public mind with political rallies, all-night vigils, demos and protest marches - in fact any large gathering of young people. Pop festivals have been happening for long enough to have established a character of their own" (White, 1972).

White was responding to a popular view held in the early seventies that the growing popularity of what were termed 'pop festivals' presented the threat of the possibility of a major incident that local authorities were not equipped to deal with.

The rise in popularity of outdoor concerts in the sixties had brought to prominence a number of frustrating problems for local authorities responsible for granting a Public Entertainment Licence (PEL). Concerns ranged from unacceptable large-scale disruption to local residents to the risk of a major crowd related incident. At least one local authority sought protection from parliament in order to overcome their fears. The Isle of Wight County Council Act (1971) was introduced following major concert events on the island in 1968 and 1970, the latter attracting an estimated 250,000 people. The Isle of Wight Act places heavy financial burdens on concert organisers in order to finance additional local services. It also restricts the number of persons that can attend an event on the island by stipulating that any event

Difficult working conditions for extracting casualties within a secondary barrier system – Oasis Hnebworth 1995

expected to attract more than 1000 people requires special permission from the local council. The Act has effectively deterred concert promoters from organising major casual concert events on the island since 1971.

Following the successful introduction of local legislation, Jerry Wiggin MP presented the 'Night Assemblies Bill' to the House of Commons in 1971. Wiggin freely acknowledged that sections 4 and 5 of the Isle of Wight Act had prompted his Bill. The Night Assemblies Bill was not intended to ban casual concert events, rather it would introduce strong measures to control them nationally. The Bill was however defeated after a lengthy Commons debate in May 1972 (Hansard 12.5.72). It was possibly this attempt to introduce legislation that prompted White to make his observations the same year.

The point that White was making of course was that major casual concert events required a unique approach to crowd risk assessment that should be separate from planning to deal with crowd disorder. Given the fact that White published his observation two years before the death of a young woman at a David Cassidy concert in London in 1974 and 18 years before a fatal accident at the Donington Monsters of Rock event in which two young men died in 1988 his view would seem to have been well founded. Public disorder, alcohol or drug abuse was not considered to be relevant factors in either of these tragic incidents. In both cases intolerable pressure loads imposed on the victims in a high crowd density situation caused death. These and other similar fatal incidents at concert events abroad suggest that there are forces that can be created by peaceful crowd activity that are perhaps not fully understood by some promoters and the leisure security staff that they regularly employ to supervise crowds.

In order to form a balanced view on crowd safety standards at a casual concert event today a broad international view of crowd related incidents needs to be taken. This would seem necessary in order to establish if a safety culture has become evident since White recorded his observations. The definition of safety culture put forward by Toft and Reynolds (1994) says that:

> "Safety culture can be defined as those sets of norms, roles, beliefs, attitudes and social and technical practices within an organisation which are concerned with minimising the exposure of individuals to conditions considered to be dangerous".

A History of Fatal Crowd Incidents

Through personal research, which explored fatal incidents occurring during the period 1974 - 2003, it was revealed that there have been at least 136 fatal accidents at concerts. Incidents such as fire, where it is known that fire exits were locked, and cases of public disorder or criminal acts were not included in the research on the grounds that the root cause of the incident had been clearly established.

The figures quoted here are not a definitive list, they are merely intended to illustrate the level and type of incidents that have occurred in similar circumstances in countries thousands of miles apart. The list includes both indoor and outdoor venue types, the common link being that the root cause of these fatal incidents has not been fully explained in scientific terms. They have all been regarded

Tower at Glasonbury, 2003.

to have been caused by the crowd itself in the form of panic or irrational behaviour.

Preliminary analysis from primary research data indicated that fatalities occurred in the following circumstances:

34 during ingress
25 at front of stage
13 falls
58 during egress
4 during egress from a public appearance by a group at a shopping mall
2 stage diving

It is interesting to note at this point that more fatal accidents have occurred during pedestrian flow into and out of a venue than in front of a stage. The egress figure of 58 does however require further explanation as 53 of these fatalities occurred at one incident in Belarus in 1999. The circumstances here were that the crowd was exited at the end of an event when a sudden storm caused a large number of people to run for shelter in a nearby subway station and a crowd collapse occurred. It might be argued that as this incident happened at a railway station it should not be included in the analysis. The rationale applied however was that as conditions where railway systems are in close proximity to concert venues are quite common this incident should be included in order to open up the crowd safety debate to include boundaries of responsibility. Similarly, the four deaths at a shopping mall occurred when a crowd of excited young women had attended a promotional appearance by a British pop group, and this type of event adds yet another dimension to the crowd safety debate.

It might be reasonable to speculate that in circumstances where a fatal accident occurs during a period of pedestrian flow the root cause might be a systems failure or venue design fault. Toft and Reynolds (2) have however warned that *"many of the popular ideas regarding the underlying causes of technological disasters are myths"*. A systems failure conclusion might therefore ignore a fundamental issue, which is that of fully understanding the needs of a particular crowd profile during their movement. In other words, we need to question established notions of unit width requirement for pedestrian flow that have long been regarded to be suitable for all crowd demographics and conditions.

If however it is accepted that a systems failure verdict is a reasonable explanation for a fatal incident during a period of pedestrian flow the fact remains that there have been 39 unexplained deaths during an event in countries globally. With the exception of two incidents of stage diving, these incidents fall broadly into two categories: highly excited crowd behaviour in front of a stage (crushing) and, highly excited crowd behaviour in the upper levels of a purpose built venue (falls).

Cultural Attitudes to Safety Management

With the benefit of hindsight it is easy to see that concert events do require a scientific approach to risk identification that is separate to that of other large-scale crowd gatherings. It would also appear that the promotion of concert events has failed to fully embrace a safety culture at international level. Clearly there are safety conscious promoters just as there are safety conscious private security companies but commercialism can outweigh safety at *some* events and the reality is that there has been little change in crowd conditions at outdoor concert events since White published his observations in 1972.

It is clear that there are three key factors that have prevented the full implementation of a safety culture into rock concert promotion. The first, and possibly the most important factor, is that rock 'n' roll originated as an anti establishment ideology that was designed to appeal to youth culture. To try now to introduce 'rules' might possibly appear to a youth audience to be contrary to a fundamental principle of rock ideology, that of complete freedom of

Personal and general security at the Prodigy Knebworth

expression. This freedom of expression naturally includes activities that youth culture enjoys, regardless of the fact that a casual observer might regard these activities to be risky in terms of personal injury to participants. The point here is that youth culture regards these activities to be perfectly normal and they believe that they are in control of risk. As Brian Toft (1996) rightly pointed out in a discussion on risk, when dealing with the actions of people, risk is subjective rather than objective. That is to say that levels of risk exist in the mind of the beholder. Some people will happily indulge in activities that others would not consider. Even crowd members who do not actively take part in these activities accept them as cultural norms, therefore the likelihood that a crowd will accept the introduction of safety rules that might ban or inhibit crowd/artiste bonding seems unlikely. The leisure security industry must therefore adopt a subtle approach to safety management not simply introduce safety 'rules'.

Secondly, it is important to remember that what is now refered to as the *'leisure security industry'* came into being initially to deal specifically with the prevention of damage to theatre seats when audiences wanted to dance to rock 'n' roll music rather than sit and watch a performance. Typical of the media coverage of this new youth attitude was a report in the *Daily Telegraph* at the time, which read:

"Police were called to five cinemas in London and surrounding districts last night to deal with excited young people creating disturbances during the film Rock around the Clock. ... as the tempo grew faster they left their seats to dance in the gangways." (Daily Telegraph 1956)

Venue operators, possibly frightened by this new youth attitude, turned to dance halls for help. Dance halls were very popular at the time and they all employed teams of ex-boxers or wrestlers to keep order. What we now call a 'bouncer mentality' was therefore introduced very early in the development of rock 'n' roll and it was encouraged further when examining fire officers insisted that audiences did not stand and block theatre gangways or stand on seats. A tendency for highly excited pop audiences in the sixties and seventies to invade the stage simply reinforced the view that strong security measures were needed. Consequently, since the emergence of rock 'n' roll in 1955 private security companies have consistently met the diverse problems created by hysterical pop fans, macho rock and anti social punk attitudes head on in the firm belief that 'rules' must be obeyed. For over four decades the leisure security industry has steadfastly maintained a policy of meeting cultural behaviour by reactive methods rather than proactive strategy thereby creating a 'them and us' situation that is proving difficult to overcome. As a crowd management practitioner with over 40 years of experience the writer has long been frustrated by the fact there are no nationally approved training programmes available to those people that wish to study peaceful crowd behaviour in a serious effort to overcome this problem.

A third factor is that it has been my experience that practitioners that conduct crowd management operations and academics that carry out research have consistently failed to come together to produce a common approach to risk analysis for peaceful crowd activity. Academic institutions have traditionally only funded research into the social causes of public disorder or evacuation systems failure. This is possibly due to the fact that crowd related incidents have generally been reported to have been caused by the crowd itself due to panic or irrational action. A panic conclusion is also convenient as it discharges responsibility to the crowd. Brealy (1992) drew attention to this misleading practice when he argued that accident and/or panic conclusions could conceal the fact that crowd management planning was fundamentally flawed and the true cause of an incident might be concealed.

This does not imply there have been deliberate attempts to disguise the

Thrust stage and secondary barrier system and pitch cover for U2 at the Feyenoord Stadium Rotterdam.

truth, rather that inquiry teams have to deal with witness accounts which can vary greatly with regard to what happened. With particular regard to the UK coroners court system, Cellia Wells (1995) has explained that, *"by the Coroners Act 1988 neither the Coroner nor the jury shall express any opinion on any other matter than who the deceased was, how, when and where she came by her death"*. It would appear therefore that a coroner's jury cannot by law express an opinion on the root cause of an incident. In other words in a crushing incident the verdict would be accidental death due to compressive asphyxia. The jury cannot speculate as to how a pressure load was created.

Research data that has been produced by studies of fatal incidents due to systems failure tends to remain on university shelves to be used only for the purpose of student argument or, become the secrets of architects who design permanent venues. On a personal level, I have found a great deal of value in traditional studies of crowds and contemporary theories on risk. In my opinion much of this theory is applicable to concert crowd activity. Sadly however much of this work is written in an academic language that practitioners find very difficult to understand; few people will read a thesis if it requires a dictionary to explain every page. Practitioners of course are equally guilty in so much as they too have their own language which academics might find difficult to understand. A consequence of a failure by practitioners and academics to come together is that the management of peaceful crowd activity has not been established as a social science, consequently no national training programmes are currently available for the private security industry. It has been my experience that the courses that are currently offered by universities seem to focus either on management of a leisure venue or a broad view of crisis management aimed at local authority emergency planning officers. Important as these courses are, in my opinion they do not address the needs of the practitioner planning for a mass crowd gathering at a greenfield site event.

Risk Assessment

An absence of practical national training programs is somewhat puzzling given the fact that every employer has a responsibility under current health and safety legislation to compile a risk assessment for their work activity. In a seminar paper on crowd safety, Graham (1993), explained the principle of risk assessment and he went on to argue that: *"the application to crowd safety may require some thought. However, there should be no difficulty in identifying the significant risks and establishing the relative priority for action"*. The principle of risk assessment is clear in terms of identifying what insurance people often call `pure risks` such as trip hazards or poor ground conditions. I would however take issue with Graham over the issue of identifying the risks associated with human behaviour, as I believe that this matter takes more than *"some thought"* as there are a number of risks that are not immediately obvious. Understanding and dealing with continually changing cultural attitudes actually requires the practitioner to conduct an ongoing research programme in order to deal with new, or in some cases, regurgitated, crowd actions.

A mass crowd at a concert event is very much a psychological crowd. That is to say that crowd attitudes are often influenced for months prior to an event by exposure to subtle media pressure in the form of radio, T.V. video, records, internet, computer games, fan clubs and magazines. Consequently a crowd can display different levels of emotion as they go through the stages of arrival, attendance and departure. They often arrive at an event in a high state of anticipation and excitement. Once the crowd is let into the venue, pressure is maintained on them by presenters and support groups on stage who constantly build excitement levels, often for a period of many hours. Normally a headline act will not appear until it is dark thereby giving maximum effect to lighting and special effects such as pyrotechnics. At the point that an act appears it is often to a high sound level. At the sudden exposure to a combination of high sound level, sophisticated light systems and special effects, a mass of people share the same experience at the same instant, and there is a contagious response that often encourages individuals in the crowd to abandon their natural self restraint. The likelihood in these circumstances is that there will be a massive energy release from the crowd in the form of a dynamic or lateral surge. In this type of situation a crowd will not respond to reason. Pleas to 'move back' or to 'stop pushing' are pointless as the whole crowd is now caught up in a dynamic of their own. None of the individuals within a crowd consider themselves to be the perpetrator of dangerous actions. People are at best simply enjoying themselves or at worst, victims of the actions of others. The crowd as a whole accepts these conditions to be 'normal' even when individuals might be frightened by their situation.

Dangerous Crowd Behaviour

Moshing

Crowd surges are not the only problem that might be experienced. Cultural behaviour at rock concerts can be a major cause for concern. *Moshing* is an American term used to describe what seventies Punk Rock culture called *slam dancing*. Moshing is therefore a dance ritual during which people literally slam into each other, although it appears to be a violent action it is not intended to be. It can nevertheless result in the participants receiving cuts, bruises or more serious injuries such as a broken bones. The act of moshing generally takes place in the *'mosh pit'*. This term is used to describe the general area that moshing takes place and should not be confused with the area in front of stage known as the *primary pit*. A mosh pit can start spontaneously anywhere in the

Crowd surfing Bon Jovi, 2000.

crowd and should therefore be regarded more as an activity and not an actual place. The term moshing is also often used in a broad sense now to refer to a number of other activities.

Crowd Surfing

Crowd Surfing is one of these activities, and it involves crowd members lifting an individual above the crowd so that the person can roll or swim their body over the heads of the crowd. Normally a surfer will move toward the stage with the intention of climbing onto the stage to stage dive. People have been known to actually bring surfboards into a show for the purposes of crowd surfing. There have been numerous injuries recorded as a result of crowd surfing. These injuries have included neck and/or head injuries to people that have been kicked in the head by the surfer, or spinal injuries caused as a result of the surfer falling, or being dropped onto the ground. There is an added danger in that a crowd collapse might then take place onto a fallen surfer causing an intolerable pressure load. There have been serious injuries reported as a result of crowd surfing. For example, Sara Jean Green wrote in the Seattle Times (2002) that the parents of 14-year-old Scott Stone reached an out of court settlement for permanent brain damage which it was claimed was the result of a crowd surfing incident in 1996. Green went on to claim that there had been 1,000 reported injuries from just 15 American concerts in 2001. In America there have also been allegations of sexual assault and even rape on female surfers who have been dragged down and stripped of their clothing by males in the crowd.

Stage Diving

Stage Diving is exactly what the term implies. It is the act of a performer or member of the audience diving from the stage into the crowd. The intention is then that the crowd will support that person above their heads while they crowd surf. Unfortunately there have been at least two fatal accidents due to stage diving. In 1994 a young man died at a club in New York as the result of what appears to have been a stage diving incident. It was alleged that a security man pushed the victim off of the stage, but the security denied the allegation and alleged that the victim was stage diving (Rogers et al 1996).

[For legal reasons, a sentence at the bottom of this page that appeared in earlier editions has been deleted.]

Pogoing

Pogoing is a seventies punk rock dance ritual, during which the crowd jumps up and down in unison, often giving gladiatorial salutes. The activity is still popular with a range of rock culture crowds. While this activity appears to be harmless, pogoing can present a problem at green field sites, particularly where there is a steep gradient toward the stage. After prolonged or heavy rain the field becomes very slippery and a mass of people all jumping up and down in unison can easily cause a dynamic surge similar to a landslide which might result in a crowd collapse.

Skanking

Skanking is a Jamaican term originally used as a term for Reggae dance and then appropriated as a term for slam dancing, or as a prelude to crowd surfing. The term is now more likely to be used to describe a mosh pit activity where a circle forms within a crowd. The crowd then moves in a circular route while they continue to slam into each other. In some respects the circle resembles a North American Indian war dance, or in extreme cases, like a whirlpool. The size and duration of this rotating circle is dependent on the number of people drawn into it. Skanking has been known to cause a crowd collapse which, as has been previously stated, can lead to intolerable pressure loads being imposed on those unfortunate enough to be at the bottom of a pile of bodies.

Taking part in each of the activities described above are considered to be fun by a youth culture that appears to have little regard for their own safety. The crowd manager therefore has then to consider a number of possible accident scenarios when he/she designs an event plan to establish maximum safety conditions.

At this point it is important to differentiate between the terms *crowd management* and *crowd control*. The American pedestrian planner John Fruin (1993) has argued that people often interchange these two terms believing them to be simply two titles for one subject when in fact they are totally separate functions. It has certainly been my experience that few people actually appreciate the difference. Crowd management is defined by Fruin to be the *"systematic planning for, and the supervision of, the orderly movement and assembly of people"*. By Fruin's definition crowd management involves the assessment of people handling capabilities of a space prior to its use. It also includes evaluation of projected levels of occupancy, adequacy of means of ingress and egress, processing procedures such as ticket collection, and expected types of activities and group behaviour. Crowd control is defined by Fruin to be *"the restriction or limitation of group behaviour"*. The United Kingdom Crowd Management Association (UKCMA) has adopted both these definitions in their approach to crowd safety planning.

The Crowd Management Plan

A crowd management plan must demonstrate a high level of knowledge on the issues of crowd management (venue design) and crowd control (cultural behaviour). While crowd control is part of a management plan, it may also occur as a crisis management response, such as a serious problem at the front of stage. In my opinion it is the inability to implement a crisis response strategy that is the weakest link at *some* concert events, particularly in front of a stage. It is important to remember that a response delay to a problem was cited as being a key factor in both the Roskilde and Sydney fatal incidents.

The Use of Technology

Given the fact that we now live in the age of the computer it is perhaps surprising that little new technology is currently being put to use to aid the management of crowds. On the spot crowd safety decisions at most casual concert events are still likely to be by visual observation conducted by supervisors who use radio contact to management and response teams. CCTV is used increasingly at major events but there can be technical problems transmitting CCTV images over a long distance and while the police often use their own sophisticated systems, including helicopter cameras, access to these pictures is often restricted to police officers who may (or may not) pass on information to the supervising security company. By adopting this attitude they (the police) are making an assumption that their officers can correctly interpret the images that they are watching. As police training focuses on reactive crowd control strategies based on their experience of dealing with public disorder rather than proactive management ones, this practice is questionable. In my view an integrated control room would seem to me to be a better system as the crowd manager would be on hand to provide the police observer with an informed opinion.

The use of radio has been common at major events since the seventies. Only the major companies have the capacity to provide the necessary dedicated equipment and train staff in its use however. Those companies that do not have sufficient equipment will hire a radio network system. The risk with this practice is that the system will clash with local mini cabs or other on-site services. I have also experienced an added difficulty when a local authority-licensing officer insisted that all 500 stewards at an event had a radio. I finally convinced him that if all 500 decided to use the network I mighty have to wait up to 2/3 hours to send a message that might be urgent! Clearly communications systems need to be tested well in advance of an event and advice sought where necessary to overcome such issues as poor signal or bleeding into other networks.

Arguably the most positive technological step forward in crowd safety planning in recent years has been the development and use of daylight screens. Initially these screens were limited to use in hours of darkness but design has now advanced to the point where they are very effective in daylight. Screens are now regularly used to create crowd shape and to aid the control of crowd density by transmitting images to all areas of a mass crowd.

It is possible to implant a computer chip into a ticket, which could provide a great deal of information such as arrival and flow rates, but such systems are rarely used at major events. Computer counting systems obviously require on-site data processing equipment and trained staff to evaluate the information received, which would involve a cost factor. The promoter has to decide therefore if the information gained justifies that cost.

Computer measuring systems (CMS) have been available to measure pressure loads created by crowds for some years. Following the Hillsborough football disaster, which claimed 96 lives in 1989, CNN Ltd introduced CMS to provide an indication of the dynamic loads imposed on barriers, fences or walls. A signal is transmitted via sensor pads to a monitor screen(s) where an operator can initiate response action, but the system is not necessarily a cure for front of stage crushing problems.

My own research indicates that a fatal front of stage accident is unlikely to occur as the result of a horizontal load imposed on people positioned directly on the barrier. A fatal crushing accident normally occurs approximately two to three metres away from the barrier. There are perhaps two reasons for this, first, those people directly in front of the barrier are using it to push themselves off in order to gain breathing space, while people behind are likely to be caught up in a dynamic surge. The victim(s) are then caught up in horizontal pressure load from two directions. Second, I would argue that most front of stage fatal accidents are the result of a crowd collapse which then imposes a vertical load on the persons at the bottom of a pile. In which case a pressure reading from the barrier is of limited value. This does not imply that CMS is not a valuable research tool. When used with CCTV to add a visual image a CMS system could provide valuable data that might enable a more scientific approach to FOSB systems design. To the best of my knowledge this type of research into barrier system design has not been tried; a decision on FOSB system type is generally generic.

Barrier Systems

The only common criteria currently used for FOSB systems are that all indoor systems should withstand a 3kN pressure load and outdoor systems should be able to withstand a 5kN pressure load. This stipulation is made to ensure that a FOSB system will not easily collapse thereby giving a pit rescue team valuable time to respond to an incident. It is left for a security company to train a pit team (or not) in the manner that they should respond to any given situation. There is no data available to my knowledge to indicate that a single parallel FOSB system is any less safe that a curved one. Although in my opinion a curved system is better as it can dissipate the load from a dynamic crowd surge and it creates better crowd viewing. The use of multi barrier systems is an option available but once again they should not be regarded as a magic

Roundhay Park Leeds Simple Minds – A pit set up showing pit deck. This would not now be used in concert promotions

panacea that will cure all front of stage problems. Multi systems are of course far more labour intensive, which in turn requires far more trained teams, and there are complications in terms of the need for medical teams to have quick access to people taken over the barrier.

The Pit Team

A pit team is only a small part of the overall team provided by a security company; there are also specialist back stage teams, search teams and security response teams. At a major event it is common to employ 500-600 staff to supervise a crowd. There are possibly only four or five companies in the UK that can provide this level of staff to an event and even these might be hard pressed if they have other work on that day. A tactic that I regularly used was to form a consortium of the best known companies who would then provide a given number of staff to work as an integrated part of the event team. There are three advantages to this system: first each company is supervised by their own managers therefore discipline is maintained; second by using a smaller number from each company the likelihood is that you will avoid casual labour in favour of staff who have attended company training and thirdly, smaller security companies were able to gain valuable experience when given an opportunity to provide a small team to work at a major event. The use of door supervisors should be limited to a security role however. They should not, in my opinion, be used in a crowd control role as door supervisor training differs from that of safety stewards. While door supervisors are licensed they are often employed as freelance individuals and it might be the case that a company discipline procedure is simply not there.

The consortium concept does obviously rely heavily on the fact that all the companies taking part will accept that they are working as members of a bigger team; there can be no company egos. The running of a major event is above all a team effort; it cannot be a one-man show. Over the years I was fortunate to maintain excellent working relationships with all of the major companies in spite of the

The pit, Big Day Out 2002.

fact that we were at all other times, competitors. Of the literally hundreds of events that I have been involved with I cannot remember a single occasion when an individual team did not give me 100% in terms of effort and support. This in itself speaks volumes for the professionalism and commitment of the management people that work in the leisure security industry.

The key to achieving better, and safer, crowd management does however lay in developing training for the role. Such training should be underpinned by a national formula for risk assessment for peaceful crowd activity and standardised risk documentation. To achieve this requires the introduction of a duel system approach to training made up of a study of quantitative measurement (pure risks) and qualitative assessment (active use of a venue).

This approach is explained further in the following models:

Quantitative Measurement Model

This relates to all those issues that can be scientifically measured and specific risk factors formed as a result.

Space: for an agreed capacity and the formation of queue systems. It also dictates crowd density.

Pedestrian flow systems: location and number of gates and lanes required for an agreed flow during ingress, egress and emergency evacuation. Search policy.

Information: provided regarding event entry conditions in all advance forms of advertising. On the day, clear signage to direct people to entry points.

Topography: arena gradient, grass or hard standing areas land drainage.

Engineering: correct type barriers for entry lanes, tolerance of temporary structures, effect of structures on sight lines. Use of daylight screens.

Lighting: for all exit routes and signage.

Communications: dedicated radio network/CCTV/Phones.

Staff: training, specialist team training, level of supervision.

Special effects: use of pyrotechnics, lasers or dry ice.

Medical: dedicated team to current standard of official guidance.

Welfare: separate to medical team able to deal effectively with people who are stranded, lost or need specialised assistance.

ELT: close to main control room, attended by emergency services and local authority officers. Ability to implement a Major Incident Plan.

Crowd Control Systems: suitability of FOSB design and barriers used for pedestrian flow systems.

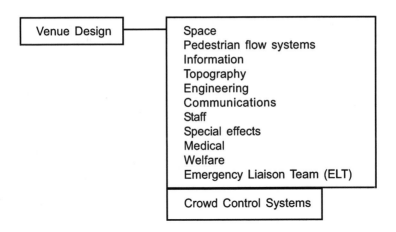

Qualitative Assessment Model

The EVA method requires the crowd manager to research previous incidents and their cause. A low frequency high intensity incident would be one that is rare but where the casualty rate is high, i.e. a fatal accident. A high frequency low intensity incident could be classified as a 'near miss' incident where casualties were low. A possible example would be nu-metal concerts where moshing occurs frequently, resulting in a large number of injuries that were treated on site but victims were not removed to hospital.

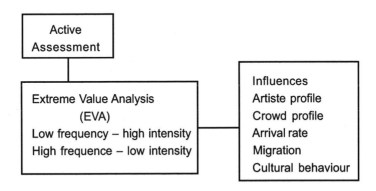

Influences: Factors include weather/alcohol/drugs/ media/web/peer presure
Artiste profile: Will the artiste ontrol or incite cultural behaviour?

Crowd profile: Age range/male/female ratio.

Arrvival rate: Will the crowd queue overnight? Will they arrive en masse by coaches or trains or can we expect the majority of people to arrive by car?

Migration: Will there be a good deal of bulk crowd movement, if so at what time(s)?

Cultural behaviour: Can we expect moshing/surfing/stage diving/pogoing/skanking.

In conclusion I would emphasise that the opinions and models that have been presented in this chapter are very much a personal view and consequently they may differ greatly from other practitioners' opinions. Such is the way of things when a common system for crowd planning and management does not exist.

Mick Upton

Mick Upton has acted as a crowd management consultant at senior level for many events. Just some of these include all Monsters of Rock at Donington, Live Aid, the Moscow Peace Festival, the V.E. Commemoration Hyde Park 1995 and Royal Ascot. He has also served on UK government sponsored Lead Bodies set up to introduce NVQ qualifications for events, door supervisors and V.I.P. protection.

He was the founder, and until January 2000, the Chairman of ShowSec International Limited. Since 1992 – he has been a regular guest lecturer on crowd safety issues at the Cabinet Office Emergency Planning College, Easingwold.

In response to their request, he has submitted study papers to Sir Greville Janner M.P. (European Security Standards), Bruce George M.P. (Standards in the British Security Industry) and the International Security Conference (Security Training Standards). He has also acted as a consultant to Bramshill Police Staff College and devised and delivered training for the U.K. police service, local authorities and foreign agencies. He has also acted as consultant to UK official published guidance on concert event crowd management.

Mick is an I.P.S.A. approved security instructor and a keen supporter of regulation of the private security industry. For his services to the entertainment security industry he is the recipient of a Silver award from the Event Services Association, unprecedented four times winner of the Live Gold Award for crowd management planning, and the recipient of a Police award for designing and delivering training for the Police Service.

In January 2002 he retired from active crowd management planning, at which time he was presented with a Lifetime Achievement Award by the Event Services Association, a Lifetime Contribution to Concert Safety Standards by *Total Production* magazine and a certificate from Mojo Barrier designers acknowledging his outstanding achievements in the field of Crowd Management.

Although retired, Mick is currently involved in a partnership with the University of Buckinghamshire to design, develop and deliver a qualification for crowd management.

10 COMMUNICATIONS STRATEGY
Iain Hill

Introduction

To run any type of event, planning, co-ordination, and the ability to react quickly to unforeseen circumstances are key factors. Event management requires the organisational ability to execute these attributes in an efficient and effective manner. In the event scenario this can be achieved by having a clear and effective communications strategy that allows those managing the event to reach all parties concerned with the running of the event. Central to event planning is the establishment of a communications centre where the rapid transmission and dissemination of information to all those concerned with the event can be focused.

In the running of large-scale events, large crowds of people both access and egress from a site in a short period of time. People also migrate on a festival site in response to a desire to see a particular band, eat, sleep and carry out other functions. As the staging of each event is different the ability to communicate with both the audience and staff can in some cases be the difference between life and death. To be able to spot a potentially dangerous incident in a crowd and to take necessary action to prevent the situation from escalating, or to alert a security officer in time to rescue an audience member from the pit, is essential. Whilst the prompt action of well-trained staff will always be a vital element in safety, without the ability to immediately communicate a situation, the best possible training could be rendered meaningless. Events such as the disaster at the Station Club in West Warwick USA, in February 2003, where the entire audience attempted to leave the venue by a single exit ending in disaster, highlights the need for effective long-term or permanent communications.

This chapter examines the existing literature and legislation on communication strategies. It goes on to focus on recent issues where shortcomings in communication strategies have given rise to an industry debate focusing on communication at events and especially the ability to raise public awareness of how safety issues could and should be improved.

Communications: The Planning Stages

The promoter is the central focus of communication during any event. The promoter is responsible and thus ultimately liable for anything that goes wrong during the period of an event; he or she is directly or indirectly the contracting party to for those contributing to the event. However, in the case of the fixtures and fittings inside a venue or the upkeep of the site, the venue manager or site manager are responsible for the safe presentation and upkeep of the venue or site. The Event Safety Guide (HSE 1999) identifies the two main perspectives in the development of successful communications strategies:

- Inter-professional communication
- Public information and communication

The development of a successful communications strategy must be established during the planning phases. The application process for a licence under the Public Entertainment Licence legislation initiates the communications procedure, it is the statutory responsibility of the local authority to contact all the relevant bodies and attend liasion meetings. At these liaison meetings, one of the factors that is discussed is what can be learned from intelligence gathered from past concert experiences? Such information details characteristics of the events and in particular the behaviour of the crowd that attended these past events. This information is crucial in enabling planning, development and contingency for untypical or potentially dangerous behaviour. In the planning stages the police have a particular role. Owing to the nature of the license application procedure, the Police have the right to object to a licence if they deem that the promotion is unsafe, will attract violent behaviour or if the promoter or the event has caused problems in the past. In 2002 the police were forced to withdraw the licence for the Homelands Festival in Winchester. This decision was based upon the police perception, through intelligence gathered, of the behaviour of the fans that accompanied the So Solid Crew and Oxide & Neutrino. The police felt that a shooting incident at a concert earlier in the year meant that they could not ensure the safety and control of a large audience comprising the bands' followers. The promoters were forced to exclude them from the line-up in order to obtain the licence for the event.

Planning and the Licence

The process of applying for a licence ensures that all parties are aware of the commercial arrangements for the event (important in the case of marketing and publicity so that any specific information can be communicated to the public at an early stage). Written records of these meetings are kept, ensuring that areas of responsibility are clearly defined and communicated to all parties at the earliest possible stage. The establishment of this formal structure of meetings and agendas is designed to establish a chain of correspondence where all parties will automatically be notified should a particular arrangement or set of arrangements change. Safety at any event is dependent upon good design as well as good management; the attention to detail that is elicited by the licence procedure and the preparation of the support documentation ensures that one allows for the other. In this sense, good communication acts as the catalyst that enables robust design to develop into good management. It is crucial that unambiguous language, the avoidance of jargon and the use of universal terminology in:

- naming of specific control points and control workers;
- labelling different types of rendezvous and collection points;
- providing unique reference labels for key locations within and around the venue;
- clear naming for conventions for categories of people involved onsite;
- compatible terminology for assessing risks and grading levels of urgency;
- clear protocols for establishing communication;

is carried out. HSE 1999: 38.

The logic behind this aspect of event planning is important. If verbal communication is key to successful event planning and management, then everyone involved has to be speaking the same language. Visual data is another key concept in the planning of events. A universal site plan showing gridded areas is needed to identify key access routes for vehicles, personnel and the public. If a universal plan is used then if grid co-ordinates are given all those involved with the event will be able to identify what is happening in which area. Restrictions on access at any given point must also be shown. At the planning stage an event organiser may appoint a network co-ordinator to ensure that the reception and dissemination of the vital elements of communication are carried out, with maximum efficiency and effectiveness.

Implementation, development and review as a continuous process is key to a successful communications strategy. Planning for an event is crucial owing to the evolutionary nature of most events, particularly large, outdoor events. Elements change as the planning process progresses and the event grows in complexity. It is vital that any new or additional detail or changes *to* the overall plan are communicated to all the parties concerned with the utmost efficiency and clarity. The myriad of documentation accumulated during the planning process (site plans, safety certificates, insurance policies, and even the minutes of meetings) must be collected and constantly updated. Pages of complex and detailed calculations provided by a stage supplier are of little use to a rigger and stage manager when on the set-up day they need immediate access to the weight that a particular point can bear. Therefore clear instructions to all those working on site must be available.

Frameworks for Efficient Communication

There are many organisation and key personnel involved in an event and the communications framework must allow effective and efficient communication.

- Within each organisation…(and)
- Between different agencies… " involved in the event. HSE 1999: 39.

The establishment of an effective and efficient framework at the planning stage should result in the smooth management of the event. Any organisation or individual needing to respond to an incident on site must be able to be contacted easily and be granted preferential access to the incident concerned. It is crucial that information regarding any incident that may have off-site repercussions is transmitted to the appropriate organisations so that they can plan effective action well in advance.

To illustrate how a successful communications strategy works on site but fails to alert offsite authorities, it is pertinent to observe a recent incident at an indoor concert reported by panel member Chris Urlings of Peter Reiger Konzertbüro, at the Safety Focus Group panel meeting at ILMC 15 in London. The incident occurred when a bomb threat was made during a concert at the Köln Arena in Germany. The capacity crowd of 8000 people was evacuated in 11 minutes, without panic or injury. This would suggest a well implemented major incident strategy. However, once the crowd had left the building, there was no single authority to take charge of crowd dispersal, which left the crowd milling around the outside of the venue with the consequent disruption (and possible danger) to traffic in the local vicinity. Although there was no further incident, if the bomb scare been real the failure to properly disperse the crowd could well have had serious consequences both to the crowd themselves and the ability of the emergency services to tackle it. At such an event it would be assumed that a more centralised communications strategy would be an established feature at indoor arena leading to efficient communication and co-ordination. However, this was not the case.

The indoor license process should indicate a procedure, which enables the venue management to have a perfectly honed communication strategy. This should include the local authorities and the emergency services so that a potential disastrous situation does not occur outside the boundaries of the concert arena. Accumulated past experience and sharing such experience with the local authorities and the police is the best form of planning and perfecting management procedures as monitoring and change are key management tools in event procedure which are constantly in flux.

It is clear from this example that the frameworks for communications had not been established successfully in order to cope with such an incident. Each individual authority had performed their duties effectively: the venue management (in conjunction with the promoter) had evacuated the building in a short space of time and there is no suggestion that the emergency services had been slow to respond to the incident. However, a breakdown in communication between the key organisations involved in the event led to a lack of responsibility for the management of the crowd once they had safely left the building. Alarmingly, a major German promoter related that there were "a significant number" of events where the management had no emergency evacuation procedure.

Communications at the Event

The Incident Control Room

The central focus of communications at any event will be the Incident Control Room. There are a number of factors to take into consideration to ensure that the control centre is able to function effectively and that efficient communications are established and maintained for the duration of the event. If the promoter has appointed a network co-ordinator at the planning stages, they will have informed all the contractors working on the event of the approved radio frequencies. The main parties, the major contractors, the local police, fire and ambulance personnel on duty or on standby at the event will also have been informed. Consultation with the Radio-communications Agency is necessary to ensure clear and efficient radio contact is constantly available. Onsite perimeter tests must be carried out to ensure blanket coverage over the area of the site is reached and that masts and antennae are positioned correctly to achieve such coverage. Ear-defending headsets must be issued to staff where the possibility of background noise would otherwise render the radio handsets useless. The network co-ordinator will need to be aware of the relevant legislation contained in The Health and Safety at Work Act 1974 regarding potential noise levels and working personnel on in the immediate vicinity of the stage. Spare batteries and adequate charging facilities must be provided.

The issue of soundproofing arises, as the Emergency or Event Liasion Team (ELT) needs to be located in a position where it enjoys good visibility around the whole of the site. The positioning of the control room at the centre of the operational aspects of the event means that it must be close to the stage area.

The Use of Radio

Radio as a means of communication is an important means of facilitating operational efficiency for the promoter and for all of the contractors involved in the event. In an emergency it becomes a vital tool for the emergency services and there may well be the need for the emergency services to have command channels at larger outdoor events where a number of different channels are being utilised. The promoter must be able to communicate with off-site emergency services by means of a telephone land-line and this must be kept secure and free at all times. The promoter will also advise any off-site services, particularly transport links, of any unforeseen changes in the schedule. It is no use ordering a series of late trains to run enabling a large crowd to disperse quickly, if the event finishes an hour later than scheduled and those trains have run at the scheduled times.

The quality of the staff using this equipment is also important. Staff must be fully trained and competent and able to use the equipment in an efficient manner. The Event Safety Guide identifies a number of prime concerns in the communications procedures that are used at any event:

- Tight radio discipline with proper use of call signs and contact protocols;
- Making the purpose / function of a message clear (is it a question, warning, request for action, command, prohibition, etc);
- Concise and precise information;
- Cross-checking that messages have been received and interpreted correctly;
- Relaying message content clearly and unambiguously;
- Keeping accurate records of communication activity;
- Keeping accurate logs of decisions and actions. (HSE 1999: 41).

Given the amount and the variety of sub-contractors that are used at any given event, and the fact that they will all have developed separate communications protocols, it is essential that the event organiser introduces a universal procedure for the acknowledgement of messages.

In the event of an incident or an emergency, the need for procedures that ensure the provision of accurate and complete information is acute. Situation reports must be given in a practised format that everyone who has a radio is familiar with, and communication patterns and chains must be logical and universally known. The immediate and essential elements are Identification, Location, Incidents and Requirements, or whom you are, where you are, what has happened and what help you need to deal with it. As the incident develops further information is given in the form of Warnings, Access, Casualties, as well as the establishment of Control Points at the incident and any other relevant information. It is key that all staff involved in potential major incidents meet beforehand to run through universal procedures and that each person involved is furnished with written, easy to follow instructions in case of problems

Models of Communication

The Guide to Safety at Sports Grounds (HMSO, 1997) provides a useful model of how communications at events can be properly implemented. As many large music events take place in sports stadiums, this analysis is wholly relevant to any event organiser, as long as it is understood that the physical conditions at a green-field site may well call for additional physical and structural planning. Essentially the guide states that there are six lines of communication that are needed. "These are:

1. communications between members of the safety management team, from the safety officer to stewards and all other safety personnel
2. communications between the safety management team and all points of entry (including the monitoring of counting systems) and all points of exit
3. communications between the safety management team and the police, other emergency services and medical agencies
4. communications between the safety management team and spectators, inside and outside the ground
5. communications between the safety management team and other members of staff
6. communications between the safety management team and officials in charge of the actual event. "

HMSO 1997: 167

There are inherent differences between indoor events, and those on greenfield sites and those that take place in sports stadia. At a live indoor event and in a stadium there is another layer of management, the venue manager. Although outdoor green field events have a site manager the venue is usually hired without a venue manager. At a large outdoor event, the promoter will be entirely responsible for the organisation of the event and the implementing of communications strategies within the overall running of the show. To this end, he will be bound by the procedures inherent in obtaining a Public Entertainment Licence to satisfy the relevant local authority that all the necessary structures (both physical and managerial) are in place. If the concert or event takes place at an established venue, the licence that governs events at the venue may be granted on an annual basis (a large indoor venue or stadium or a purpose built outdoor arena). This assumes that the management of the venue will have implemented the necessary systems and procedures. A safety certificate or occasional licence may be needed in a stadium which will (theoretically) ensure that the systems and the means of communications conform to the relevant British Standards or Codes of Practice, but existing communications structures and systems will already be in place. A modern stadium will almost certainly have an internal telephone communications system which the staff there will have been trained to use and will be used to having as their main links in many of the lines of communication outlined above.

The touring production personnel who are part of the artiste's entourage, as well as the promoter's production personnel, may well favour the radio set means of communication, partly for the standardisation that it provides in any venue of what may be a long tour. It is vital, however that the *means of communication* that are adopted at a particular venue, are never allowed to block or interfere with the *lines of communication* outlined above. The existence of more management structures in established venues may well have a tendency to complicate communications strategies, unless the appropriate consultation takes place. Whatever the real causes behind the earlier example given of the evacuation of the Köln Arena, it is clear that despite adequate communications with the public *inside* the Arena which allowed for such an impressive evacuation, the system of communication with the public, once they were *outside* the venue had not been properly established.

The Role of the Police

This problem is identified and dealt with specifically in the *Guide to Safety at Sports Grounds* and, although it reflects the greater involvement of a further management tier (that of the police) at many sporting (and in particular football) events, it really emphasises the need for consultation between the parties involved. It must be made clear in the context of a live event that the *Guide to Health and Safety at Sports Grounds* deals with a different scenario to that of the *Event Safety Guide*. In the *Guide to Health and Safety at Sports Grounds* the contextualisation of the audience and performer is viewed differently from that of a live concert and that any advice given from the guide must be done so bearing in mind the inherent differences between these two publications. It must be clarified here that in an event where an established venue is used, the venue manager is responsible for the fixtures and fittings, internal communication links, services and the health and safety of the venue itself. The promoter is responsible for all aspects of the promotion entering the venue. This includes extra communication links and the health and safety of the audience in regards to all the equipment brought into the venue by contractors. This is similar to the greenfield site where the owner or site manager is responsible for the state of the site when hiring it out to promoters.

"if the police are on duty in the control point, there should be a clear, unequivocal understanding of the division of responsibilities between their personnel and the ground's own safety management team. This understanding should be recorded as part of the written statement of intent..."
HMSO, 1997: 169.

From a different perspective, the police cannot and do not want to manage sports and music events. Stadium management and promoters cannot (and do not want to) be responsible for any acts of public disorder (or simple infringements of the law) in the vicinity of a venue that are caused by a crowd that has been attracted to the area (or even the city) by wanting to watch an event, therefore liaison and communication are vital.

The recent (and continuing) debate over the granting of a licence to the Glastonbury Festival provides a high profile public example of issues occurring in the granting of a licence for an event. The first refusal of the licence by the Local Authority (in 2001) was instigated by the local police force. This was the result of the danger to the public safety that arose from large numbers of the people able to gain access to the site without a valid ticket. This was achieved by various means including over, through and under the perimeter fence. The festival was re-established in 2002 by taking the necessary measures to counteract the problem with the necessary financial investment in an 'impenetrable' perimeter fence and effective dual management between

Michael Eavis in conjunction with the Mean Fiddler Organisation. However the application for a licence was again contested in 2003 by local residents from the surrounding towns who claimed that the problem had been transferred to them as frustrated crowds who could no longer gain access to the venue, committed crimes and created congestion in the surrounding area. The ongoing success of the Festival will to a certain degree depend upon the success of the ability of the organisers and the police to persuade people who do not have a valid ticket, not to travel to the area in the hope of gaining entry, and in policing the activities of those who do.

Communicating with the Public

The example of the Glastonbury Festival provides an introduction to the another key area of Communications Strategy, communication with the public. Whatever the conclusions drawn from any analysis of the concert industry, there is an important debate about the need for legislation or regulation designed to *improve* public safety and lead to a decrease in the number of injuries and deaths at concert events. The industry may claim that it can improve safety through self-regulation. However all parties agree that the analysis of the safety factors explicit in the investigations into recent crowd disasters at concerts all point to the ability to be able to communicate rapidly, effectively and efficiently with the public.

Thus the next section will look at the factors involved with communication with the audience and the vital importance that this plays in the success of crowd management strategies and therefore in crowd safety.

The UK's Guide to Safety at Sports Grounds, identifies eight major Means of Communication:

a. radio communications
b. telephone communications (internal and external)
c. public address systems
d. closed circuit television systems (CCTV)
e. scoreboards, information boards and video boards
f. signs
g. written communications (via tickets, signs and printed material)
h. inter-personal communications (HSMO 1999: 168).

The first two elements, radio and telephone communications, are pertinent to the 'internal' means of communication at the organisational and management levels of any event. The remainder are the means of transmitting information to the public, an area which is being seen as increasingly important to the safe management of any crowd, and which is also being seen increasingly as being the root cause of many of the incidents that do occur. The central debate in the concert industry as far as crowd safety is concerned, is to what effect the communication element inherent in crowd management needs to be improved. More specifically, whether the means of improving these should be voluntary or whether they should be subject to enforcement by law.

Public Address Systems

Public address systems have provided a central means of communication with the public. They are particularly effective in enclosed stadia and at sporting events where the noise of the crowd is the only major aural distraction. In such an environment, public address systems will be the primary means of communication with the public, outside of direct personal contact with staff and stewards. Any system employed must to be audible, clear and intelligible and must be able to be heard under normal conditions by all members of the public that are in attendance at the event. There may be the need at larger events to have various systems that are 'zoned', particular with respect to those members of the audience that are inside and outside the perimeter of the premises where the event is being held, be it a stadium or a greenfield site. It must also be made clear here that new technology has enhanced the Public Address system enabling delay techniques that enable all customers to hear the same message at the same instant if needed. However zoning is also important in venues where the action taking place has been compartmentalised. Delay techniques are especially important in an emergency where it may be necessary to impart different information to different sections of the crowd. Conversely, in circumstances where the size and the scale of the event prevent proper zoning by the public address systems, the communications strategy must take into account the dangers that may arise from information 'leaking' into the wrong parts of the audience and creating confusion.

A back-up power supply and the use of back-up loud hailers in the event of a system failure, inspection tests and the existence and use of override facilities are all essential elements in the successful use of a public address system. The technical specifications of the public address systems that are selected for use are governed by the need to adhere to the relevant British and European Standards. In addition to this, the specific technical points that need to be taken into consideration in the installation of a public address system in a stadium are governed by the publication: *Stadium Public Address Systems* published by The Sports Council. A 'Code of Practice' which defines the specifics of the maintenance of the systems and that is specifically designed as a guideline for the approval by these systems by licensing authorities, is also available from the Institute of Sound and Communications Engineers.

The operation of the public address system as a means of communication with the public is every bit as important as its technical quality. The event organiser needs to take into account the following factors:

- The location of the operator and the provision of a separate booth. The question as to whether the public address system should be operated from the Communications Control Point is a contentious one. The operator needs to have a clear view of both the stage and of the public and yet needs to be able to carry out the communication function without the continued distraction of the other activity that is a perpetual feature of the Control Room. In a stadium, there may be the money and the design features available for a separate facility which must then have provision for communications (ideally through a land telephone line) between the two points as well as an unmistakable visual warning for the operator when that communication is about to take place. In a green-field concert environment, it may well prove more practical to effect the separation by means of a (preferably clear and sound-resistant) panel or divider.

- The need for a previously agreed operational policy for the use of an override system in the event of an emergency. At music events, the organisers must balance the correct point at which to cut the noise of the music to make an announcement where a decision to override a band's performance at the wrong time, may give rise to more crowd management problems than it solves.

However, in the case of many large events the control room is behind the stage and the operator has to rely on CCTV footage or at worst auditory stimuli. This question of override and of the interruption of a performance is one of the most contentious of all the contemporary issues in the practice of crowd management at major concerts. It has a direct connection with a related issue, which is that of the role of the artiste in communication with the audience. The artiste has a responsibility not to incite the audience to violence against itself and against others and the property of others. However, this responsibility has to a great extent run counter to the culture of concerts and in particular to some of the more extreme (though no less popular) sub-cultures of popular music. *USA Today* published a survey of concert injuries and deaths which showed an alarming escalation in 1999 to a world-wide total of 19,723 injuries at all concerts and festivals during the year". (*USA Today*, August 8th 2000). The escalation was identified with the growth in popularity of the activities of 'crowd-surfing' and 'moshing'. The example of the tragedy at the Roskilde Festival provides evidence of how very serious this issue had become and the reactions and statements concerning the behaviour of the band in the immediate aftermath give an illustration of how emotive the issue will always be.

Emergency Scenarios

Emergencies provide a special and heightened role for communication with an audience. In an emergency, communication is very often simply the only means by which the organisers (and even the emergency services) can prevent further injury or death. Emergency public announcements can mean the difference between panic in a crowd and the smooth evacuation of a crowd from premises. The timing as much as the content of an announcement in these circumstances, is vitally important. Persuasion time is defined as the period where the audience is made aware of a situation and of the need to evacuate the premises. *The Event Safety Guide* summarised the key points for emergency announcements:

- Early warning / timely information is essential.
- Persuasion time must be added to movement (evacuation) time.
- Clarity and quality of announcement delivery are crucial.
- Consideration should be given to whether an audience will respond better to an empathy figure making certain announcements.
- Live, directive messages relating to the circumstances are more effective than those that are pre-recorded.
- Reasons for messages (the nature of the problems) should be given where possible.
- Key message elements and sequencing should be pre-planned.

St John's Ambulance nerve centre, the National Bowl, Milton Keynes at the Robbie Williams concert.

- Announcements should be reinforced by message displays where possible.
- Sectoring facilities can help public announcements be targeted effectively.
- Positive statements and instructions are preferable to negative ones.
- Key items should be repeated (location of problem, required destination, required route etc).

To ensure safe egress from an event in the case of emergency evacuation a code is perceived essential to alleviate panic, although some recentr research point to the need to inform the audience of the real problem. Through careful planning and the correct use of codes the audience can be oblivious to the danger, whilst all staff are fully aware. This creates confidence in the procedure and alleviates danger. (HSE, 1999: 45)

The Role of the Performer in the Communications Strategy

Youth subcultures have often provided manifestations of behaviour that are totally desirable and acceptable within that culture (widespread and heavy use of drugs, 'pogo dancing', 'crowd-surfing', stage diving and 'moshing'). However many of these appear totally irrational and damaging to themselves and others. Therefore, the question that has to be asked to what extent society needs to regulate and control those activities within the confines of a concert where the participants are (to a large extent) both aware and supportive of the activity itself and of the risks involved?

If this last paragraph appears a convoluted explanation, then the point of phrasing it in this way is to focus on the dilemma that faces the artiste in the concert situation; also, to a lesser extent that which confronts the promoter in terms of how to deal with the audience exhibiting such behaviour. The gradual corporatisation of the music business has distanced the promoters' direct cultural identification with the audience. (This is a generalisation; the 'rave' culture was a recent and important exception to this trend.) The same is not true for the artistes. No matter how successful the artiste becomes, it is very difficult for them to cease to identify and interrelate with the sub-culture that gave rise to their initial popularity. A rock band may become as 'corporate' an entity as the business that nurtures it, but this is unlikely to change its public image. Performing live in front of a large audience creates the only personal interface between the artistes and the audience and it is the control of this interface that is the key to the behaviour of the audience. To what extent do the theatrical qualities that enable performers to 'excite' an audience preclude that performer from playing a rational role in 'controlling' that audience from a health and safety perspective? In another context, does the 'euphoria' that unites a performer with his audience preclude that performer from playing a role in controlling the crowd in order to assure its safety?

The answer to this must in the main is "yes". We have seen how Pearl Jam were exonerated by the investigation into the events at Roskilde, their manager speaking of "the band's devastation over the tragedies that occurred...during their performance" (Kelly Curtis quoted on Dotmusic, 20th July, 2000) and "their long history of attention to fan safety" (ibid.). It is natural that any human would react in a similar way when confronted with such events, but to assign a performer with a responsibility for communicating with the audience on matters of safety other than in the most extreme emergency, is not a viable communications strategy.

In the same way, and given the heightened states of excitement that are the feature of many concert performances, the use of the PA system as a means of communication and the consequent overriding and interruption of that show, needs to be treated as a means of last resort. This 'loss' of a major means of communication with the audience is perhaps the salient difference in crowd management between a sporting and a musical event, irrespective of the physical conditions under which the event is staged.

If the current feeling in the industry is that more has to be done to communicate essential safety information to the public, then what are the means by which this communication should be undertaken? Perhaps by the development of music messaging boards similar to a scoreboard in a soccer stadium where important information is shown on the giant screens when an emergency arises. It is clear that everyone in the audience is focused on the boards and information would thus be relayed effectively and efficiently.

Further Means of Communicating with the Audience

Advance and logistical information is possibly the easiest type of information to convey as it has the active interest and participation of all the members of the audience. Everyone attending will want to know when the event is taking place and what the best way to get there is. Most of the audience will actively seek this information out and the event organiser has many means of ensuring that the arrangements that have been made for the smooth arrival and dispersal of the audience, is properly disseminated. These requirements are part of the licence procedure and the methods are largely complementary with the

Triple screens at Cypress Hill, the National Bowl, Milton Keynes 2003.

marketing process and tied in with traffic planning. Publicity material and tickets are especially helpful. Tickets have the disadvantage of being limited in space as a means of carrying information but are essential in ensuring that each individual accesses the venue through the appropriate entrance. The customer needs the ticket to gain entrance and it is only logical that the ticket gives the information as to where and how. Further advantages of using the ticket as a means of conveying essential safety information is the fact that many fans will view it as a personal souvenir of the event and are therefore likely to study it in detail. Publicity material has more scope for logistical information and maps; web-sites and fan club sites are even more useful for logistical information. Other media such as radio and television has its part to play but its role tends to be limited by cost. Information needs to be attractive; websites and publicity materials would be good vehicles for this but they need to be interactive and carry the correct information in an easily assimiable form.

Route marking and signs are essential to re-enforce and interpret the information that has been disseminated in advance. The signs need to be made in conjunction with the transport authorities (the AA and the RAC play a vital and unheralded role here) and keep the public directed and well orientated. This is particularly helpful in minimising problems with the surrounding neighbourhood of the event.

Notices and information displays giving audiences instructions fulfil the same function in the immediate vicinity of the venue as well as inside the venue itself. A well-informed crowd is more likely to remain focused and well behaved; certainly the converse rings true. A crowd that lacks information is more likely to get angry and frustrated. This is also apparent in crowds where either the gap between artistes is too long or information on the lateness of an act has not been imparted to the audience. This often culminates in bottle throwing or fighting to relieve boredom or tension.

The Psychology of Communicating with the Audience

Maintaining and enhancing the feeling of audience well-being is an essential role of the staff working both within and external to the venue. Stewards that are visible, recognisable and helpful are important in establishing a rapport with the audience. Similarly, well trained, well informed and friendly staff are the best means of transmitting important safety information and minimising any frustration that may occur through lack of knowledge. At the barrier, the relationship is even more important. Staff need to be alert for signs of build up of pressure and must have a rapport with the audience in the vicinity. They must command respect in order to be able to organise the movement away from the pressure build up and they must be able to gain the audience's assistance in removing people in distress that they may not be able to reach.

Staff need to maintain the balance between being perceived by the audience as figures of authority or empathy. Success will depend upon their ability to be both. It must be recognised that there is an inherent need for the training of staff and stewards in all aspects of crowd management, and control as well as the need for further research into areas of crowd psychology that enable and the balance between authority and empathy.

The Use of Video Screens

An important means of disseminating information is the video screen and (in a sports stadium) a scoreboard. The reason for this is that advances in technology have made these both more sophisticated and more accessible. Scoreboards at stadia are capable of carrying a greater variety of and capacity for information and are far more versatile and easy to programme than 25 years ago. The cost of video screens at outdoor events has dropped dramatically concomitant with the ease of access and the number available, and the problems associated with their use in daylight have been overcome. This makes them a fixture at most major events. Both video screens and scoreboards can be used as a means of transmitting important safety information in advance and during an event. If an incident occurs during an event the screen or scoreboard is seen as less of an intrusion in a concert than the extreme measure of overriding the PA system and interrupting the performance itself to make an announcement.

Used as a way of conveying a message to the crowd, it could be a means of dealing with any build-up of crowd pressure before any incident develops into an emergency. It is the newness and the neutrality of the video screen that is so appealing. Any message that is read out over a PA system is often seen as an intrusion by 'authority'. The music has been interrupted as a necessity in getting the message across. With the video screen it is not the same as there is far more scope for a creative and non-intrusive presentation. By non-intrusive it could mean a message, where the presentation (through the use of graphics, for example) is made in terms that the audience readily identifies with. The artiste or performer could also deliver important safety information by the means of pre-recorded video performance. The performer is able to achieve two things by this method. Firstly to be seen as one step removed from the dynamics of the performance on the day. Secondly, to be able to remove themselves from the need to deliver a message within performance, which may detract from the show. From the artiste and management perspective attention should be focused on the immediate needs of the artiste's own performance on the day of the show. An example of this could be where a performer delivers a video message before a show about the dangers of stage diving or crowd surfing and are shown not to condone this behaviour and thus the crowd gets a clear message before the start of the show.

It is this ability to maintain the element of non-intrusion that is the key to the success of screens and scoreboards where the presentation of safety information increases public awareness of key safety issues and thus reduces both injuries and deaths at major concerts. The details of how to make the best use of this medium will inevitably be the subject of much future research and further debate.

The industry has had a rude awakening with the events that unfolded at the Station Club in West Warwick on the 21st February 2003. However there is no doubt in the industry that audiences need to be more aware of the potential dangers they are facing whilst attending an event and of the means that are available to them to avoid these dangers. The recent forum of the Safety Focus Group at the ILMC 15 (March 2003) talked about introducing compulsory "airline style" briefings on crowd safety as a condition of the granting of a licence for an event. The logic is inescapable; it is likely to be far more useful than previous methods. The chances of survival for any individual in a concert audience facing an emergency, providing that they are able to carry out an orderly evacuation of the premises, are far greater than the chance of surviving an aeroplane crash no matter how much you know about the safety procedures.

If safety procedures at live music events are to be improved, communication is a key factor. Event organisers need to be able to contain the effects of crowd behaviour; they need to be able to adapt to the changes that new cultural movements bring. Dangers may change with the customs and the cultures but the causes of injury and death in a crowd remain the same: crushing, asphyxiation and physical trauma. Communicating to a crowd the best ways of avoiding these is the major challenge facing the concert industry.

REFERENCES

HSE (1999) **The Event Safety Guide**. A guide to health, safety and welfare at music and similar events. HSE, London.

HMSO (1999) **Guide to Safety at Sports Grounds**. Fourth edition. HMSO, London

Wertheimer P. (1980) **Crowd Management Report of the Task Force on Crowd Control and Safety**. City of Cincinnati.

HMSO (1989) **The Hillsborough Stadium Disaster. Interim report** HMSO, London.

John J. Fruin, (1993) **The Causes and Prevention of Crowd Disasters**. (Originally presented at the First International Conference of Engineering for Crowd Safety, London).

Anthony DeBarros, (2000) **Concertgoers push injuries to high levels**. Published in USA Today, August 8th, 2000.

Websites
www.dotmusic.com
www.crowdsafe.com
www.glastonburyfestivals.co.uk
www.festivalnews.com
www.ilmc.com

Iain Hill

Iain Hill acted as agent and promoter for Spandau Ballet from 1982-89. Iain Hill Presents also promoted UK and international tours for Sade, Animal Nightlife and Eighth Wonder. In the 1990's Iain Hill Presents turned to artist management and enjoyed international success with Matt Bianco, Sarah Jane Morris and Kym Mazelle. Iain Hill returned to promoting in the UK with 11 sold out shows at the Royal Albert Hall for the Spanish flamenco star, Joaquin Cortes, and continues to promote Joaquin Cortes in the UK as well as introducing new flamenco artists to a world-wide audience. Iain also works as senior lecturer in music industry management at Buckinghamshire Chilterns University College.

11 AN INSIGHT INTO THE WELFARE OF THE AUDIENCE
Penny Mellor

"When a pop festival takes place a population gathers which is equivalent to a good sized village or more often a small town. Those who come will produce many of the symptoms of a more stable population but some will also bring with them a wide variety of personal problems and will also create many more. It is to be expected that many will arrive unprepared for all that occurs; some will be lonely, hungry, cold, ill; some will be broke; some will be compromised; others will wish to retain contact with the outside world to benefit by the experience that the festival brings them and build upon it." *(Department of the Environment Advisory Committee on Pop Festivals (UK), 1973: 81)*

Introduction

Information tent, Knebworth Park, August 2003

This chapter aims to present an overview, pose questions, stimulate discussion and promote further research in a number of areas of event management concerned with audience needs. The term 'further' research is actually rather misleading, as very little research has been carried out in the specific area of audience needs i.e. those beyond the expectation of entertainment and the satisfaction of basic functions by provisions such as toilets, water, food, security and other elements associated with the total experience of an event.

Audiences have not generally been the subject of in-depth study. Crowds have been studied in relation to public order or in emergency situations (Home Office Emergency Planning College, 1992), but studies of 'peaceful' or 'non-confrontational' crowds are much rarer (see Managing Crowds Safely, HSE, 2000). From observations, the exploration of aspects of audience needs and the highlighting of areas where study may fruitfully assist in expanding our understanding of events will be the focus of this chapter. Such exploration will enable services to be provided that are of more effective benefit to the management of safe events.

For nearly 25 years, having worked 'in the field' of outdoor events on a range of greenfield or stadia sites throughout the UK, the author has a wide range of experience from which to draw. In size these events have ranged from a few hundred people on a rough mountainside celebrating 'magic mushrooms', to 50,000 'heavy metal' fans in a purpose-built amphitheatre, and 125,000 people adoring Robbie Williams in the grounds of a stately home. Over the years, while entertainment and production technology have changed, and event management has become more sophisticated, it can be observed that audience needs have remained relatively constant.

It is a statutory requirement in the UK under health and safety legislation to provide for the needs of workers. Performers needs are usually well met without question through the system of riders associated with live artistes. However, the need of the audience has often been a neglected area, given little consideration or budget. This chapter will explore the premise that without adequate and appropriate provisions for their needs, the audience has a more negative experience of events, which has consequences for both safety and event development.

Drinking water, Knebworth Park, August 2003

Why Audiences Have Needs

"It will be readily accepted by most people that personal crises are a fact of life; each person experiences crises and in general deals with them effectively, or at least sufficiently well to carry on with their lives. There are, however, times when a crisis seems so intense and overwhelming to the individual that the usual efforts to deal with it are thwarted and the person cannot carry on". *(Leiba, 1999: 13)*

Audience needs arise from three sets of factors, which are not mutually exclusive. Firstly, audience members may have pre-existing problems or anxieties when they attend an event; secondly, the event can itself give rise to needs due to poor event planning and management, lack of facilities, unreasonable restrictions, sheer size, etc and thirdly, just being a member of a crowd can produce problems.

One question which is often overlooked when planning for events is the fact that people attending events may arrive with pre-existing medical conditions such as asthma, or may suffer physical injuries, accidents or illnesses as a result of attending. However, provisions are usually made in the event management plan to deal with these occurrences. The same cannot, however, be said for non-medical, emotional and psychological problems that people may bring with them. For example, someone may have suffered a bereavement of a family member recently, or failed their exams, or be anxious about a seriously ill relative. These emotions will affect how they feel while at the event.

Considering that "At any one time one adult in six suffers from one or other form of mental illness. In other words mental illnesses are as common as asthma" (Foreword by the Secretary of State for Health, UK National Service Framework for Mental Health, NHS, 1999), it is to be expected that a proportion of the audience could suffer mental illness, depression, or even a serious breakdown whilst at an event. What will happen if there are no services on-site to cope with this? Why does event management sometimes fail in providing support? Is it perhaps because audience needs are not taken seriously? Or because "Mental illness is not well understood. It frightens people and all too often carries a stigma." (NHS, 1999: 1)

No such mitigation is available for distress caused by poor event planning. Lack of facilities, such as no safe place for the care of lost children, causes tremendous anxiety in parents whose child has gone missing. Young people may have missed the last bus home because there was no Information Point to tell them when it was leaving.

People are more likely to be in a relaxed and contented frame of mind if they are effectively managed and the venue is comfortable and pleasant, with adequate facilities, such as toilets, food, drink and information points (HSE, 2000 p17)

Sometimes inappropriate restrictions are imposed on the audience, even for supposed safety reasons, causing distress. For example, at an outdoor stadium event in 1999 the audience were stopped from bringing in plastic bottles of water. A few obscured taps provided drinking water, without cups or containers and some bottled water was on sale inside the arena at highly inflated prices. As it was a very hot day, it resulted in dehydration and anger in the audience, which led to tension and anxiety that could manifest itself in both physical (fainting) and mental (worry) distress.

Many events are attended by young people - often as their first event. They are inexperienced in event attendance, which often leads to a naïve outlook with regard to what they bring, what they expect to find and how to avoid the potential hazards.

There is something almost ritualistic about going to your first music festival or concert; it is considered part of the growing-up process. This experience includes experimenting with social relations, surviving away from parents or guardians without authority figures to control behaviour or make decisions on your behalf. This is a major part of the motivation for attending and part of the thrill. The downside occurs when things go wrong. Young people at their first event have no 'event survival skills' to fall back on. The consequence is a very rapid change from a sense of high excitement to a feeling of deep despair and fear. At this point, young people seek help from more experienced people, to offer support in a 'loco parentis' role. Many things can go wrong, some that might appear trivial in other settings. But at events, these can become overwhelming where clear information with regard to micro environmental factors, including finance, geography and technology are essential to survival.

At weekend events, the noise and vibrancy of the camping experience where a combination of lack of sleep, fatigue, poor eating, exhausting activities and possibly the consumption of intoxicating substances, combine to form a challenging physiological and psychological environment. After several days, the result can be the inability to think clearly, to cope with difficulties, and even, in the extreme, to paranoia.

In the exploration of social psychology and behaviour studies some light can be shed on how people behave both in large crowds and small groups. It is clear that most people attend events in small groups, sharing resources. Becoming separated from the group is one of the most common causes of distress at events. While being in a crowd can cause problems, for example, by increasing the likelihood of separation from your social group, on the other hand, the overall homogeneity of the crowd at an entertainment event may mean that other individuals and groups are prepared to help the isolated individual. However, they may not be able to give sufficient assistance – hence the need for support services.

> "Experience indicates that when persons are generally happy and content, then incidence of accidents and illness decreases. Conversely, when people are angry, upset or depressed, they tend to have more accidents and illnesses. Therefore the medical team should be concerned not only with the elements relating to the operational planning of the medical facility, but also with the planning of the festival as it relates to the overall emotional climate. A negative emotional climate at a festival can create as many problems for the attendees and medical staff as physical hazards can." (Dubin, 1974: 17)

Audience members are not passive beings, attending only to absorb the entertainment. They are there for the total experience of enjoyment and sociability (the 'emotional climate'), as a special occasion above and beyond everyday life experience. The audience expects their needs in this respect to be provided for. If these needs are not satisfied owing to a lack of appropriate services, this will at best lead to individual distress. Cumulatively there are serious implications for crowd management, for compliance with safety procedures and people's attitude towards attendance at future events if such distress is felt on a wider scale.

In addition to the basic requirements of water, food, security and the demand for quality entertainment, what other provisions might the audience need?

Types of Welfare Services Needed at Events

Services are required to prevent, alleviate and assist audience members in distress. They vary depending on audience type, but some basic services are required at all events. The UK Event Safety Guide (Health & Safety Executive, 1999: 135) suggests that the type and level of services be determined by the risk assessment for the event.

Audiences need access to information, advice, support, care, comfort and practical assistance with lost property, a meeting place and message system

Meeting point, Glastonbury festival 2003

for missing people, lost children's area, left luggage/cloakroom, public telephones, banking facilities and perhaps a sanctuary for animals, depending on the event. In the UK, these services are grouped together under the term "welfare". In addition, facilities for people with special needs (disabilities) are considered in this context (Mellor, 1994a). If these basic services are not provided, members of the audience have to exist for the period of the event outside their comfort zones, which may lead to minor or major distress.

Information is especially important and can influence the attitude of the audience to the event:

> "People experiencing difficulties in obtaining information may feel unsatisfied, discontented or even aggressive. It is our belief that people in a contented mood are more likely to comply with instructions. Widespread aggressiveness may also lead to public order problems. (Au, Ryan, Carey, Whalley, 1993: 6-60)

There are serious safety implications if people are not provided with the information they need, as recognised in the Canadian Emergency Preparedness Report where: "Reduction of uncertainty in spectators reduces the tension that can lead to behavioural problems." (Hanna, 1995: p45).

As mentioned earlier in this chapter, most people attend events in a group and can easily become separated from each other, especially in large crowds.

Therefore, a message system and a meeting point are crucial to provide the mechanism whereby people can be reunited. People are often dependent on their companions for food, money, warm clothing, a lift home, and feel stranded and disorientated when they are alone. The placing of such a facility is vital to the welfare strategy.

A lost children's point is essential at all events, even those where children are not expected. No one can take risks with children's safety, so 'screened', competent workers must be available to operate a safe haven for any lost children, or vulnerable young people. Parents who have lost a child are usually distraught, not thinking clearly and need considerable comforting. They have to be easily directed by stewards to the lost children's point.

Lost property is often overlooked but has practical implications if people lose items – they may be stranded, with no money, travel tickets, keys, warm clothes, mobile phones with which to communicate with others outside the concert arena, etc. The potential for losing things can be reduced by having left luggage/cloakroom on site. It can ruin someone's experience of the event if there is nowhere to go and check if their missing property has been found.

The Event Safety Guide (Health & Safety Executive, 1999) and Cabinet Office Emergency Planning College seminar paper (Mellor, 2003) describe in more detail other services that should be considered.

Concerning provisions for people who may be under the influence of drugs, this is rather contentious in the UK, although the situation has improved recently, especially at club or dance events. (See Safer Clubbing, Home Office/London Drug Policy Forum, 2002). Event organisers are in a difficult position in so far as they cannot be seen by the authorities to admit that some audience members may experience drug problems at their event, for fear their licence application would be refused, therefore the provision has been discouraged. If there is a drug service on site, this has been taken to indicate that there is a problem at the event. Additionally, services on site might be a visible 'target' for police observation; therefore, audience members could be reluctant to approach. Drug support is often best provided as part of a mixed welfare team, taking the approach that people are seeking help, no matter what the cause of their problem.

One of the recommendations in Safer Clubbing (Home Office/London Drug Policy Forum, 2002) is for event organisers to produce a drug policy, which provides "the chance to consider carefully all the key issues which affect the safety of their customers who take drugs." It can also "serve as a checklist to ensure all areas of concern are addressed". The policy should help to create a safer physical environment, and outline measures to tackle drug dealing and reduce the harm from drugs.

The Methods of Providing Welfare Services

The provision of a range of services therefore forms an important safety net to help people if things go wrong. The services must be an integral part of the event, incorporated early in the planning stage.

Part of the problem for the event organiser is that they are often unfamiliar with the welfare needs of the audience and the provision of appropriate services. Whilst the type and level of welfare provision should be determined by the risk assessment for the event, there is little practical guidance on how to do this. Risk assessment is not always straightforward, even in well-documented areas, as Turner and Pidgeon argue:

> "The application of risk assessment is rendered particularly problematic when we consider that the concept of risk itself is highly contested. In many circumstances risk assessment will be tricky to conduct, very context-sensitive, and likely to be constructed and interpreted differently by different stakeholders." (Turner, Pidgeon, 1997: 184)

Event organisers are unsure how to assess the level of necessary/acceptable/ desirable provision. Indeed, some event organisers have shown reluctance to consider welfare needs, believing that to provide for them is a sign that they are expecting a troublesome event.

> "As with any gathering, it can be assumed that some people will encounter distressing situations. Organisers need to see that this does not necessarily imply that their event is "bad", but that these situations are almost inevitable and that it is not difficult to make provisions for them." (Mellor, 1994b).

Mobile phone recharge point, T in the Park

Other organisers in the UK are seeing welfare provision more positively, almost as another form of insurance to cover themselves if things do go wrong. Welfare staff may have to do very difficult jobs at the event, such as supporting someone who finds out that a close relative or friend has died or become seriously ill, while they are at the event. The event organiser has a responsibility to ensure that they provide sufficient support for the welfare providers.

The organiser is ultimately responsible for the range, level and quality of welfare services at their events. There are various methods of delivering these services. Firstly, by the event management staff themselves; secondly, as an add-on to other services such as stewards or medical; or thirdly by specialist teams. By what criteria or measurement (other than financial) can an event organiser assess which method would be most appropriate?

The first method is most suitable at small events, where a general combined welfare service is sufficient. It enables direct control of the service, close liaison, information exchange and direct, rapid feedback from the welfare staff to the event organiser if serious problems arise for members of the audience. The disadvantage is that the staff may not have adequate training or expertise in the provision of welfare services. They may also be called upon to deal with event management matters should a crisis occur in the organisation.

The second method of providing welfare as an 'add-on' to another service has the benefit of an integrated approach. Welfare can merge seamlessly into the functions of medical services, for example, by providing rest and recuperation for someone following an accident, or caring for the child of a sick member of the audience. Stewards may often provide an 'outreach' welfare service anyway – directing and giving information to the audience. The disadvantages of the 'add-on' service are the same as when provided by the event management team - i.e. the staff may not have appropriate skills or could be taken away from welfare duties if there is an unexpected demand for the prime service provision.

The third method of welfare service can be provided by a specialist agency set up to provide sympathetic support relevant to the audience. It requires the service provider to be familiar with the characteristics of the audience, their potential needs and to be culturally and ethnically sensitive. There are very few agencies specifically set up to provide welfare services at events as a full-time, permanent activity. The author was co-ordinator of Festival Welfare Services (FWS) a small national voluntary organisation in the UK funded for 19 years by the Home Office to promote welfare provisions at festivals by volunteers. The funding was stopped in 1995 and the agency was unable to survive solely by financial support from event organisers (Mellor, 1995). So far, no other agency has taken on this role, partly because of the resources required and lack of finances to sustain it.

The Management of Welfare Services

Whichever agency provides the welfare services, they need to be carefully managed, as the people who use the service may be vulnerable and their safety needs assuring and protecting. The services must be accessible for anyone, including people with special needs, such as a disability (physical or psychological) and for people from culturally and ethnically diverse backgrounds. This may involve producing information in several languages or having interpreters.

The services can be provided by volunteers, paid staff specially trained for the event, or by professionals from relevant agencies. There may be cost implications in the provision of service, but this should not affect the quality.

Welfare workers need training, regardless of existing skills. Working in an event setting is different from any other. Professionals may have the advantage of expertise in relevant skills, being qualified and employed in these disciplines e.g. as social workers, advice workers, childcare workers, helpers for people with special needs. However, they still require specific preparation and briefing to transfer their skills to the event setting. Some professionals have found it difficult to adjust to the difference between working in a permanent building with considerable resources and a management hierarchy to advise on more complex issues, to working in a field with basic facilities and more flexible working arrangements. Volunteers have the advantage of enthusiasm for event work, but need more training and support for what can be very demanding and distressing work.

Most teams involve people with a range of skills and experiences. Their valuable qualities are flexibility and the ability to reassure someone that they are safe and with people who will do their best to help. The advantage of a team of people with mixed skills is to provide a broad range of welfare help. There may however, be management issues when 'experts' from different disciplines are working together as part of the same team. They may have different work methods e.g. social workers, psychologists, tourist information staff, and need to be able to adopt a common teamwork approach in the event setting.

Event welfare work is usually crisis work – searching for immediate solutions to alleviate distress. Welfare at events cannot provide long-term support. This must be arranged outside the event. This can be difficult and frustrating for workers used to 'case-work' where they would normally follow through an individual's care over a much longer period.

The motivation of workers is very important, particularly the desire to help others in an event *Lost property and left luggage point, T in the Park Festival, 2003* setting – the priority is to want to help, not to be a spectator at the show, as these are often mutually exclusive activities. Recruitment and selection of appropriate staff is important to make sure people enjoy and feel rewarded by the work. But what makes a good welfare helper? Where do helpers come from? What selection criteria are to be used? How can equal opportunity principles be applied to ensure the team composition is appropriate and reflects the event audience? Are there any qualifications available? Who is able to train and brief staff ready for the event and manage the teams on site?

Some parts of welfare provisions are quite specific to the event setting – for example safe systems and procedures have been devised to operate a lost property system or look after lost children. Events have great potential to provide a brilliant setting for training welfare workers, enabling them to learn new or enhance existing skills, including multidisciplinary teamwork and shared learning with colleagues from other services.

The skills of the welfare teams will be invaluable in assisting if a major incident occurs and this contribution should be recognised and incorporated into emergency plans. Welfare workers have the potential to play a significant role in providing information, advice and support, provided this is planned.

The Location and Signposting of Welfare Services

Site planners have to understand the function and requirements of welfare services and incorporate them into site plans and designs so that they are positioned in the most appropriate and effective places. At some event sites the services (such as the meeting point) are identified as necessary, and a suitable and eye-catching structure designed. However, the position is often so out-of-the-way that no one can find it, or if they do, no one uses it because it is too isolated and dark to feel comfortable or safe waiting there. Conversely, some meeting points are at a central crossroad of main tracks across the site. These areas can be busy with flows of people through them that they can be almost impossible to spot anyone if you are waiting there. At one very large event, two identical meeting points (without message facilities) were sited at opposite sides of a crowded site. People who had arranged to meet friends spent much of the afternoon going between these meeting points, getting more irritable as they were unable to locate their friends. Doubling of facilities for large events is not always appropriate.

For an information/welfare point, positioning is crucial to ensure that it is easy to find and accessible for people who are distressed, but also in a quiet enough place where staff can make themselves heard and calm agitated people, without the stress of shouting above loud noises.

The location of welfare services will also be influenced by the position of other services, such as medical services, with whom they will work closely. Welfare services use site radio communications (therefore cannot be in a radio black spot), and a landline telephone, a water supply, toilets, electricity, etc must be provided. The structure housing the welfare area should be on a relatively flat area for positioning tables and chairs and be accessible by wheelchair users.

Facilities should be marked on site plans, and stewards and other site workers informed or apprised of locations. The challenge of exploring a site to discover where things are is part of the excitement of the event experience for the audience, but sufficient pointers must carefully balance this, to lead people easily to where they want to be if the occasion becomes an urgent need.

The positioning of welfare services can be a difficult decision for event planners. Welfare is not an obvious income-generator, unlike a food concession, so competition for positions can cause displacement to inappropriate sites. Obviously, seeking advice of an experienced welfare provider will enable appropriate positioning in relation to the other activities on the site. It is hoped that the increasing understanding by event organisers of the role of welfare in the safety culture will lead to a more thoughtful inclusion within site design.

Just as welfare services should be placed appropriately in the environment, they also need to be planned within the time dimension of the event.

The Timescale for the Provision of Welfare Services During the Event

The question of 'when' relates to the boundary concepts of an event. Just as we can ask 'Where does the event site end?' (Is it outside the arena, outside the car parks, beyond the nearest shuttle bus or public transport access etc?'), we also need to address the question 'when does the event begin and end?' (Is it from when the first people arrive outside the gates until the very last person has left the arena, or the last car has left the carpark?) Demarcating the boundaries of the event is a crucial decision for the event organisers, as it helps to define their sphere of responsibility as well as defining a temporal element.

At many events in the UK a licence is granted for the event, prescribing safety conditions only for the times when the music is performed on the main stage and for the entertainment arena, not the ancillary campsite. The event organiser obviously has responsibilities outside these times and places, but it is usually a matter of negotiation as to where and when these stop.

When addressing audience needs, the provisions for them should, at a minimum, be made available for the total time period that the majority of the public is on site. This usually means from when the site gates open to the public until people have left the immediate area after the show. Welfare services

Wheelchair accessible toilets and washing point on the campsite, WOMAD Festival, 2003

have to be ready to operate when the gates open. In the past, if a management decision has been taken to open the gates early, welfare services have sometimes not been informed of this, causing problems because the teams were not ready. In terms of planning, welfare services need to be given a realistic show opening time and contingency time to be prepared for. Any costs of staffing the services have to be included for the whole period of the event.

From experience it is clear that many of the most difficult welfare problems are encountered by audience members towards the end of the event. People are tired (including staff) and want to go home, but fatigue makes people less able to deal with difficulties or crises. This is exacerbated in the dark, if people are inebriated, cold, hungry and in an unfamiliar location far from where they live. For people who have lost the friends they travelled with, have missed the last bus or can't find their car, the event turns into a nightmare. Without support services, these people will at best leave the event with very negative feelings towards the experience and may become a 'never-going-to-an-event-again' casualty. At worst, young or vulnerable people may be put at risk of serious harm.

The aims of welfare services are to enable distressed audience members to leave the site in safety, feeling more positive about the experience. This may mean advising someone to catch the last bus home, even though they can't find the friends they travelled with. If this is not carried out, there may be audience members left on site when the event has ended. In 1999, during an event, the author had to assist a 16-year-old deaf mute girl on her own who had become separated from her companions and could not find them to travel home with. This sort of experience takes time beyond the official end of the event.

The end of the event has been a neglected aspect of event management, although this is now receiving more attention. There has been an insistence on people leaving the site quickly, which has led to crowding at exits, irritation as drivers queue to leave car parks, people trying to drive before recovering from the effects of alcohol or excitement, potentially leading to more road traffic accidents. Giving people more time and assistance when leaving might help alleviate some of these problems.

However, welfare services cannot remain on site forever, and a decision has to be made to close the service at some point. There may still be audience members requiring longer-term support well past the end of the event. In this case, welfare services have to be able to refer people on to services in the locality. The difficulty with this is that many events are held at weekends when local services have limited resources or access. Advance liaison with local agencies should be established, rather than having to try to do this in the middle of the night from the event site.

Despite these difficulties, the event organiser's responsibilities to the audience have to be incorporated in the risk assessment so that realistic plans can be made.

Areas for Further Development

Much can be done to increase our theoretical understanding of welfare aspects of event management and to improve organisation and planning of them. Some areas for a 'wish-list' that could be explored, given funding and resources, are:

Statistics on welfare needs

Festival Welfare Services originally gathered basic statistics showing the range of welfare problems, age, length of enquiry for different events, although mainly rock festivals and concerts. This could be extended to gather information for a range of event types, to reach a better understanding of appropriate services to meet the needs of different audiences.

Training for event organisers/event staff.

In the context of this paper, this would be around understanding welfare needs specific to events, (welfare risk assessment) and quality criteria for selecting welfare services

Investigate links with other academic areas

For example, from sociology (crowd and group behaviour, communications with the crowd, especially regarding safety messages); psychology (e.g. effects of sleep deprivation/fatigue on decision-making); risk behaviour; crisis theory (how people behave in a crisis and cope with stressful situations).

Connect with social/cultural changes affecting audiences

Organisers obviously already research the type of entertainment that will be popular with the target audience and the changing market. Welfare provision should similarly reflect changes in social/cultural/economic environment e.g. drug use patterns, improved accessibility by people with special needs, multicultural populations, mental health issues.

Technological advances

Event production technology has changed enormously. There is great potential to make better use of this technology by welfare services to assist audience needs. One obvious area is electronic messaging, which offers exciting prospects for using electronic displays to contact members of the audience. Also, computerisation of lost property has been successfully piloted at some events.

Education for (first time) attenders

People seem to be coming to events better prepared. This is partly due to excellent websites being developed with festival information and advice. There is a need to assess the most effective ways to provide this advice – what works to make the first-time concert/festival goer's experience more pleasurable and safer, without spoiling the element of discovery and exploration?

Audience needs is a rich and under-explored territory, full of interesting connections and potential for further study.

Conclusion

It is clear that providing for the needs of the audience is an important, but neglected, aspect of event planning and management. It is an exciting and challenging area for both researchers and event managers. The discussion raises fundamental questions, not least regarding the extent of the event manager's responsibility to the audience. While the Event Safety Guide states that 'The event organiser, whether an individual, collective or local authority, has prime responsibility for protecting the health, safety and welfare of everyone working at, or attending, the event.' (Health & Safety Executive, 1999: 1), it is still unclear quite how to apply this to audience needs. There is no doubt that a better understanding of audience needs will provide an enhanced event safety environment, lead to increased audience satisfaction and the prospect of healthy attendance levels - surely the aim of good event management?

REFERENCES

Au, S.Y.Z., Ryan, M.C., Carey, M.S. (1993) **Key principles in ensuring crowd safety in public venues**. In: Smith, R.A., Dickie, J.F. (eds.) *Engineering for Crowd Safety*, Amsterdam. Elsevier Science Publishers

Au, S.Y.Z., Ryan, M.C., Carey, M.S., Whalley, S.P. (1993) **Managing crowd safety in public venues: a study to generate guidance for venue owners and enforcing authority inspectors**. HSE Contract Research Report No. 53/1993, London: HMSO

Department of the Environment Advisory Committee on Pop Festivals (1973) **Pop Festivals Report and Code of Practice**. London: HMSO

Dubin, G.H. (1974) **Medical care at large gatherings: a manual based on experiences in rock concert medicine.** U.S. Department of Health Education and Welfare

Hanna, J.A. (1995) **Emergency preparedness guidelines for mass, crowd-intensive events.** Emergency Preparedness Canada

Health & Safety Executive (1999) **The event safety guide.** HSG 195. London: HSE Books

Health & Safety Executive (2000) **Managing crowds safely.** HSG 154. Sudbury: HSE Books

Home Office Emergency Planning College (1992) **Lessons learned from crowd-related disasters.** Easingwold Papers No.4, Easingwold: Emergency Planning College

Leiba, T. (1999) *Crisis intervention theory and method.* In: Tomlinson, D., Allen, K. (eds.) *Crisis Services and Hospital Crises: mental health at a turning point.* Aldershot: Ashgate

Mellor, P. (1994a) **Do you have a social conscience?** *Event Organiser,* 4, Summer

Mellor, P. (1994b) **Coping with emotion and distress in crowds.** *Event Organiser,* July, 8.

Mellor, P. (1995) **Which way now for welfare arrangements?** *Event Organiser,* 23, December.

Mellor, P. (2000) **Welfare Arrangements.** Unpublished paper presented at the Safety at Festivals & Mass Gatherings seminar, Cabinet Office Emergency Planning College, Easingwold, 6-8 October 2000.

NHS (1999) **National Service Framework for Mental Health - modern standards and service models.** London: Department of Health

Turner, B.A., Pidgeon, N.F. (1997) **Man-made disasters.** 2nd Edition. Oxford. Butterworth Heinemann

Penny Mellor

Penny Mellor has worked in the UK events industry for nearly 30 years. She was co-ordinator of a charity, Festival Welfare Services, funded by the UK Home Office, for 18 years, working at a wide range of festivals, concerts and outdoor events throughout Britain. She advised event organisers and local authorities on welfare-related aspects of event planning, assessed conditions at and made recommendations for specific events and co-ordinated and trained local welfare agencies and volunteers to provide services on site. She produced publications and guides, such as Organisers' Planning Notes, Security Charter, Welfare Charter and a Survival Guide to Festivals, and has written articles on welfare and outdoor events, promoting the provision of adequate and appropriate services.

Since 1996, she has been a freelance consultant. From 1996-99 she worked on the 'Event Safety Guide' (Guide to Health, Safety & Welfare at Music & Similar Events) with the Health & Safety Executive and a consortium of event industry professional associations. She visited Italy to advise the Italian Promoters Association and government ministers on the production of an Italian event safety guide, and was adviser to the Health & Safety Executive on the revision of their guide 'Managing Crowds Safely' and to the Home Office on the revision of their guidance for drug safety in clubs and at dance events 'Safer Clubbing'. She contributed to the 'Core Cities (local government) Group' development of a model entertainment licence application form and was involved in the event associations' response to government proposals for entertainment licensing reform.

She is presently involved in several projects, including the development of technical and vocational qualifications for the 'entertainment industry' and is working with the International Live Music Conference's Safety Focus Group to develop pan-European event safety guidance. In 2003 she arranged welfare provisions at outdoor concerts and festivals in the UK and has also made research visits to outdoor events in Denmark, Hungary, Spain and Slovakia.

Penny lectures at the Emergency Planning College (Cabinet Office) and on several universities' event management courses. She also runs training workshops on event health, safety and welfare, risk management and crowd management.

In 1995, she received The Event Services Association Award for outstanding contribution to the events industry and in January 2003 received the Total Production 'Unsung Hero' award.

HEALTH AND SAFETY ASPECTS IN THE LIVE MUSIC INDUSTRY

PART 4
CASE STUDY:

This case study is presented as a detailed account of perceived anti-social bahaviour at rock concerts and will of course present contoversial and difficult conclusions. It must be stated that these conclusions stem from the work carried out by Holly Marshall and are in no way indicitive of the consensus of the authors in this book.

Introduction to Case Study

The Introduction to this book mentions the encroachment of a "compensation culture" on the Events Industry and how the investigation into any "accident" at an event will inevitably centre on the need to find the cause and to apportion the blame (and hence the liability) for the consequences of the incident. Compensation has a silent partner in insurance and the economic necessities of increased involvement of the insurance industries will inevitably lead to a tightening of the rules of the game, either through good practice and self-regulation or, in its absence, through legislation.

These are the facts of life for any emerging industry: as a society we no longer question the need to carry insurance in order to drive a motor vehicle, and the need to have passed a test (on both driver and the condition of the vehicle) in order to validate that insurance. The Event Industry is undergoing a similar process. Self-regulation through the Public Entertainment License and the publication of operational procedures such as outlined in The Purple Guide, have done a great deal towards showing maturity in the industry and have prevented the need for interference at a national legislative level. European legislation aimed at the standardisation of working practices is set to have an even greater impact on the touring industry, as it will in any industry where there are a large number of self-employed individuals and small firms. Increased costs for insurance are a major problem that results from this imposed legislation.

The other area that is indicative of a "maturing" industry is in the field of training and education. It can be argued that the Events Industry as we know it was born with the advent of the 1896 Olympic Games in Athens, and major sporting events in purpose-built stadia and arenas have been around for the past hundred years or so. The music based Event Industry is much younger; bands have toured in the United States since the 1930's but the live concert phenomena with amplification and arena size audiences is a product of the Rock and Roll era that dates from the mid 1950's. Given that this new industry spent a large part of its nascent period as a "counter-culture", the reality is that it has a business history of not much more than 30 years. Yet in that time the industry has grown exponentially both in terms of its economic value and the technological advances that have been brought to it. Education and even training that is not gained through work experience, is a relatively new introduction. This book is designed to help fill the gap in educational literature that is directly relevant to the concert industry: it is a textbook written for those working in the industry and students participating in events-related programmes of study at schools, universities and colleges by experts who have worked in the industry and are still active in it.

When the task of compiling the book was in full flow, it was felt that there was a need to find some means to draw attention to the growing role of education in the industry. The problem was how best to go about this. Last summer, the authors were marking a dissertation submitted by a third-year student who had chosen a specific (and polemical) area of crowd management, that of perceived anti-social behaviour. There was never any doubt as to the academic quality of the work (it received the best mark ever awarded by the Faculty for a student dissertation). What became increasingly apparent, however, was the fact that the project itself had a direct relevance to the attemped achievement of the book: to bring a contemporary academic analysis to a topical issue in the industry, that of crowd management. It does this in a way that gives a unique perspective as Holly Marshall the author writes from the perspective of both a producer and consumer. What is more, in an area of crowd management that deals with issues that are as controversial as 'moshing' and 'crowd surfing', Holly achieves a balanced and considered debate having thoroughly researched the existing literature on the subject and combined it with her own observations and those of industry professionals.

The project is printed in its original format and with only the most necessary editing. As such it stands out from the other chapters in its length, which results from the inclusion of the academic underpinning necessary for the completion of such a project. This is justified by the fact that it illustrates the processes of education and research that are part of an academic institution, in this case one that dedicates part of its resources to teaching courses that are specifically designed for the music industry. This chapter is a fine example of what can be achieved in this field.

12 PERCEIVED ANTI-SOCIAL BEHAVIOUR AT ROCK CONCERTS: A Detailed Study

Holly Marshall

Introduction

The main focus of any audience participant in a live music event is one of enjoyment. To the audience member the event commences when the event is communicated by the promoter through a media outlet. This may take the form of a music magazine, SMS text, the Internet, word of mouth or a secondary outlet from friends who have communicated the event. The temporal element connected to an event can last for many years as the substance of the artiste or the event itself may be iterated on many occasions in an almost folkloric reverence.

Therefore there are several key concepts which govern the delivery of discourse surrounding the event. The first is how the band performed at the event. The second is how well the event was managed, although this may be measured in terms of how easy it was to obtain alcohol or how clean the toilets were. Thirdly, how safe the event was which will often be described in terms of where the participant stood during the event, or how easy or difficult it was to gain access to the site. The first two are arbitrary measures that are inconsequential to the enjoyment of the event as the performance of the artiste is not usual measured by how close the performance is to a CD of the artiste but by more emotive measures including what was said between tracks, how the artiste engaged with the audience and what the light show was like.

The management of the event is measured in the audience experience of what they could add as value to their experience, what free gifts were available and how cheap the beer and merchandising were. The third element of safety is of paramount importance to the audience member because if they feel threatened or unsafe the event experience becomes tainted and could either end in tragedy or in a refusal by the audience member to go to further events.

At a concert the audience stands facing the stage and exerts a force on the barrier parallel to the stage. At various times during the event the audience pushes forward trying to be closer to the action. The music event is an inherently dangerous place; medial, lateral and circular motion takes place, people crowd surf, some where possible stage dive and others push in all directions, destabilising the mass of people. In this study the effect of movement in the mosh pit on those attending concerts will be identified, observed and analysed. The genre of music to be analysed is rock in its many parallel and sub genres.

Collins (2002) and Hamm (1995) described Rock as a style of pop music with a heavy beat. Unlike many musical genres, such as manufactured pop, middle-of-the-road (MOR) and R'n'B, which are mostly consumed in a 'second-hand' circumstance (i.e. consumption via visual or audio media), rock is noted for its association with the 'first-hand' consumption in a live context. Live rock is commonly associated with a plethora of social practices and traditions. As expressed by Hansen & Hansen (1999), Hargreaves & North (2000) and Longhurst (1995) these include the physical appearance of the artiste and audience; signs and codes used as communication between artiste and audience; and behaviour of the audience as a group. Concentrating on the latter, this research project is based generally upon the traditional audience behaviour displayed at live rock concerts.

The actions of group behaviour performed within the audience at live rock concerts are often perceived as 'anti-social' by non-participants, such as concert promoters, security team members and the concert attendees' parents. The

actions do, however, represent a highly important tradition and culture, which has grown and developed to become a significant component of today's live rock industry. These acts of cultural behaviour have been defined by many previous researchers, such as Ambrose (2001: 3) and Upton [n.d.], and include 'stage diving', 'crowd surfing' and 'moshing' (refer to appedix A definition of terms)

Unfortunately, due to its apparently aggressive and dangerous nature, this cultural activity has become the source of blame for serious injuries and fatalities caused at past rock concerts, such as at Roskilde 2000 and

Girl being helped from the pit, Metallica 2001.

at Big Day Out 2001 (Dotmusic, 2002 and Crowdsafe, 2001). In relation to these incidents, many promoters (i.e. Michael Eavis, Glastonbury Festival and Stuart Galbraith, Clearchannel) and venues such as Birmingham Academy and The National Bowl have chosen to take actions with a view to reducing the likelihood of further tragedies occurring. To alleviate the likelihood of further tragedies behavioural policies have been created that prohibits the aforementioned cultural activity. As a result of this action, the enforcers involved have been perceived to undermine the importance of cultural activity. Consequently this has caused an eruption of outrage amongst both members of the rock audience and artistes, across the globe, protesting that an important component adds to the performance, atmosphere and total experience of rock concerts, and has been removed without any consultation.

Many industry officials and anti-moshing representatives argue that the perceived anti-social act of moshing is merely a fad, and that by prohibiting it, live rock music consumers will eventually accept this notion and develop an alternative method by which to consume rock concerts. This argument, however, was highlighted as being merely an opinion for when the term 'moshing' was entered into the Yahoo Internet search engine, 28,400 results were produced, showing that this cultural activity is a highly developed and recognised concept. Moshing is a form of dancing, indulged in by live rock concert consumers, just as line dancing is performed by Western music consumers. By attempting to prohibit this cultural activity, the industry is effectively attempting to prohibit a socio-cultural act of tradition.

Previous research has been conducted, illustrating both the positive and negative aspects of the cultural activity, as valued by concert attendees, artistes, promoters, venue representatives and concerned bodies alike (Ambrose, 2001 and Crowdsafe, 2002). Research has also presented insights into how and why individuals act differently when in a crowd, and how this is important to social behavioural traditions (Hargreaves & North, 2000 and Haralambos & Holborn, 1995). Past research has also been conducted into the methods of crowd management that can be undertaken in order to control audience behaviour at sports and similar events (Frosdick & Walley, 1997 and Crowd Dynamics, 2002). Very little research, however, has attempted to find a solution to effectively control a rock concert audience, without causing the demise of the aforementioned cultural activity indulged in by live rock concert consumers. In the few instances where specialised controls have been devised, the actual practice of such measures has been minimal, localised to specific concerts, and generally overlooked by the industry as a whole.

As an alternative to simply ignoring this issue altogether and allowing the dangerous activity to be conducted in an unmodified environment, or by following the assumed easiest alternative by prohibiting the cultural activity at rock concerts altogether (as many promoters and venues have previously practised and continue to do so), this research project offers an important revised addition to previous research by shedding new light on the issue. In essence, it will seek to find a modified method (or series of methods) by which the audience members participating in such acts of perceived anti-social behaviour can be protected from serious injury, without eliminating the element of traditional behaviour from rock concerts altogether. By finding a practical solution to this problem, which can then become an industry standard practise at live rock concerts worldwide, all parties concerned with the promotion and attendance of rock concerts will benefit. Concert attendees will be permitted to resume their traditionally practised behavioural acts that socially represent an important culture, and concert practitioners will be rid of the legal concern of personal injury and fatality occurring within the audience, previously caused due to lax and improper, non-specialised safety practices.

A Review of Literature

The live performance of rock, as expressed by Shuker (1994: 206), is essentially physical. The raw, highly energetic sounds of punk rock in the mid-seventies drove rock concert attendees to express their aggression, individualism and profound lack of connection to other forms of music at the time, through a form of dance, referred to in the present as 'moshing' (Ambrose, 2001: 1, & Malavenda, 1995). The ritualised and furious physical display combines real violence with displays of emotion and...

"...induces euphoric displays of affection and hostility between its usually male participants". (Ambrose, 2001: 1)

The frantic displays of energy expressed by these rock concert attendees are still practised at live rock concerts worldwide, having become a highly significant component of the 'Total Experience' of attending a rock concert, as perceived by many performers and audience members alike. Participation in this cultural activity is purely voluntary, and is never indulged in by the entire audience at once. As defined by Ambrose (2001: 2) and Malavenda (1995), the activities indulged in by many rock concert attendees, commonly perceived by onlookers and outsiders as acts of anti-social behaviour, collectively referred to as 'moshing', include 'moshing'; 'crowd surfing'; 'stage diving'; 'slam dancing'; 'skanking'; and 'pogoing' (refer to Appendix A for definition of terms). Such activities are usually undertaken in a semi-circular space directly in front of the stage, described universally as the 'moshpit'. Barron (1994) noted that:

"… a concert without a mosh pit today is basically a historical anachronism".

Ambrose (2001: 3) maintained that, to the outsider (i.e. anyone unfamiliar with the internal psychology attached to such activities) these cultural activities appear to be out of control, terrifying and highly dangerous – guaranteed to create scores of casualties. There exists, however, a highly structured sense of community within the environment. (Ambrose, 2001: 3)

"Moshing generally is a considerate sport, though. Most moshers protect, watch out for and support fellows pit dogs (moshpit participants). If one goes down, the crowd backs away and assists the individual." (Malavenda, 1995)

Ambrose (2001: 5) maintained that the acquirement of minor injuries such as bruises, broken noses and ankle sprains as a result of participating in this cultural activity, is inevitable. It is often the very presence of these risks that drives the individuals to participate, further providing them with a sense of belonging, fraternity and harmony. A consistent message maintained by participants, Ambrose (2001: 5) detailed is 'If you don't want to get injured, don't go into the pit'.

"Concerts are about pleasure, the assertion of the values of the music, and solidarity in a community of companionship". (Shuker, 1994: 207)

Crowd Management Strategies (2002) maintained that, to date, the rock concert industry has done nothing to establish specialised safety guidelines for the cultural activities performed by audience members at rock concerts. As a result of this, past fatalities and serious injuries sustained at rock concerts have been wrongfully attributed to the effects of this cultural activity, due to its perceived aggressive, dangerous and anti-social nature. Dotmusic (2000) stated that, during Denmark's Roskilde rock festival in 2000, nine concert attendees were crushed to death as a result of a serious crowd surge.

"It's believed that this hectic form of dancing could have contributed towards the death of the nine people at the Danish festival during Pearl Jam's set." (Dotmusic, 2000)

The following year, BBC (2001) reported the death of a sixteen-year-old girl at Sydney's Big Day Out festival, due to a crowd of 70,000 surging forward towards the stage. In recent light of these tragic events, along with many other serious injuries reportedly sustained at rock concerts, concert promoters worldwide have been issuing moshpit prohibition regulations in a naïve attempt to prevent future repetitions of these incidents. In reply to an email querying their behavioural policy regarding this cultural activity, a representative of the National Bowl at Milton Keynes stated:

'Moshing' is strictly prohibited at the Milton Keynes Bowl. … Any person who is found to be 'MOSHING' or 'CROWD SURFING' will be ejected from the venue". (rw@gaming-international.com, November 2002)

Prohibiting the cultural activity at rock concerts, however, possesses highly complicated implications, which ultimately affect the macro-environmental factors surrounding the concert promotion. Concert attendees may become dissuaded from attending a particular performance or venue due to the restrictions, which causes financial loss implications to the promoter, venue and to the artiste. Groups of like-minded people will no longer be able to enjoy the same 'Total Experience' associated with attending rock concerts, causing social implications, as they will have to develop new means by which to express their enjoyment of the concert experience. This may in turn lead to legal implications, as the prevention of partaking in certain activities, which is normally commonplace to certain social groups, commonly leads to rebellious behaviour. Kemp (2000: 156) reported an incident whereby a rock concert audience was prohibited from 'stage diving'. This consequently caused a strong negative reaction by audience members, resulting in physical and verbal abuse targeted at the security, crew and staff in the moshpit. "This incident proved that trying to stop these antics was more dangerous than allowing it to continue." (Kemp, 2000: 156)

Security dealing with an incident, Metallica 2001.

On 6 July 2001, Crowd Management Strategies published a list dating 1990-2001, displaying every concert safety related death caused due to lax or improper concert crowd management (Refer to www.crowddynamics.com/main/crowddisasters.html). Of the two hundred and nineteen victims listed, only ten persons were reported to have died as a result or part-result of 'moshing'. The majority of deaths shown were caused due to crowd crushes, suggesting that the prohibition of this cultural activity does not pose a viable solution to the preventing the occurrence of fatalities at rock concerts. Instead, adequate and specialised safety planning techniques and strategies are the real solution to creating safe environments at rock concerts.

The purpose of this research project is to discover a solution to this strongly debated issue. Simply prohibiting the cultural activity alone clearly does not pose a viable solution to preventing future tragedies from occurring within rock concert audiences. Not only does this prohibition fail to address the need for effective, specialised crowd management, it also denies concert attendees the choice to participate in this highly developed, meaningful, united cultural activity.

"Should moshing be banned because it's too dangerous? No. Should it be regulated and made safe? Maybe, in the best of all possible worlds, it should be." (Ambrose, 2001: 229)

The unique addition of this project to existing knowledge, which has failed to fully recognise and tackle this issue, will attempt to uncover specialised safety devices and regulations, which can potentially be put into practice at rock concerts worldwide, as a matter of legal requirement (or at the least, by strong recommendation). The crowd management guidelines will both accommodate perceived anti-social behaviour at rock concerts, and create a safer environment for the audience.

In order to gain a fuller understanding of the reasons and concepts surrounding the cultural activity indulged in by audience members at rock concerts, and thus to analyse how this activity may become successfully accommodated, managed and controlled, it was necessary to interpret these actions from sociological and psychological perspectives.

Ralph Linton, cited by Haralambos & Holborn (1995: 3), defined the culture of society as the way in which its members collect, learn, share and transmit ideas and habits.

"Without a shared culture, members of society would be unable to communicate and co-operate, and confusion and disorder would result." (Haralambos & Holborn, 1995: 3)

Haralambos & Holborn (1995: 12) ascertained that shared values which define what is important, worthwhile and worth striving for by a particular culture, are the key to integrated social cultures. They form the basis for social unity or solidarity, as individuals often identify and feel kinship with those who share the same values as themselves. As action is meaningful to those involved, an understanding of people's actions requires an interpretation of the meanings people give to their activities.

Crozier (2000: 67) maintained that the enjoyment of music, particularly in a live context, is essentially a social experience. The action of dancing (which the cultural activity is ultimately defined as) portrays a...

"... reciprocal relationship where music influences, and is influenced by, social behaviour". (Crozier, 2000: 67)

Crozier (2000: 67) further explained that dance is governed by the values and norms that have evolved over time, and that conformity to these rules is essential for the activity of dancing to continue. Davidson (2000: 219) noted that audiences, which are comprised of individuals who have generally never previously met, uniting to experience a single performance, also function as a group. The individuals comprising this group have a tendency of acting in a unified manner, which can lead to both pro and anti-social behaviour.

Crozier (2000: 73) cited a report by Hansen & Hansen (1991) which stated that social identity adopted by supporters of rock music is often evident...

"...by the violent and 'bizarre' gestures and behaviour that are often exhibited at rock concerts". (Crozier, 2000: 73)

Crozier (2000: 73) also cited a statement made by Singer *et al* (1993) which suggested that rock is associated with...

"...challenging styles of dress, rebellious behaviour, and delinquency". (Crozier, 2000: 73)

Both studies highlight the fact that the cultural activity indulged in by many rock concert audience members are generally perceived as acts of anti-social behaviour by non-participants.

Bilton *et al* (1996: 621) suggested that the individual's choices concerning which goals to pursue and which actions to undertake are...

"...decisively influenced by the wider social context of norms and values in the society". (Bilton *et al,* 1996: 621)

Social behaviour is monitored by conscious thought, which operates through symbols learnt in a social context. Members of particular social groups create perceptions and expectations of each other, designing appropriate patterns of action in a certain situation. At a rock concert, for example, audience members would expect each other to either stand back and watch the performance, or participate in the previously mentioned cultural activity.

Haralambos & Holborn (1995: 5) maintained that the ways in which members of a particular society behave are dictated and defined by their culture. As these definitions vary from society to society, considerable misunderstanding between different members of different societies can be generated. Haralambos & Holborn (1995: 892) noted that the members of different social groups often interpret actions with differing, sometimes conflicting meanings. The members of the social group who comprise the audience at a rock concert, who choose to partake in such previously outlined cultural activity, interpret this activity as an act of cultural conformity and as a form of interaction with the music, the performers and with each other, i.e. pro-social behaviour. The members of other social groups, such as concert promoters or venue representatives, however, often portray a conflicting interpretation of the audience members' actions, describing their behaviour as dangerous, aggressive and anti-social. Michael Eavis, organiser of Glastonbury Festival, told The Observer newspaper:

"Mosh pitting is one of the most dangerous aspects of putting on a festival and clearly we try to stop that kind of behaviour". (Dotmusic: 2002)

Rogers *et al* (1995: 162), however, maintained that onlookers of such perceived aggressive behaviour...

"...cannot afford to assume that they understand the aggression of another by simply viewing aggressive acts as outsiders".

Like aggression, Smith & Bond (1998: 91) noted that culture also mediates the format of helpfulness, pro-social behaviour and the...

"...willingness to help one another in situations where some distress or difficulty has arisen". (Smith & Bond, 1998: 90)

Alongside the acts of perceived anti-social behaviour and aggression that are performed by consenting audience members at rock concerts, is a sense of untidiness, well being and compassion. Ambrose (2001: 3-4) described this notion as a form of 'Moshpit Etiquette';

"... a common law shared by those who take the moshpit seriously, ... people look out for one another and react instantly when they see something going wrong". (Ambrose, 2002: 3-4)

Waters (1994: 3) maintained that event organisers must understand the targeted audience by learning the content of satisfaction they obtain from attending the venue, event, or activity. Grainger-Jones (1999: 120) expressed that customers posses certain expectations when attending an event, and become angered when conditions are otherwise than expected. Leisure provision, Waters (1994: 4) explained, is concerned with meeting people's needs – providing them with their anticipated experience. The cultural activity participated in by audience members at rock concerts worldwide, is not simply an act of aggressive behaviour, but is culturally significant and highly important to rock concert audience members and performers alike. The activity *alone* does not present a significant threat to the personal welfare of its participants, as has previously been assumed, but specialised crowd management practices do need to be introduced at rock concerts to properly protect moshpit participants and the audience as a whole.

As Frosdick (1998: 202) quoted from the Crowd Safety Guidance of the Health & Safety Executive (1996):

"…ensuring crowd safety is a basic responsibility of venue managers, owners and operators".

Bodwin *et al* identified that the assembly of large numbers of people will inevitably lead to hazards; these however, they will vary according to the nature of the event. It is therefore vital to create specialised crowd management strategies, which pay particular attention to the crowd psychology and dynamics portrayed at the specific nature of the event.

Crowd Dynamics [n.d.] maintained that the initial task in controlling a crowd disturbance is to isolate those creating the disturbance from those not actively involved. HSE (1999: 50) recommended that, at large events, it is potentially effective to subdivide the audience by employing the use of barriers to reduce the effects of crowd sway and surge. In light of the recent tragic events sustained at 2000's Roskilde festival and 2001's Big Day Out festival, a fresh attempt to control crowd behaviour was devised and brought into practice at the 2002 Big Day Out festival in Sydney, Australia. The device employed the use of a 'D-barrier' system surrounding the moshpit, which was used to isolate the area from the rest of the crowd and to monitor its entry and exit points (Refer to Appendix B for diagram). Roadogz (2002) expressed the opinion that the device was a great success, effectively localising an identified crowd surge, which occurred during System Of A Down's set, within the 'D-barrier' area. The barrier system also prevented the outward expansion of the moshpit, which also could potentially have caused a catastrophic crowd surge. Malavenda (1995) also suggested the employment of a specialised 'T-barrier' system, which employs the use of a double barrier that extends out into the middle of the crowd. This then allows the security team safe access to the middle of the moshpit area to monitor the audience. The system, Malavenda (1995) maintained also physically separates the audience into two smaller, more manageable groups so that any identified incident that requires immediate attention can be accessed and dealt with more quickly and easily.

The Department of Culture, Media and Sport (1997: 119) recommended the use of a continuous crush barrier configuration for areas of standing accommodation. This type of barrier configuration, used at a large rock concert would significantly reduce the effects of a crowd surge by localising that surge to a smaller, more manageable area. The Department of Culture, Media and Sport (1997: 88) further provided specifications for the horizontal imposed loads for such crush barriers. Because many outdoor rock concerts are held in fields where viewing areas are located on sloping ground, such specifications and crowd management methods could potentially be applied effectively to this type of event.

Kraus & Curtis (1990: 365) maintained that there should be a regular, consistent approach to providing all recreation participants with an adequate understanding of the inherent risks involved:

"They must be helped to understand the nature of the risks that are involved, unsafe acts and their consequences, and hazards to be avoided." (Kraus & Curtis, 1990: 365)

Crowd Dynamics [n.d.] also expressed the need for efficient communication between event organisers and crowd members as it is essential to achieve the best possible control and to maintain goodwill among audience members.

"People tend to be more understanding and co-operative when they know why." (Torkildsen, 1999: 386)

Both issues, as suggested by Kraus & Curtis (1990: 365) and Grainger-Jones (1999: 121) can be achieved by posting advice and rules, including the reasons for why such rules have been enforced, in noticeable positions surrounding the moshpit area. Regular public announcements regarding regulations, their reasons for implementation, and advice to moshpit participants concerning their safety and welfare may also be provided. This would effectively create a promotion of safety and a real understanding of the dangers inherent in the environment.

HSE (1999: 50) maintained that the careful positioning of stewards, employment of CCTV and/or the provision of raised platforms will enable the monitoring of audiences for signs of distress, crushing, sway and surge. If existing and/or potential hazards can be detected early on, the necessary course of action to be taken can be deployed with immediate effect and minimal disruption to the performance and audience as a whole will occur. In practice, however, the use of CCTV and raised platforms has yet to be efficiently employed at the vast majority of rock concerts, possibly due to the inherent costs. Security personnel are employed as a matter of course to monitor and control the section of the moshpit immediately in front of the stage, by operating from behind the front of stage barrier. This type of crowd monitoring, however, neglects to attend the most dangerous, central section of the moshpit, where injuries can potentially be sustained and remain unnoticed. This neglect has consequently led to avoidable concert tragedies in the past, which will continue to occur until effective crowd monitoring is established.

Goodwin [n.d.] noted that there is currently no mandatory or legal requirement to train security staff for specific moshpit management. The fact is that the security teams hired at rock concerts have little knowledge of, and…

"…little sympathy for the culture of rock gigs or their pits". (Ambrose: 2001, 85)

Having been trained in "martial arts and the criminal drug underworld", these professional security teams tend to regard rock concert attendees as moronic, and often refuse to act when informed about incidents that require attention. Ambrose, (2001: 85) and Warne (1997: 191) further expressed the importance of sensitivity towards crowd psychology in understanding crowd behaviour. Moshpit security teams therefore require specialised training in rock concert audience psychology and dynamics, and how to deal with the specialised needs presented by audiences at this specific type of event.

HSE (1999: 50) and Malavenda (1995) maintained the need for emergency contingency planning at rock concerts. Effective leisure management, according to Torkildsen (1999: 386) requires the ability to make emergency decisions in crisis situations, which require clear, quick and precise thinking and decisions. If crowd problems cannot be eliminated at the time of their occurrence, the necessity to end the performance immediately should become a legal requirement. BBC (2002) argued that the tragedy which occurred at the Big Day Out festival in 2001 could have been prevented if the promoters had taken light of such guidelines:

"Michalik's death could have been prevented if the promoters had stopped the show … security staff 'just stood back and did nothing … they did not appear to recognise the signs that people were distressed and needed to be removed'." (BBC, 2002)

Prior to the performance of any concert, a single authoritative figure should be appointed with sole responsibility concerning the decision to end the performance, should a serious situation arise. This would effectively eradicate any misunderstanding or uncertainty regarding such action, consequently reducing the possibility of a tragic occurrence.

Crowd Management Strategies (2002), in an attempt to initiate the process of creating specialised rock concert planning, produced a list of techniques which, if implemented, could potentially help to prevent the occurrence of death and injury within rock concert audiences. The list, titled 'Mosher Friendly Guidelines' included the following recommendations:

- Isolate the moshpit from the general audience and limit its capacity
- Ban alcohol, cigarettes and certain types of clothing and accessories in the moshpit
- Provide stationary special first-aid assistance near the moshpit
- Restrict moshing to those aged eighteen years and above
- Ban stage diving and crowd surfing
- Provide specially trained security
- Provide padding on the floor and all on hard surfaces, e.g. barriers
- Provide moshpit safety announcements in advance and during shows
- Gain assistance from performers in managing the moshpit

In recognition of the latter recommendation, Shuker (1994: 213) noted that audience members perceive performers in an iconic perspective and are therefore more likely to respect, understandingly, a performer's wishes, and comply with their requests. By adopting compliance from performing artistes as a matter of course at rock concerts, the management of the cultural activity indulged in by audience members will be made much easier. Assistance from performers can be employed to calm crowd mentalities, issue behavioural policies, monitor the audience, and to halt the performance if perceived necessary. Malavenda (1995), who further supported this notion, suggested making such compliance by performers with assisting crowd management a contractual agreement.

The fact that the live music industry needs desperately to develop crowd management strategies and safety regulations specifically designed for rock concerts, which also accommodate the cultural activity of 'moshing', is evident. Although many basic guidelines and suggestions have been produced to elevate the problems (detailed above), the actual employment of these guidelines within the industry is, at present, minimal and generally ignored. It is inevitable that planning a rock concert in the future, by taking heed of necessary safety precautions and strategies, will require a great deal more advance preparation and care, more staff working the event, more energy and commitment, and more money for security, staff and equipment. If, however, the problem is not tackled with serious commitment, the live rock industry as a whole will suffer, and tragedies will continue to occur.

Methods Utilised in the Study

The purpose of this investigation was to discover how the cultural audience activity of 'moshing', often perceived as anti-social behaviour by non-participants (such as the concert promoter), could become more safely accommodated at rock concerts. Primary research collection targeted rock concert attendees and rock concert practitioners (promoters, venue managers, stage managers, etc.) to discover their views in regards to various topics, which were deemed necessary to analyse and appraise, in order to create an effective and valid investigation.

The investigation had two main aims: firstly to discover the nature of a rock concert audience's psychology and dynamics; and secondly to recognise and understand the management of crowd control at rock concerts, discovering methods by which concert audience environments can be made more safe. The investigation adopted both quantitative and qualitative research approaches in order to generate both a descriptive and numerically supported study. Although the articulation of the two research paradigms often proves difficult, it was perceived that a combination of approaches was needed to create a fully implemented and accurate research approach.

Quantitative research was employed in order to create an accurate sample of views held by concert attendees and therefore an accurate reflection of the views held by the population of this social group as a whole.

"The logic of quantitative sampling is that the researcher analyses the data collected from the sample, but wishes in the end to make statements about the whole target population, from which the sample is drawn." (Punch, 1998: 105)

As Silverman (2000: 2) suggested, quantitative research objectively reports reality. This scientific, representative approach enabled the collection of facts and the study of the relationship of these facts with each other via cross-tabulation. It was then possible to draw valid conclusions and make reasonable decisions based upon the analysis. If, however, a qualitative approach had been adopted to research crowd perceptions, this would have generated a limited and highly opinionated response, consequently not reflecting the perceptions and dynamics of this social group as a whole.

Qualitative research was employed to gain a more intimate acquaintance with the perceptions, motivations and opinions of a select few individuals. By employing the use of qualitative research, it was possible to generate a more in-depth understanding of the views regarding this topic, held by concert promoters, venue mangers, stage managers and other concert practitioners. As Bell (1996: 6) explained, the adoption of a qualitative perspective is concerned with understanding the individual's perceptions of the subject.

"(Qualitative research is) concerned with how the social world is interpreted, understood, experienced or produced. ... (It is) based on methods of data generation which are flexible and sensitive to the social context in which data are produced. ... (It involves) understandings of complexity, detail and context. Qualitative research aims to produce rounded understandings on the basis of rich, contextual, and detailed data." (Mason, 1996: 4)

Quantitative research collection, which is based on numbers and statistics, was not used in this instancee as it would have generated a response which was limited in knowledge. The use of qualitative research for this purpose therefore generated a more detailed and descriptive response and an intimate understanding of the knowledge held by industry officials.

To enable the conductance of quantitative research, a questionnaire was constructed, targeting rock concert attendees (page 216). A correlational survey, which as Punch (1998: 78) explained, seeks a wide range of information, and the different pieces of which are studied individually where variables are not involved, would have been an inappropriate method of data collection for this particular research investigation. Instead a questionnaire was developed as is seeks information, which includes...

"...measures of attitudes, values, opinions or beliefs." (Punch, 1998: 103)

This research method posed the most efficient and effective way by which to uncover a significant sample of the range of views held by those occupying this social group, which may reflect the population of this group as a whole.

"...surveys aim to describe or explain the characteristics or opinions of a population through the use of a representative sample." (May, 1998: 82)

The questionnaire was distributed to individuals who regularly attend rock concerts, with a response rate of one hundred persons. The use of questionnaires, as opposed to interviews, enabled the collection of relevant information without having to employ the aid of an interviewer. The simple question and answer format is thus much more time efficient in generating a large response.

The majority of questionnaires were distributed and collected at a live rock concert staged at The White Horse live music venue in High Wycombe,

Buckinghamshire on January 17th 2003, where individual concert attendees were requested to participate, prior to the evening's performance. The remaining questionnaires were distributed among students of Buckinghamshire Chilterns University College, cinema attendees at the UCI screens in High Wycombe, Buckinghamshire, and to email respondents worldwide who requested copies of the questionnaire in response to various messages posted on different Internet website 'message boards' (such as www.worldwidepunk.com and www.tjs-newport.demon.co.uk).

The questionnaire featured twelve questions in total: ten open-ended and two closed-ended, which were specific and condensed enough to enable the collection of all relevant information required by the study, in a quick-to-complete format. The questions in closed-ended form were employed to create a format that was easy to read and understand, and quick and simple to answer, making it more appealing for candidates to participate.

"The 'fixed-alternative' question provides respondents with a selection of answers, … from which they have to make the choice which best reflects their answer to the question." (Ackroyd & Hughes, 1992: 105)

Due to the answers having already been categorised by the questions, it was then quick and easy to interpret and categorise the answers, entering the resultant data into a graphical format so that it may be easily read.

The closed-ended questions, asking respondents to provide a description of their conceived perceptions (i.e. questions one and four), provided candidates with a variety of answers from which to choose, including a generalisation of every possible perception conceivable. This enabled the researcher to categorise the answers quickly and easily. If, however, an open-ended question format had been used in this instance, the interpretation and categorisation of answers would have proven much more difficult and time-consuming.

The two open-ended questions were employed to generate a more personal, specific and accurate response from candidates. Question twelve in particular, allowed respondents to express their opinions, experiences and beliefs, an account of which a closed-ended question could not have achieved.

"The 'open-ended' item allows respondents the freedom to provide an answer in whatever form they choose." (Ackroyd & Hughes, 1992: 106)

- Question one *"What is your perception of moshpits at live rock concerts?"* aimed to discover how rock concert attendees regard this cultural activity. Although the question limited replies to a choice of eleven responses, it enabled an accurate reflection of pre-conceived opinions, which may be positive, negative, both or neither.

- Question two *"How important to you is being able to mosh at a rock concert?"* was a vital addition to the justification of conducting of this investigation. It aimed to enhance the hypothesis, which states that this cultural activity is regarded as a highly important component to the experience of rock concert attendance (refer to Introduction and Literature Review).
- Question three *"Have you ever encountered regulations that prohibit moshing at rock concerts?"* aimed to create an impression of how widespread the precautionary method of prohibiting this cultural activity is being practised, as opposed to introducing safety methods that can accommodate it.
- Question four asked respondents to describe their reaction when faced with the prohibition of this cultural activity. The aim of this question was to discover whether the majority of candidates were in favour or against this idea, and whether or not they would resort to taking action, such as rebellion or leaving the concert, in order to emphasise their displeasure. The replies to this question would therefore highlight the apparent effectiveness of this method.
- Question five *"Have you ever been badly injured in a moshpit?"* was intended to highlight the extent to which such environments pose a threat of danger to their participants, therefore supporting the apparent need to introduce safety methods to protect participants.
- Questions six and seven asked those who replied *"Yes"* to question five, whether or not they had become dissuaded from continuing to participate in the cultural activity, and if so, for how long. The questions aimed to discover whether a sustained serious injury would have a long or short-term effect upon the willingness to participate in the cultural activity, and when compared to the answers given to question one, if such an injury had also affected the particpants' perceptions of the activity.
- Question eight aimed to discover the level of respondents' support regarding previously devised and practised safety and security methods for rock concerts, and whether or not they thought such devices would form a valuable addition to concert safety. The importance of gaining concert attendees' response to this topic was supported by the fact that such devices are ultimately devised to promote *their* safety.
- Questions nine *"Have you ever encountered any of these, or similar*

safety devices for moshpits?" and ten *"If yes, what was the device(s)?"* aimed to discover the extent to which the industry has already adopted safety methods to protect moshpit participants, and therefore, which devices are more popularly used or disregarded.

- Question eleven *"Did the device(s) appear to work effectively?"* aimed to discover the level of validity and efficiency of such methods, as perceived by those whom the methods were designed to protect, therefore indicating whether or not these methods pose a valuable addition to the solution of this problem.

- Question twelve aimed to create an opportunity to collect further ideas concerning possible methods of safety and security promotion, that would otherwise have been neglected from the research. The question also offered candidates an opportunity to expand on previous responses or make comments that they felt to be relevant to the subject.

To enable the conductance of qualitative research, an interview schedule was constructed, targeting promoters, venue managers, stage managers and other rock concert practitioners (See page 225). The interview format was employed because, as Punch (1998: 150) indicated, it formed the most efficient method by which to access people's perceptions and the meanings and definitions they give to situations and constructions of reality.

"Interviews yield rich insights into people's experiences, opinions, aspirations, attitudes and feelings." (May, 1999: 109)

The use of a case study was not employed for the purpose of qualitative data research, as this approach would be unable to formulate a guide to answering the research question. As Punch (1998: 150) maintained, the basic principal of adopting a case study is to study in detail a single case (or a small number of cases), the objective being to create an in-depth understanding of that case. This investigation has already considered previous cases in relation to concert safety (i.e. the tragedies of Roskilde 2000 and Big Day Out 2001 and the safety methods deployed by Big Day Out 2002, Crowd Management Strategies (2002), etc), therefore using such cases as a starting point for further investigation. The simplest and most accurate method by which to answer the questions under investigation was to ask directly those who represent the crowd and concert management for their knowledge and perceptions. The adoption of a case study would have also generated a biased result based upon the researcher's individual capacity of knowledge, experience, opinions and observations.

Another qualitative research approach discarded by this investigation was the method of observation.

"...participant observation ... requires researchers to involve themselves in the lives of those being studied – looking, listening, recording, and so on." (Ackroyd & Hughes, 1992: 127)

Although this research method would have generated a highly accurate result, given the restraints of time placed upon the conductance of this research project, the approach would have proven to be too time-consuming.

The concept of documentary analysis is a further form of qualitative data research that was not adopted by this particular investigation. As Mason (1996: 71) described, documentary sources can include already existing documents and specifically generated documents. Such documents can be text based, such as: Acts of Parliament, insurance policies, diaries, and shopping lists or non-text-based, such as: photographs, film, television, drawings, and pictures. This type of data collection was deemed inappropriate to this particular investigation, as the primary aim was to generate 'real' facts by interfacing directly with concerned parties, rather than attempting to interpret facts from documentary sources. This type of analysis would also have required more time and skill than was readily available.

The open-ended question structure of the interview schedule posed the most efficient and effective method of data collection to enable the compilation of perceptions, opinions and new ideas held by industry practitioners. It was then possible to compare and contrast the responses given by different candidates, referring directly back to the research title "How can perceived anti-social behaviour be accommodated at rock concerts?"

Different questions were adopted by the interview, compared to those employed by the questionnaire, as the aim of the interview was different from that of the questionnaire (i.e. to discover the knowledge, experience and perspectives from a management point of view). It was important to investigate the perceptions held by both the crowd and the management of rock concerts, so that a solution to accommodating both crowd dynamics and crowd management at rock concerts might be found.

The interview was conducted using two different methods. The question schedule was distributed via email to various live music venues, promoters and industry officials following the acquirement of email addresses from The White Book, the Music Week Directory and from some of the websites accessed during the conductance of secondary data research. This distribution method generated twelve responses from different authorities (refer to Results). The interview was also conducted via face-to-face meetings, employing the aid of a Dictaphone, with: Pernilla Holl – Venue Manager of London's Highbury Garage on January 23rd 2003 at 1600hours; Brian Wheeler – Venue Manager of London's Electric Ballroom in Camden on January 30th 2003 at 1600hours; and with Josh – Stage Manager of London's Brixton Academy on February 6th 2003 at 1300hours. The face-to-face meeting format also allowed for the request of further elaboration on responses, enabling the accumulation of in-depth information.

The interview schedule featured nine questions that were tailored so as not to be persuasive in generating an expected response.

- Question one *"What is your perception of moshpits at live rock concerts?"* aimed to discover the nature of opinion concerning the cultural activity as perceived by industry officials. This enabled the comparison and contrast of given responses with each other, and also with the responses given by rock concert attendees to question one of the questionnaire.

- Question two *"Have you ever considered or practised the prohibition of moshing at live rock concerts?"* aimed to discover the density of such a prohibition and for what reasons the enforcers give to justify doing this. It was then possible to compare and contrast the answers to this question to the answers given to questions one and four of the interview and to question three of the questionnaire.

- Question three *"If you have ever prohibited moshing at live rock concerts, how successfully was it conducted?"* aimed to discover how industry officials perceive the audience's reaction to the prohibition of this cultural activity. The answers to this question were then compared and contrasted to the answers given to question four of the questionnaire.

- Question four aimed to collate an insight into the general perceptions held by industry officials regarding the safe accommodation of the audience's cultural activity at rock concerts, indicting the level of seriousness such persons devote to the needs of concert attendees. It was then possible to compare and contrast the answers generated from this question to the answers given to question eight of the questionnaire.

- Question five *"Have you ever considered/practised the use of such regulations/devices? If so, please describe."* aimed to discover the degree to which venues are already employing measures, which are not actually required in order to obtain a Public Entertainment Licence, that create a safer environment for concert attendees. By comparing the responses to this question to the answers given in response to questions nine and ten of the questionnaire, it was possible to estimate the level of commitment that the industry is already devoting to the needs of audience members.

- Questions six and seven asked how successful the conductance of previously and currently practised methods had been, and how the audience had appeared to react in conjunction with the application of these methods. When assessed and then compared and contrasted to the answers given in response to question eleven of the questionnaire, it was possible to detect the extent to which such methods pose a viable solution to the question of how the cultural activity can become more safely accommodated at rock concerts.
- Question eight provided a vital opportunity by which to collate further ideas, otherwise neglected by the question schedule, that could potentially be practised in conjunction with creating a safer rock concert environment.
- Question nine asked interviewees if they wished to make any further comments concerning the subject. This provided a chance for further elaboration on previous answers, or to discover important, related information that would otherwise not have been provided in response to the questions asked previously.

When all primary research had been completed, it was then possible to analyse the quantitative data using mode and cross-tabulations as this method of data analysis formed the best method by which to discuss the type of data collated. The methods of data analysis used in relation to the qualitative data collected were comparison and abstraction, due to the nature and type of the data. It was then possible to compare and abstract the data collected from the quantitative research with that of the qualitative research and with the secondary research presented within the literature review.

Results of the Study

Questionnaire
The questionnaire used in conjunction with this study is included in the text and then the results shown.

Questionnaire targeted at rock concert attendees

Please answer the following questions truthfully.

1.   What is your perception of moshpits at live rock concerts?
Please tick <u>any</u> that apply.

(a)	Positive	(b)	Negative
(i)	Vital	(v)	Dangerous
(ii)	Fun	(vi)	Antisocial
(iii)	Exciting	(vii)	Intimidating
(iv)	Sociable	(viii)	Should be banned
(c) Neither (Indifferent)			

2.   How important to you is being able to mosh at a rock concert?
Please tick the <u>one</u> that applies.

(a)	Vital	(c)	Preferable
(b)	Important	(d)	Not at all important

3.   Some venues and promoters are introducing regulations that prohibit moshing at rock concerts. Have you ever encountered such regulations?
Please tick the <u>one</u> that applies.

(a) Yes		(b) No

4.   If yes, what was your reaction? If not, what would your reaction be?
Please tick <u>any</u> that apply.

(a)	Against	(b)	Supportive
(i)	Anger	(vi)	Understanding
(ii)	Rebellion	(vii)	Relief
(iii)	Illegal action (e.g. rioting)	(viii)	Pleased
(iv)	Wouldn't attend concert	(ix)	Indifference (doesn't affect
(v)	Left concert		you)

5.   Have you ever been badly injured in a moshpit (i.e. worse than bruises and sprains)?
Please tick the <u>one</u> that applies.

(a) Yes   (b) No

6.   If yes, did this dissuade you from continuing to mosh?
Please tick the <u>one</u> that applies.

(a) Yes   (b) No

7.   If yes, for how long?
Please tick the <u>one</u> that applies.

(a) Minutes   (d) Months
(b) Days   (e) Years
(c) Weeks   (f) Forever

8.   In order to prevent the prohibition of moshpits, but also protect the welfare of moshpit participants, some solutions are being devised and practised at live rock concerts as a solution to this issue. Do you think that any of the following devices could provide an acceptable alternative to the prohibition of moshpits? Please tick <u>any</u> that apply.

(a)   Padded flooring and barriers..
(b)   Properly trained moshpit security team (not just front of stage)..............
(c)   Segregation system, separating moshpit from the
        rest of the audience ....
(d)   CCTV monitoring the moshpit, surveying potential hazards..............
(e)   Limit moshpit capacities (i.e. no. of people in the given space)..............
(f)   Banning alcohol and cigarettes in the moshpit................................
(g)   Banning bags, spikes and other potential harm-causing items in the
        moshpit..
(h)   Banning stage diving...
(i)   Banning crowd surfing..
(j)   Assistance from performers in managing moshpits...........................
(k)   Providing special ventilation and drinking fountains for moshers.............

(l)   Banning certain clothing and accessories in the moshpit (e.g. chains)........

(m)   Restricting moshing to those 18 years of age and older..................….…....

(n)   Providing special first-aid assistance near the moshpit at all times...........

(o)   None of these...

9.   Have you ever encountered any of these, or similar safety devices for moshpits at rock concerts that you previously have attended?

Please tick the <u>one</u> that applies.

(a)   Yes   (b) No

10.   If yes, what was the device? Please describe.

11.   If yes, did the device(s) appear to work effectively?

Please tick the <u>one</u> that applies.

(a) Yes   (b) No

12.   Do you have any ideas for other possible methods that can be introduced at rock concerts to protect both the audience and the culture of moshing? Do you wish to make any further comments regarding the subject?

The results obtained from the questionnaire targeted at rock concert attendees have been presented by employing the use of tables, bar graphs and pie charts as these methods of data presentation create a clear and concise document.

Figure 1.1 presents the results collated from question one of the questionnaire, which asked candidates to affirm any of the given descriptions that applied to their perception of the cultural activity. As it can be observed, the majority of responses reflect a generally positive perception of the activity as 74% described it as "Fun", 56% described it as "Exciting", just 22% described it as "Dangerous" and only 1% believed that it "Should be banned".

Figure 1.2 (Appendix C) provides a summary of the results displayed in Figure 1.1, showing that 61% of respondents perceive the cultural activity as positive, 7% have negative perceptions, 30% perceive the activity as portraying both positive and negative attributes, and 2% neither regard it as positive or negative.

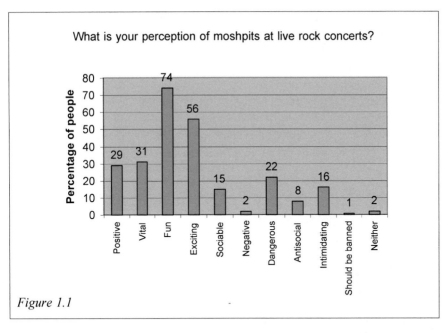

Figure 1.1

Figure 2 presents the results collated from question two of the questionnaire. In summary, 72% of all respondents answered that they would ideally like to be able to participate in the activity (i.e. they answered "Vital", "Important" or "Preferable") and 28% replied that the ability to participate is "Not at all important" to them.

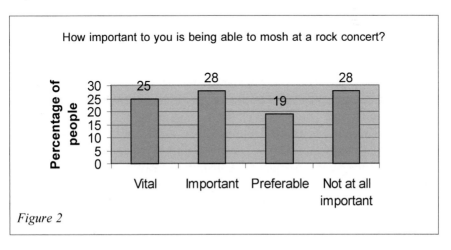

Figure 2

Figure 3 (Refer to Appendix C) presents the results obtained from question three of the questionnaire. As the pie chart indicates, 27% of all respondents replied that they had previously attended a rock concert where the cultural activity had been prohibited and 73% replied that they had not.

Figure 4 presents the results derived from question four of the questionnaire. As presented by the bar graph, 42% replied that they would/did experience an emotion of "Anger"; 27% replied that they would/did experience a feeling of "Understanding"; 35% replied that they would/did act rebelliously; and 13% replied that they would be prepared to/did resort to illegal action (e.g. rioting).

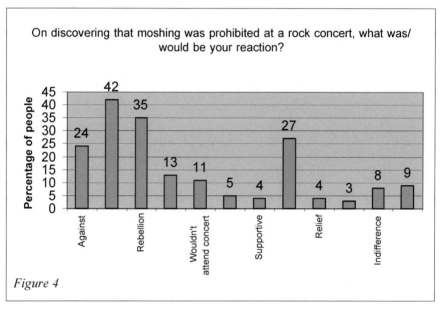

Figure 4

Figure 5 (Refer to Appendix C) presents the results obtained from question five of the questionnaire. As the graph indicates, 37% of all respondents replied that they had previously been seriously injured in a moshpit and 63% replied that they had not.

Figure 6 (Refer to Appendix C) presents the results derived from question six of the questionnaire. Of those who answered "Yes" to question five, 46% replied that their injury had dissuaded them from continuing to participate in the cultural activity and 54% replied that it had not.

Figure 7 presents the results collated from question seven of the questionnaire. Of those who answered "Yes" to question six, 47% replied that they had become dissuaded from participating for a period of "Minutes" only; 5.9% replied that they had become dissuaded from participating for "Months"; and 29.4% replied that their injury had resulted in them never participating in the activities of a moshpit ever again.

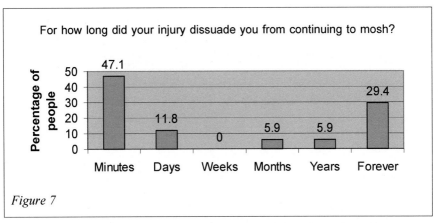

Figure 7

Figure 8.1 (Refer to Appendix C) summarises the perceptions of the cultural activity as portrayed by the respondents who answered with purely negative replies in response to question one. Figure 8.2 (Refer to Appendix C) shows that 100% of those respondents replied to question two that the ability to participate in the activity was "Not at all important" to them. Figures 8.3, and 8.5 show that, of those who perceive the cultural activity as purely negative; 86% had sustained serious injuries in a moshpit. One hundred per cent of those people had become dissuaded from continuing to participate in the cultural activity; 83% of whom had become dissuaded from participating "Forever" and 17% had ceased to participate for a matter of "Years".

Figure 9 presents the results obtained from question eight of the questionnaire. As the data exhibits, the most popularly supported devices for crowd safety at rock concerts included: the provision of special first-aid assistance (N) with 62% of respondents voting in favour of this method; the prohibition of potential harm-causing items in the moshpit (G) with 52% of those voting in favour; and the provision of a properly trained security team (B) with a support rate of 47%. The least popular device was the installation of CCTV surveillance (D) with a mere 7% support rate by respondents. Eight per cent of all respondents, however, replied that in their opinion, none of the suggested devices could provide an acceptable alternative to the prohibition of the cultural activity.

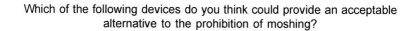

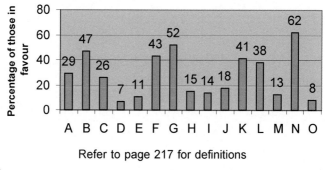

Which of the following devices do you think could provide an acceptable alternative to the prohibition of moshing?

Refer to page 217 for definitions

Figure 9

Figure 10 (Refer to Appendix C) presents the results obtained from question nine of the questionnaire, showing that 30% of all respondents had encountered safety devices for moshpits at rock concerts they previously had attended, and 70% had not.

Figure 11 presents the results derived from question ten of the questionnaire.

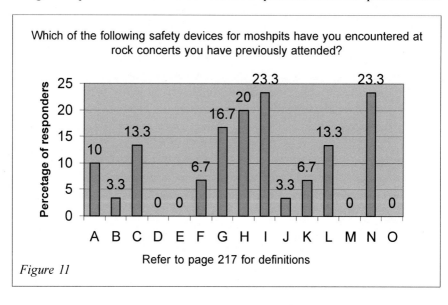

Which of the following safety devices for moshpits have you encountered at rock concerts you have previously attended?

Refer to page 217 for definitions

Figure 11

As the graph exhibits, of those who answered "Yes" to question nine, 23.3% answered that they had encountered a prohibition of crowd surfing (I) and 23.3% replied that they had encountered a provision of first-aid assistance near the moshpit (N). Not one of the questionnaire respondents, however, had ever encountered a provision of CCTV surveillance (D); a limit on moshpit capacities (E); or an age restriction placed upon moshpit participants (M).

Figure 12 (Refer to Appendix C) presents the results collated from question eleven of the questionnaire. Of those who answered "Yes" to question nine, 56.7% replied that the device(s) had appeared to work effectively; 20% replied that the device(s) had not appeared to work effectively; and 23.3% did not reply to the question.

The table below presents a summary of replies given in response to question twelve of the questionnaire. The replies have been grouped in relation to their content summary.

Do you have any further ideas for methods which could be introduced at rock concerts to protect moshpit participants? Do you wish to make any further comments?

1 Security who understand and sympathise with the psychology of the crowd

2 Security who treat moshpit participants with respect and care

3 Security should be able to see into the entire moshpit because it can get very dangerous at larger concerts

4 Security personnel should stand at a higher level to the crowd so that they can monitor the entire area

5 Moshpits can be very dangerous as security can't see what's going on in the moshpit, only at the front of stage barrier. I nearly died in the Red Hot Chilli Peppers' moshpit at Reading Festival, 1999 when I was trampled and couldn't get up and only survived because fellow moshers pulled me up. Big gigs and festivals definitely need surveillance and protection for moshers and strategies to get people out quick

6 Moshpit security should be trained in first-aid

7 Every venue should have adequate first-aid on stand-by

Do you have any further ideas for methods which could be introduced at rock concerts to protect moshpit participants? Do you wish to make any further comments? (continued)

8 Make participants safety conscious

9 Warn people of the dangers before entering a segregated moshpit

10 People should be educated of the dangers

11 Don't allow people who are too young or fragile into the moshpit

12 Encourage participants to act friendly and non-violently, and look out for and help each other

13 People should be friendly and help each other out

14 Moshpits can be really fun, people are just there to enjoy the music, but there's always one person out to hurt people on purpose

15 Good ventilation should be provided as it gets too hot in the moshpit

16 Much cheaper or free water should **always** be available and easily accessible (i.e. you don't have to queue at the bar for ages to get it)

17 Cigarettes should be banned in the moshpit because I hurt my eye on somebody's cigarette and had to go to hospital

18 Media overhype moshing

19 Make sure the band look out for and control the crowd (e.g. Dave Grohl of the Foo Fighters at Reading Festival 2001)

20 The bands should have more common sense and not play too many hardcore songs in a row. They should play some slower songs so people can calm down

21 Deftones stopped their performance once and refused to re-start until an audience member who had fallen over was helped up

22 You can't ban moshing - it's impossible to delegate how people will respond to music

23 Banning moshing creates a negative atmosphere and has a negative effect on rock culture

24 Moshing is part of rock culture

25 People who mosh choose to be there

26 Moshing is just a form of dancing, a way of enjoying the music - dancing is not banned at other types of music concert so why should it be banned at rock concert?

27 Segregation systems ruin the atmosphere of the moshpit

Interview

The interview questionnaire is included in the text and then the results from the interviews are presented.

Interview schedule targeted at promoters, venue managers and other rock concert promotion representatives:

1. **What is your perception of moshpits at live rock concerts?**
   Positive or negative? Please elaborate.

2. **Have you ever considered or practised the prohibition of moshing at live rock concerts?** If so, Why? How would/did you conduct and regulate this?

3. **If you have ever prohibited moshing at live rock concerts, how successfully was it conducted?** What was the audience's reaction?

4. **Moshing is generally perceived by audience members as a major component to the total experience of rock concerts. Many participants also perceive moshpits as dangerous but still choose to participate. What are your views regarding the introduction of safety and security regulations and devices, which allow audience members to participate in moshpit activities in a safer-than-usual environment?** (e.g. padded flooring and barriers/ segregation systems/limiting moshpit capacities/prohibiting crowd surfing/ providing ventilation and drinking fountains for moshpit participants/etc)

5. **Have you ever considered/practised the use of such regulations/devices?** If so, please describe. If not, would you be prepared to consider the introduction of such measures?

6. **If yes, how successfully were they conducted?**

7. **If yes, from the experience that you have had, how did the audience react to these regulations?**

8. **Do you have any further ideas concerning possible devices/regulations that can be practised at rock concerts to protect both the welfare of the audience and the culture of moshing? Please describe.**

9. **Do you wish to make any further comments regarding the subject?**

For the benefit of the reader and in order to avoid confusion, the fifteen respondents to the interview have been referred to in alphabetical form, each respondent having been allocated an individual letter (for example, a former head of security has been allocated and referred to as "Respondent D"). The table below identifies the rospodents' positions in the industry and their allocated respondent letter.

Respondent #	Respondent name and authority/location
A	Venue Manger of London venue
B	Venue Manger of London venue
C	Stage Manger of London venue
D	Former Head of Security for company
E	Representative of Crowd Studies company
F	Representative of Exeter venue
G	Student Union Entertainment Representative
H	Venue Manager of University Student Union
J	Representative of Crowd Management Focus Group
K	Marketing Manager / Promoter of Newbury venue
L	Representative of Poole venue
M	Managing Director of Promotion company
N	Booking Manager of London venue
P	Representative of Birmingham venue
Q	Entertainment Manager of University Student Union

The data collected in response to the interview has been grouped firstly by the responses given to each individual question (proceeding with question one), and secondly according to the nature of response (e.g. positive or negative).

Question One
- In response to question one "What is your perception of moshpits at

live rock concerts?" Respondents A, B, C, M and N replied with generally positive perceptions. Respondents A and C exclaimed that a highly populated moshpit represents a good concert atmosphere and customer satisfaction. Respondents B and M described the cultural activity as an effective outlet for expression. Respondents N and Q described their perceptions as "positive", so long as participants are sensible and the necessary safety precautions are taken. Respondents A, B and M indicated the activity's apparent risk factor but suggested that the resultant injuries were not of a serious nature.

- Respondents D, E and H replied with generally negative responses. Respondent D stated that this was because he had witnessed many injuries to crowd members caused by the activity. Respondent E suggested that the activity was dangerous because there is no education concerning the inherent dangers. Respondent H described the activities as "the product of too much alcohol going in to over-aged teenagers".
- Respondents J, G, J, K, L and P did not indicate that they held specific positive or negative perceptions in regards to the cultural activity. Respondent F exclaimed that participants support each other's modes of expression and that dangers only arise when older participants enter the environment with an aggressive attitude. Respondent G replied that moshpits are a potential disaster, but add greatly to the atmosphere of a concert. Respondent K replied that the activity is something that concert attendees expect to be able to do, it should therefore be accommodated and made "an acceptable risk". Respondent L stated that the activity is not negative so long as the performing artiste is comfortable with its conductance and that it is safely accommodated.

Question Two
- In response to question two, Respondent H alone replied that he had actively prohibited the cultural activity at rock concerts. Respondent H explained that the security at his represented venue possess the authority to request the artiste or DJ to "calm things down". Subsequently, if this does not happen, the security personnel have the authority to end the concert. Respondent L described a number of moshpit prohibition systems that he had previously encountered at live music venues in London and Manchester which featured signs indicating the prohibition; security personnel who enforced the prohibition; and requests made by performers, discouraging audience

members from participating.

- Of those interviewed who replied that they do not prohibit the cultural activity, the majority of respondents stated that they would evict audience members who acted inappropriately. Respondent K further exclaimed that prohibiting the cultural activity would destroy the atmosphere of the concert, and Respondent B stated that the injuries sustained at his represented venue were not of a serious enough nature to justify prohibiting it.

Question Three

- In response to question three, Respondent H replied that the audience's response to the prohibition of the cultural activity had been extremely negative but that audience members had been behaving "more sensibly" at succeeding concerts. Respondent L replied that, at the concerts he had attended where moshpits had been prohibited, the audience's reaction had been mixed. Audience members appeared to be more concerned with being able to listen to the music and watch the performance, rather than participating in the cultural activity.

Question Four

- The general response received in connection to question four was positive. The exception was Respondent H, who questioned "why bother" to attempt to create a safer environment for rock concert audience members when it is simpler to prohibit it? Respondents A, B, C and N exclaimed that the promotion of safety by creating a safe-as-possible environment was essential. Respondents E, P and Q enforced that educating participants of the cultural activity's inherent dangers was imperative. Respondent E further insisted that a ban should be placed upon mediated images, which promote the cultural activity as positive, instead promoting it as dangerous by highlighting the injuries.

- Respondent L suggested that additional security team members are always an advantage, but only if they realise that their purpose is to oversee the audience's safety and not to prevent the activity or act boisterously.

- Respondents A and K responded favourably to the implementation of segregation systems, which separate the moshpit from the rest of the audience. Respondents B and D, however, were not in favour of such systems, Respondent B implying that such systems simply concentrate the problem to one area. Respondent D exclaimed that segregation systems would not work at larger concerts, as it is impossible to predict where moshpits will initiate within a large audience.

- Respondent A suggested that the installation of padded flooring and barriers would work effectively, Respondent D implied that they would only work effectively at smaller venues, and Respondents B, C, G, K and M expressed that padded flooring was a bad idea. Reasons for this included the resultant instability under-foot and the fact that the device may delude participants into thinking that they can behave even more extrovertly.
- Although UK Public Entertainment Licences restrict concert attendance at the majority of events to those aged fourteen years and above, Respondents A, P and Q suggested limiting concert attendance to those aged eighteen years and above.
- Respondents D and P suggested that the prohibition of crowd surfing was a good idea and that those who do not comply should be evicted from the premises. Respondents A and C, however, implied that it would be extremely difficult to enforce such a regulation.
- Respondent F exclaimed that the performing artiste has a major role to play in controlling the moshpit.
- Respondent A suggested implementing a prohibition of alcohol and cigarettes within the moshpit and placing a limit upon the moshpit capacity, although she implied this would be difficult to regulate in a small venue.
- Respondent J ascertained that, as a whole, "the industry is not interested in raising the level of concert safety". Respondent J further claimed that the answers to creating a safer environment for cultural activity participants already exist, "they are simply not applied by many promoters, venues and bands because they make money allowing reckless environments".

Question Five

- In response to question four, Respondents H and M stated that they had never considered or practised the use of safety devices and regulations designed specifically to accommodate the cultural activity.
- Respondent N did not answer the question and Respondents F and J could not due to their lack of involvement in this particular area.
- Respondents B and D stated that they implement the use of **padded**

barriers.

- Respondents C, F, K, L and P all claimed that they employ (or plan to employ) the use of **properly trained security**. Respondent C exclaimed that "security are actually there to save you from hurting yourself" and Respondent F explained that the security personnel at his represented venue are well informed of the inherent risks.

- Respondent D affirmed his involvement with the use of **multi-barrier systems** and Respondent C declared that his represented venue implements the use of a **crash barrier system**, similar to those used on football ground terraces (Refer to The Department of Culture, Media and Sport (1997: 119), due to the venue's sloping floor.

- Respondents A, C and Q stated their involvement with the employment of systems that enable the entire **moshpit area** to be **monitored**. Respondent A explained that her represented venue has a DJ booth built-in to the wall to the side of the dance floor, which is slightly raised, enabling her to survey the moshpit for existing or potential hazards so that they may be dealt with immediately. Respondents C and Q both stated that they employ "spotters" who are positioned on the venue's balcony above the audience, who survey the entire audience and will contact the security behind the front of stage barrier immediately, via the use of radio communication, should an incident occur.

- Respondent C stated that his venue actively **prohibits** audience members from taking large bags, chains and other **potential harm-causing items** into the moshpit.

- Respondents B, C and K claimed that they **disallow the conductance of stage diving** and Respondents D, K and P stated that they **prohibit crowd surfing**. Respondent D detailed a system deployed at the Lowlands festival held in Holland each year. The system, which prohibited crowd surfing, included "announcements from the stage, safety message of security tee shirts and a wrist band system that took you into a side tent (sort of sin bin) for a short period to calm down. After which you were allowed back into the audience. If you were taken out a second time your wristband was exchanged for a red one and your wrist marked. If you were taken out a third time you were thrown out of the festival."

- Respondent C explained that, prior to any performance, the **band are consulted** and informed that they are not permitted to stage dive during their performance. The performing artistes are also encouraged to calm down the audience between songs and request that they make space to prevent crushing.

- Respondent L alone envisaged the provision of a **ventilation system**. Respondent L also stated that he would **provide audience members with water** and Respondent C stated that the pit security personnel at his represented venue "feed" audience members with water from sports bottles in order to prevent dehydration.
- Respondent B stated that he **limits the age of audience members** to those aged sixteen years and above, and Respondent P stated that her represented venue implements an age limit of eighteen years and above by asking standing patrons to present proof of their age prior to admission.
- Respondents A, B, C, G, L and Q claimed that they always **provide stand-by first-aid assistance**. Respondent C explained that his venue provides a first-aider at the front-of-house position and one backstage in a specific first-aid/recovery room. The venue also hosts two ambulances on-site for every concert, the majority of the venue's staff are medically trained, and all "pit" security team members have performed basic first-aid training so that if an accident occurs, it can be dealt with immediately.
- Respondent B stated that he positions **security staff amongst the audience** to prevent the moshpit from becoming unsafe and/or violent.
- Respondents A, C, D and P claimed that their venues **remove and eject** audience members who display inappropriate behaviour.
- Respondent L stated that he would **reduce the capacity of the venue** for rock concerts, and Respondent C stated that when concerts that appeal to an audience of a lower age group are staged, the venue capacity is limited to give concert attendees more space.
- Respondents D and P claimed that they have experienced involvement with concerts that **provide information and advice** to audience members, which highlight the dangers caused by participating in the cultural activity.

Question Six

Of those to whom it was applicable, in response to question six, Respondents A, B, C, D, F and K claimed that the devices with which they had been involved, had operated effectively and successfully. Respondents G, N, P and

Q did not provide an answer to the question, but no respondent replied that their implemented devices had not worked successfully.

Question Seven

- In response to question seven, Respondents B, C, D and K stated that the implemented devices had received a generally positive reaction from the audience as a whole. Respondent C explained that audience members are often unaware of such devices and generally regard security personnel in a positive light, often thanking them for their assistance.
- Respondent F stated that the audience's reaction to the provision of security personnel had been generally negative, regarding their presence as an infringement of audience members' rights.
- The question was not applicable to Respondents A, E, H, J, L, M and Q. Respondents G, N and P did not answer the question.

Question Eight

- In response to question eight, eight respondents provided suggestions by which audience safety controls at rock concerts can be further developed. The suggestions have been listed below:
- Respondent D – "Peaceful crowd safety ... The way forward is for practitioners and academics to come together to consider the wider implications of marketing (crowd psychology), laws of dynamics (pressure loads), venue design (crowd control) and licensing of the private security industry (trained teams)."
- Respondent E – Education of the risks may limit the potential to participate.
- Respondent F – Properly trained security personnel should always be provided. "When I saw Slayer in Switzerland ... the situation was inadequate. The security were all kid volunteers who were watching the band while people came crashing headfirst over the barrier. They were ... distributing water by hurling full bottles into the audience."
- Respondent G – Have vigilant staff in the "pit" who monitor the crowd the entire time, even between each artiste's performance.
- Respondent J – Concert attendees should understand the dangers of the moshpit environment.
- Respondent K – "Experienced and understanding security, decent crowd control barriers, a good door policy, i.e. with the emphasis on

people who are there for a good time and not to make trouble."

- Respondent L – "…it is important for artistes to be aware of the issues and safety implications. At outdoor/festival gigs where the ground can often be extremely uneven (Glastonbury for example), I would suggest that flooring could be placed over the ground in order to provide a more stable standing area."
- Respondent N – "It's a culture of 'respect' for each other … this can only be developed by the music press, good security, etc."

Question Nine

- Seven candidates provided comments in response to question nine, which have been listed below:
- Respondent A – Crowd surges can occur at concerts other than those of the rock genre, which do not actually feature a moshpit.
- Respondent B – "I don't think moshing's gonna go away although I do think there's gonna be a lot less of it."
- Respondent C – Moshpit participants should be much more considerate of each other. If they plan to crowd surf they should not wear heavy boots or kick. They should also help security personnel when they are lifted over the front of stage barrier.
- Respondent D – "The management of crowds must be recognised as a social science. This would enable the practitioner (or venue manager) to gain a recognised qualification that indicates to local authority officers the level of their expertise. The current system whereby anyone can, and often does, claim to be an 'expert' is totally inadequate and dangerous."
- Respondent E – "…education would highlight the problem. As there appears to be a 'promotion' of moshing from the media (TV adverts showing moshing etc) then this should be removed … perhaps a poster campaign at venues highlighting the issue would help … this is a very important issue and you can help to promote the safety."
- Respondent G – "I don't think the pit is a place where regulations would work. It's all about experience, preparation and thinking on your feet."
- Respondent J – "The concert safety issue you are addressing is important."

Discussion of the Results

The primary research adopted by this investigation studied four main areas in relation to finding a safer method by which to accommodate perceived anti-social behaviour at rock concerts. This section, in which the results of the primary research data collection are discussed, has consequently been divided into four main sections, in which the following matters will be discussed in turn:

- What are the perceptions of the management and crowd in relation to rock concert safety?
- Should the cultural activity - 'moshing' - be accommodated at rock concerts?
- How can rock concert safety be improved, without prohibiting the cultural activity and spoiling the concert environment?
- Is it economically viable to allow the conductance of this cultural activity?

What are the perceptions of the management and crowd in relation to rock concert safety?

The initial questions posed to concert attendees and concert management representatives during the conductance of primary research, concerned the individuals' personal perceptions of the cultural activity – 'moshing'. It was necessary to investigate this concept in order to justify the case presented by this research project, which indicated that the cultural activity is regarded a highly important component to the experience of rock concert attendance and therefore needs to be safely accommodated.

The replies received in response to questions one and two of the questionnaire supported this notion, confirming the importance of this cultural activity as perceived by concert attendees. The fact that 74% of all questionnaire respondents described the cultural activity as "Fun", and 56% described it as "Exciting", compared to a mere 8% who perceive it as "Antisocial" and 1% who believes it "Should be banned", highly corroborates the fact that the crowd regard this activity as a highly important component to the culture of rock concert attendance. One questionnaire respondent summarised a statement made in the literature review, stating that "moshing is a part of rock culture". Another respondent stated "banning moshing creates a negative effect on rock culture".

The findings also reflected the notion implied by the literature review, indicating that, although many concert attendees (61%) perceive the cultural activity as purely positive, many (30%) are aware that the activity portrays negative factors in addition to positive ones. This indicates that concert attendees are generally aware of the inherent dangers presented within such an environment. The indication, however, that 72% of all concert attendees prefer to be able to participate in a moshpit environment suggests that some may be compelled by the inherent risks to participate, and some may perceive such dangers as an acceptable risk. They are therefore more concerned with being able to participate, than they are about receiving an injury.

Of all questionnaire respondents, only 7% described purely negative perceptions in relation to the cultural activity, regarding the ability to participate as "Not at all important". From the findings it was further ascertained that of those 7%, 86% had sustained serious injuries whilst previously participating in the cultural activity, 83% of whom had consequently become deterred from participating in a moshpit environment for the rest of their lives. This fact strongly indicates that the negative reflection held by those persons in regard to their perception of the cultural activity had been influenced by their sustaining a serious injury. Therefore, prior to their injuries, they probably perceived the activity with equal importance, as do the majority of this social group's population. In reflection of this concept, it was ascertained that the significant majority of all rock concert attendees have, at some point in their existence, regarded 'moshing' as an important component to the total experience of attendance. These persons, it was established, generally will only become detached from this positive portrayal upon receiving (or observing) a serious injury as a result of experiencing the extreme negative effects of the cultural activity.

Although the literature review suggested that the cultural activity is often perceived by industry practitioners as anti-social, the results of the qualitative research collection suggested that concert practitioners generally understand the importance of the activity to participants, but are also very aware of its inherent dangers. Therefore, they are possibly more inclined to regard it as a dangerous act, rather than as an act of anti-social behaviour. Twelve of the fifteen interviewed industry officials, as did 30% of all concert attendees, indicated their awareness that the cultural activity portrays both positive and negative characteristics. From the findings it has been ascertained that concert practitioners generally perceive the cultural activity as an acceptable risk. They understand that dangers can arise from accommodating this type of environment, but are also aware that by prohibiting it, a negative concert atmosphere is likely to manifest, which consequently can result in a loss of business.

Respondent H appeared, however, to posses a generally negative view in terms of his perception of the cultural activity, expressing its existence as being a result of foolish individuals who are under the influence of alcohol, uniting in the intent to act childishly and rebelliously. Respondent H consequently failed to recognise the fact that a significant proportion of those persons whom regularly attend rock concerts regard the activity with importance, indicating that by prohibiting its procedure he was (and is) effectively undermining the valued importance of this culture. It is possible that many other concert practitioners who practice the prohibition of this activity, also retain similar views, assuming that by completely prohibiting the conductance of the activity, the possibility of audience members acquiring serious injuries will be completely eradicated.

As the findings suggested, supported by the literature review, the prohibition of this cultural activity can induce rebellious and possibly even illegal behaviour by concert attendees. Furthermore, the indication that 11% of all concert attendees replied that they would not attend a concert if they were aware, prior to the event, that the cultural activity would be prohibited, indicates that the concert practitioners who enforces such a regulation will lose potential business. This could ultimately decipher the difference between a promoter 'breaking even' on a production, or making a loss.

From the findings, it was also ascertained that concert attendees are generally unaware of the 'real' dangers presented within a large capacity, rock concert audience. A mere 22% indicated an awareness of the dangerous aspect of this activity, suggesting that the majority of concert attendees are ignorant of the fact that tragedies, such as those sustained at Roskilde 2000 and Big Day Out 2001, can occur within such an environment. It may be the case that, due to participation in the activity having become a vastly popular cultural tradition, the general attitude held by concert attendees, is one of misleading confidence (i.e. 'if so many people are joining in, it must be safe'). In solution to this problem, Respondent E suggested that there should be provided to audience members and concert practitioners alike, an adequate degree of education concerning the inherent risks sustainable within such an environment. Even if this precautionary method does not dissuade concert attendees from participating altogether, it will at the very least make them more aware and able to identify potential and existing hazards.

Respondent J further made a provocative statement, suggesting that the live music industry is not interested in raising the level of concert safety because it makes money from allowing "reckless behaviour".

Should the Cultural Activity - 'Moshing' - be accommodated at Rock Concerts?

The prohibition of this cultural activity has become a strongly debated, controversial issue among concert attendees, concert practitioners and industry officials alike. From the perspective of concert management, the prohibition of this activity will cause a significant decrease in rock concert-related injuries, but will also create significant macro-environmental costs to the concert as a whole (such as economic loss and legal implications, due to irate concert attendees resorting to riotous behaviour). It is important to remember that very few tragedies sustained at past rock concerts were caused as a result of the conductance of this cultural activity (Refer to www.crowddynamics.com/Main/crowddisasters.html). The majority of tragedies were actually sustained as a result of crowd surging and consequential crushing – situations that can occur at any type of staged entertainment which accommodates a large capacity, highly concentrated audience and features a single centre of attraction.

From the perspective of the crowd, the prohibition of this cultural activity effectively denies audience members the freedom to choose whether or not to participate in this form of dance, which has become a traditional aspect of attending rock concerts. The enforcement of this prohibition also prevents the activation of an important form of interaction between each individual audience member, and between the audience and the performing artiste, meaning that the resultant experience of rock concert attendance becomes detached from its anticipated form.

The responses generated from question three of the questionnaire indicate that almost one third of respondents (who represent the population of rock concert attendees as a whole) had encountered regulations that prohibit the cultural activity. This supports the suggestion made by the literature review, which indicated that many promoters and venues are adopting the perceived easiest method by which to eliminate injuries caused within the moshpit environment, by prohibiting the activity altogether.

Respondent B claimed that his venue simply has no justification in prohibiting the cultural activity, due to the injuries sustained at this particular venue being not of a serious enough nature to induce such an enforcement. This case is generally commonplace to all small capacity venues, due to the fact that the activity *alone*, which, in its simplest definition, involves people bumping and slamming into each other, does not generate serious injury and certainly not death. It is only when large numbers of people are tightly packed into a relatively small area, the type of situation typical of large capacity concerts, where tragedies resulting from exhaustion, crushing and trampling really occur.

Respondent K acknowledged that prohibiting the cultural activity would adversely affect the rock concert atmosphere. This notion influenced the speculation that concert practitioners who regard the cultural activity with positive perceptions and do not advocate the prohibition of this activity, are in fact individuals who appreciate the type of music that influences this type of reaction (i.e. 'moshing') and/or appreciate and understand the crowd psychology evident at rock concerts. Those who retain opposing views, it was speculated, may be involved with the business simply for the monetary gain alone and therefore do not or cannot appreciate or relate to the crowd psychology.

Of the fifteen industry officials interviewed during qualitative research, one respondent alone exclaimed that his venue practices the prohibition of the cultural activity, outlining an apparently effective method by which to enforce it. A further five respondents stated that they actively prohibit the conductance of crowd surfing and/or stage diving as a safety precaution. Respondent L also stated that he had previously encountered prohibition systems at live music venues in Manchester and London. Respondent H admitted, however, that prohibiting the cultural activity had created an extremely negative reaction from the audience, which further enhances the need to accommodate it.

The responses received in connection to question four of the questionnaire further enhance the implications faced to the industry if the cultural activity is prohibited at rock concerts. In representation of the social group as a whole, 42% of respondents replied that they would feel angered if this was the case, and a worrying 13% replied that they would be willing to resort to illegal action. As Respondent C indicated, the conductance of this cultural activity is extremely difficult to control and/or prevent, therefore, by executing a prohibition policy; this effectively means that a large proportion of concert attendees will have to be evicted from the venue, unless, as Respondent H suggested, the performance is cancelled altogether. This will ultimately result in a huge loss of trade to the venue, concert practitioner and artiste, caused by the reduction in bar sales, merchandise sales, future ticket sales, etc. As 'Word of Mouth' is the most powerful communication tool in terms of PR (public relations), the implications presented by enforcing a prohibition of the cultural activity are therefore catastrophic to all parties involved with promoting a rock concert.

Those persons who had encountered prohibition policies and especially those who had been evicted from a venue would proceed to inform others of this situation, who in turn would inform others, and so on and so forth.

One questionnaire respondent stated, in reply to question twelve, that 'moshing' is a form of dancing, supporting the literature review which argued that because the act of dancing is not prohibited at other types of music concert, it is unfair to prohibit it at rock concerts. Prohibiting the cultural activity therefore does not provide a logical solution to enhancing audience safety at rock concerts, as it will inevitably result in loss of business, a bad reputation, a negative concert atmosphere, and potentially even property damage. In support of the literature review which made reference to a situation outlined by Kemp (2000: 156), preventing a culturally important activity can cause more negative implications than positive outcomes.

How can rock concert safety be improved, without prohibiting the cultural activity and spoiling the concert environment?

From the findings it was ascertained that the cultural activity - 'moshing' - should be accommodated at rock concerts to prevent the inception of a negative concert atmosphere and related macro-environmental costs to the concert practitioner (such as loss of trade and legal implications). The findings also accentuated the seriousness of this matter, concerning the lack of provision of rock concert safety devices. The questionnaire results indicated that 37% of all rock concert attendees have, in the past, sustained a serious injury whilst participating in a moshpit environment. This strongly suggests the *need* for the industry to greatly increase concert safety for cultural activity participants. The realisation that 54% of those injured were not at all discouraged from continuing to participate, and that of the 46% who were, 47% had ceased to participate for a matter of "Minutes" only, further indicates and enhances the valued importance of the culture, as regarded by rock concert attendees.

During the conductance of both primary and secondary data research, a number of safety regulations and devices were uncovered which, if brought into practice effectively and with commitment at rock concerts, could significantly reduce the dangerous aspects of attending a rock concert. The regulations and devices accounted for during secondary research, displayed within the literature review, were presented to concert attendees within the questionnaire with the intention of discovering their perceptions in terms of whether or not they believed that the devices could help to promote concert safety. Concert practitioners and industry officials were also asked for their views regarding the introduction of such methods; if they had experienced involvement with the implementation of such methods; and if they had any ideas for as-yet unaccounted-for methods which could help to promote rock concert safety.

The indication that 92% of all questionnaire respondents (who represent the population of rock concert attendees as a whole) replied that one or more of the listed devices/methods by question eight could help to accommodate the cultural activity more safely, further suggests that the industry is not applying enough dedication to increasing concert safety. Crowd Management Strategies (2002) and Respondent J (further supported this suggestion), exclaiming that safety devices designed to protect rock concert audiences already exist but are simply not applied by many concert practitioners. Again, this problem is highlighted further still due to a mere 30% of all questionnaire respondents stating that they had previously encountered safety devices designed to accommodate the cultural activity.

The concert safety device most popularly supported by the questionnaire respondents was the provision of specialised first-aid assistance, located in close proximity to the moshpit. The recognition that 62% of questionnaire respondents replied that special first-aid provision could help to accommodate the cultural activity more safely, suggests the apparent lack of dedication to supplying adequate attention to the specific requirements of a rock concert audience, in terms of coping with related injuries. According to the interview results, provision of specialised first-aid was apparently the most commonly applied precautionary method by the interview candidates, six of whom claimed that they have or would use this precaution. Respondent C, however, was the only respondent who described a highly substantial degree of first-aid provision. In exception to Respondent C, the findings suggest that many venues and concert practitioners may be providing the adequate but limited degree of first-aid provisions that are necessary to acquire a Public Entertainments Licence. Such licences, however, which are legally required by every venue providing public entertainment, do not make specific requirements for rock concerts in terms of first-aid provision, even though concerts of this nature generate more injuries than most other types of entertainment. As the Health & Safety Executive (1999) sets out, the level of first-aid provision required by any venue, staging any type of event is dependent upon the number of persons present at the venue alone. From the findings, it has been ascertained that rock concert practitioners, possibly as a method by which to reduce costs, or in ignorance of the specific needs of a rock concert audience, generally supply the minimal level of first-aid provision, neglecting to cater for the specific needs of a crowd with this profile.

The secondary data research identified a number of systems that employed the use of crowd barriers to separate the moshpit from the rest of the audience, or to divide the audience into smaller sections. As Respondent B observed, a segregation system of this nature would be difficult and costly to implement at a smaller venue. At concerts with larger audience capacities, however, of perhaps five thousand persons and above (judged by the fact that Brixton Academy, a five thousand person capacity venue – has successfully implemented the use of a crash barrier system), such a system if implemented correctly and successfully, could dramatically reduce the force of crowd surges caused by the cultural activity, and the resultant effects of crowd crushing, by localising them within the designated area. The findings indicated that 26% of concert attendees support the notion of this type of device. One questionnaire respondent, however, argued that segregation systems ruin the atmosphere of the moshpit. But so long as the reason for the implementation of such a device is explained to the audience, highlighting the potentially life-threatening dangers if such a measure was not taken, then a larger percentage of concert attendees may be supportive of this concert safety method. As Torkildsen (1999: 386) stated, people are generally more accepting of measures when they are aware of the reasons for their existence.

In terms of the actual practice of implementing a segregation system, Respondents A and K expressed their support for such a device, but only Respondent C had actually experienced involvement with implementing such a device. The current lack of industry involvement with implementing segregation systems, designed to separate the moshpit from the rest of the audience, may be due to the fact that such a system is still experiencing the early stages of development, or for the fact that implementing such a device can be costly. Respondent C's represented venue features a permanent crush barrier system, meaning that a single installation cost would have been incurred. Such devices when installed at festivals, however, cannot be permanent features, meaning that every time a rock concert is staged at this type of venue, an installation cost will be incurred. Respondent B commented that the implementation of a segregation system is not a good idea as it simply concentrates the problem in one area. This concept however, neglects to recognise the fact that this type of system prevents the problem from spreading to the rest of the audience, involving patrons who do not wish to become involved with the moshpit environment. Respondent D stated that such a system would not work effectively at large concerts, as it is impossible to predict where a moshpit will initiate. Although this statement is true, the majority of all moshpit activities are always concentrated to the semi-circular area directly in front of the stage, meaning that such a system installed at this location will still work extremely effectively, by decreasing the dangers presented within such an environment. The installation of this type of device, as indicated by the literature review, will also enable the crowd to be monitored more easily. Dangerous incidents will also be more easily accessible and can be dealt with more quickly than would otherwise be possible, should this device not have been implemented.

The implementation of a segregation system would also enable a control to be placed upon the age of moshpit participants – as suggested by Crowd Management Strategies (2002) and by 13% of all questionnaire respondents. As Respondent B indicated, the licences for indoor concert venues generally restrict the age of patrons permitted on the premises. Such a control, however, without the aid of a segregation system, would otherwise be virtually impossible to regulate at festival concerts where audience members of all ages can enter the environment. A segregation system and age limit on moshpit participants would ensure that those involved with the cultural activity definitely wanted to be there and that they were physically and mentally strong enough to cope with the minor hazards inherent within such an environment (assuming that crowd crushing was successfully prevented). It is important to note that Jessica Michalik was just sixteen years of age when she was tragically crushed to death during a major crowd crush at 2001's Big Day Out festival in Sydney.

Respondents A, P and Q suggested limiting moshpit participants to those aged eighteen years and above. Only Respondents B and Q, however, stated that their represented venues restrict audience members to those aged sixteen (in Respondent B's case) or eighteen (in Respondent Q's case) years and above. From this indication, it was ascertained that concert practitioners, in general, do not recognise or value the degree of seriousness to which the dangers inherent to the cultural activity are presented to its participants, particularly those of a young age and/or fragile build. The enforcement of an age limit placed upon moshpit participants was only supported by 13% of concert attendees, probably due to the fact that those aged below the enforced limit would effectively be prohibited from participating in the cultural activity.

The implementation of a segregation system would also enable a limit to be placed upon the capacity and density of the moshpit itself, as suggested by

Crowd Management Strategies (2002), so that the effects of crowd surging and crushing could be significantly minimised and localised within the specific moshpit area. Without the implementation of a segregation system, the limitation of moshpit capacities would be virtually impossible, meaning that venues which do not implement such a device, are limited to controlling the capacity of the entire audience, not just the moshpit area. Although Public Entertainment Licences limit venue capacities as a matter of legal requirement, Respondent L stated that he would reduce the capacity of the venue for a rock concert, and Respondent C stated that his represented venue reduces the entire venue capacity when artistes who appeal to audiences of a younger generation perform at the venue. However, not a single interview or questionnaire respondent stated that they had implemented or encountered a limitation placed on the moshpit capacity, most definitely due to the fact that segregation systems, which completely separate the moshpit from the rest of the audience, currently, are rarely implemented.

A mere 11% of all concert attendees were in support of a limitation being placed upon the moshpit capacity, possibly due to the fact that such a method effectively formulates their otherwise spontaneous actions. Furthermore, those who are not admitted into the moshpit environment are likely to feel angered, which again could potentially affect the macro-environmental factors surrounding the concert in the same way that prohibiting the cultural activity altogether can cause further excalation of problems (detailed above).

A segregation system would further enable easier access by security and medical teams to those in the audience who require attention (as observed by Malavenda, 1995). The system would also enable security personnel to use their discretion concerning the admittance of individuals into the moshpit environment (as performed at the Big Day Out 2002 using the 'D-barrier') and to prohibit potential harm-causing items from being taken into the environment (as suggested by Crowd Management Strategies, 2002), which, at festival concerts, would otherwise be virtually impossible.

On reflection, the installation of a moshpit segregation system at a large rock concert could help to significantly increase concert safety. The not-so-simple but highly structured and effective device, which has been seriously overlooked and disregarded by the industry in general, could play an important role in significantly reducing the number of related injuries and fatalities at rock concerts.

The installation and operation of CCTV surveillance systems, which monitor the entire audience, could potentially help to increase safety at large concerts of festival or arena size, which otherwise are difficult to monitor due to the crowd's immense size and density. The implementation of CCTV would enable the detection of hazards, which otherwise would remain unnoticed, so that they may be dealt with quickly, preventing the occurrence of a serious incident. Although none of the questionnaire respondents replied that they had ever encountered the provision of CCTV surveillance at a rock concert, this does not necessarily indicate that such a device had not been installed at any concerts they previously had attended. Instead, the cameras could have been discreetly positioned within the venue, meaning that they would have remained unnoticed by audience members. However, as none of the interview candidates had implemented such a device, this suggested that such a system is generally disregarded by the industry as a whole, possibly due to the great expense that such a system would cost to install and operate. Simpler, more cost effective devices, such as those practised by Respondents A, C and Q, which monitor the audience from a position above head-height also offer the same type of service and safety precaution. The use of such devices would be particularly beneficial to smaller venues where income is more limited.

Although just 7% of concert attendees indicated a supportive attitude towards the installation of CCTV surveillance, the possibility of such a system remaining unnoticed by audience members is great. As stated earlier, so long as patrons are informed of the reasons justifying the implementation of this safety and security device, they are likely to be more accepting of such a device than they would be, had they not been informed. Furthermore, the realisation that the audience is being constantly monitored may also discourage individuals from behaving unnecessarily violently, as many questionnaire respondents indicated is often an issue of concern.

Many concert attendees, in response to question twelve of the questionnaire, also commented that security should stand at a higher level to that of the audience so that they can survey the entire crowd, not just those at the front of stage barrier. Respondent C was the only interviewed concert practitioner who actually indicated that the security at his venue do just this. One respondent in particular detailed a life-threatening incident where he/she had been trampled and crushed in a festival audience, but had to rely upon the help of fellow audience members to survive, as the security team simply could not see what was happening. Serious incidents, similar to this one, are occurring at rock concerts everywhere on a regular basis, but the industry is still neglecting to recognise and deal with this fact. Until it does, however, tragedies such as those sustained at the Roskilde festival in 2000 and at the Big Day Out festival in 2001, will continue to repeat.

A huge response was generated from questionnaire respondents, who suggested that rock concerts should always provide a properly trained security team, who respect the audience psychology and behaviour, and are there solely to promote safety, not to prevent them from participating in the cultural activity. This would consequently create a safer concert environment and would maintain a more positive atmosphere. This notion, supported by the literature review, indicated a lack of specialised rock concert security training, suggesting that many concert practitioners are not currently employing security personnel who have been trained properly to deal with this specific audience profile. Respondents C, F, K and P all claimed that their venues currently employ properly trained security, however, only Respondent C gave real reason to suggest that his security personnel really understand the needs of a rock concert audience in terms of psychology. The remaining candidates simply stated that their security teams were 'properly trained' – not offering a description of how or why this was the case. This lack of knowledge suggests that concert practitioners generally do not employ security teams who have been trained to protect the safety and dynamics of this particular audience profile. Such team members' boisterous and neglectful attitudes (as illustrated within the literature review) can create a negative concert environment and can also lead to incidents that should have been dealt with remaining ignored, leading to avoidable injuries.

Respondent C alone stated that his represented venue's front of stage security team is additionally trained in basic first-aid. This quality of service indicates the venue's level of commitment and professionalism in terms of promoting concert safety, unlike venues that do not provide this commendable level of service. Ultimately, the difference between hiring a security team whose members have been trained in first-aid, and hiring a team whose members are not, could mean the difference between a serious injury not being dealt with in time resulting in death, and a person's life being saved.

Not one of the interview respondents supported the idea of installing padded flooring at a rock concert (as suggested by Crowd Management Strategies, 2002), reasoning that it would deteriorate quickly due to spillages and that it would cause severe instability under-foot. In light of this reasoning, such a device, although breaking people's falls, could potentially result in audience members falling much more often than they normally would do and therefore sustaining more injuries than would normally be anticipated, given the environment in which they are populating. Respondent L, however, suggested the installation of temporary flooring at outdoor concerts, due to the ground often being uneven. Such a provision could potentially help to prevent audience members from falling and becoming crushed by the weight of the audience, as the majority of fatalities listed by 'The Rock and Roll Wall of Shame' (Refer to www.crowddynamics.com/main/crowddisasters.html) were caused.

A serious danger of attending any type of concert where the crowd is tightly packed in, is that of becoming dehydrated and suffocated. Within this type of environment at indoor venues, oxygen is sparse, the temperature is very hot and water is very difficult to access. However, not one interview respondent indicated their involvement with the operation of a ventilation system, and only Respondent L envisaged that he would provide a ventilation system when promoting a concert of this nature. The lack of provision by the industry in terms of this device could be due to the fact that such a system would be costly to install. In addition to this reasoning, outdoor venues do not need to implement ventilation systems, and neither do smaller indoor venues due to the fact that moshpit participants can escape the environment quickly and easily as there are fewer audience members to negotiate around. A ventilation system, however, installed at an arena sized indoor venue would significantly reduce the danger of moshpit participants suffocating and collapsing, as is it is difficult to exit the environment quickly.

Respondent C alone stated that audience members at his represented venue are provided with water by the front of stage security team. Of all questionnaire respondents, 41% replied that ventilation systems and drinking water should always be provided at rock concerts, however, only 2% of all respondents replied that they had previously encountered ventilation systems and/or the provision of water at rock concerts they had previously attended. One questionnaire respondent noted that water is often difficult to access at rock concerts (one often has to queue at the bar in order to obtain it) and is often charged at a high price. He/she reasoned that water should *always* be cheap or free of charge, and should *always* be available and easily accessible. The huge oversight by the industry, especially by smaller venue practitioners (larger concerts, particularly festivals, often provide water to audience members in plastic cups) regarding this provision, can lead to dehydration, even though drinking water costs virtually nothing to provide.

Numerous questionnaire respondents identified the need for performers to play a role in monitoring the audience, controlling audience behaviour and to act if hazards occur. This notion was also identified by Malavenda (1995) and by Crowd Management Strategies (2002) in the literature review. Malavenda (1995) suggested that such co-operation should form part of the contractual agreement for the artiste's performance. In exception to those questionnaire respondents who described cases where artistes had helped to control the audience (one respondent outlined an incident where Deftones had refused to continue with their performance until a particular audience member had been helped to his/her feet), Respondent C alone explained that he employs this precautionary method.

Many artistes of the rock genre are able to relate to their audiences, understanding and anticipating their behaviour. They are therefore able to detect signs of danger and are in such a powerful position, in terms of the crowd's perception of them, that they are able to effectively control the crowd, the members of which will generally respect their wishes, as Shuker (1994) noted. The indication that a mere 3% of concert attendees had witnessed the assistance from performers in controlling the crowd suggests that this method of safety promotion is currently not being implemented effectively. As Malavenda (1995) and Respondent C suggested, an extremely effective method by which to control audience behaviour would be to seek the artiste's co-operation in assistance, prior to any performance.

Many questionnaire respondents, interview respondents and those identified by the literature review identified the need for education concerning the dangers involved with participating in the rock concert cultural activity. None of the questionnaire respondents, however, replied that they had ever encountered notices or had received education concerning the inherent risks at rock concerts they previously had attended. Only two interview respondents stated that their represented venues provide such information and advice to audience members. This nature of education, which could be achieved by posting notices around the venue or making public safety announcements, could help to significantly reduce related hazards. If concert attendees were made more aware of the inherent risks of this type of environment, especially at large rock concerts, this would encourage a more sensible attitude and an awareness, so that people may behave more responsibly and will be able to identify hazards. The indication that, even though such a provision, which can be achieved virtually at no cost or effort, currently is not being implemented by the general industry, highlights even further still the industry's lack of commitment towards protecting concert attendees' welfare.

Respondent E insisted throughout his response to the interview questions that the media's promotion of the cultural activity as being positive should be banned and instead replaced with a promotion of its inherent dangers. This could initially be achieved by a poster campaign targeting concert venues and may consequently reduce the number of concert attendees willing to participate in the activity, therefore reducing the number of those at risk of becoming injured. Only when the industry really begins to recognise and value this concert safety issue and attempts to create an awareness of this problem by striving to minimise the dangers, will rock concerts become an enjoyable experience and less of a safety hazard for all parties involved.

Cigarettes were highlighted by Crowd Management Strategies (2002) as being a safety hazard within the moshpit environment, enhanced by one questionnaire respondent who stated that he/she had sustained a serious injury to the eye caused by a cigarette and, consequently, had to be treated at hospital. This type of hazard, however, is not specific to the nature of rock concerts, as injuries caused by cigarettes can be sustained at any type of public venue where smoking is permitted. Within the public bar environment, for example, people often tend to be packed into a small space, meaning that, as smoking often comes hand-in-hand with drinking, injuries caused by cigarettes burns can be commonly acquired.

The prohibition of cigarettes within the moshpit would be extremely difficult to regulate, especially at concerts with large capacities. The only method of realistically achieving this would be to prohibit smoking entirely within the venue. However, as the vast majority of live music venues host public bars, where people expect to be able to smoke, the inevitability and feasibility of concert practitioners enforcing such a regulation is extremely small, just as the prohibition of smoking in any other type of venue or bar would be. This fact, therefore, further supports the need to educate concert attendees, enabling them to become more diligent, responsible and considerate towards each other. It would also make good sense, as suggested by many questionnaire respondents, that concert attendees are advised and educated on the rules of 'Moshpit Etiquette', as outlined by Ambrose (2001) and Malavenda (1995).

The prohibition of 'stage diving' (Refer to Appendix A for definition) was suggested by Crowd Management Strategies (2002) as a method by which to increase crowd safety at rock concerts. As a general rule, however, to the implementation of front-of-stage barrier systems and 'pit' security teams at live music venues, which disable and disallow the conductance of this behaviour, mean that the act of 'stage diving' has become prohibited and/or prevented at the majority of rock concerts. The reasoning behind prohibiting this activity is due to the fact that the activity presents a threat of danger and personal injury to the audience members whom the 'stage diver' lands upon, after leaping from the stage into the crowd. Those audience members, who do attempt to stage dive at venues that prohibit this type of activity, as Respondent C indicated, are generally warned not to behave in such a fashion and/or are evicted from the venue. Therefore, as many venues already do not condone this type of behaviour, it was ascertained that this regulation does not form a valid addition to this research.

The act of 'crowd surfing' (Refer to Appendix A for definition); another cultural activity classified under the umbrella description 'moshing', is also prohibited at many live rock concert venues, as the activity can cause injury to those audience members who are used to support the individual whilst that person indulges in the activity. The indication that just 14% of concert attendees supported the notion of prohibiting this activity is possibly due to the fact that they perceive such an enforcement as an infringement of their rights as concert attendees, just as it was indicated that they do when 'moshing' is prohibited altogether. However, 23% of questionnaire respondents indicated that they had previously encountered a prohibition of this nature, suggesting that, as many venues are resorting to enforce this regulation, concert attendees may become more familiar and therefore more accepting of this regulation. Again, it cannot be stressed enough that, in order to acquire full co-operation and understanding from the audience, it is imperative that the reasons supporting such enforcement are explained fully to the audience.

Respondents D and P suggested that the prohibition of crowd surfing was a good idea and that those who do not comply with this regulation should be evicted from the venue. Respondents D, K and P all stated that their venues prohibit the activity, further suggesting that this type of measure is popularly implemented by concert practitioners. Respondents A and C, however, implied that such a regulation would be difficult to enforce and would result in many concert attendees being evicted from the venue – an action which again could potentially initiate a negative concert atmosphere and a loss of trade; the same sort of result that prohibiting the cultural activity altogether would cause. Respondent D, however, detailed a particularly effective system by which to prohibit crowd surfing, which employed the use of a wrist band system. Audience members who chose to crowd surf were warned not to and if they were caught doing it a second time their wristband was exchanged for a red one. If they were caught crowd surfing a third time they were then evicted from the festival. The system, which also included announcements from the stage, allowed audience members to become fully aware of the regulation, meaning that audience members were only evicted when they were found deliberately defying the enforcement.

Although the prohibition of crowd surfing is a commonly enforced regulation, it does not provide a solution to increasing concert safety overall. It will inevitably create a reduction in sustained minor injuries, but this will only be achieved if the activity is prevented entirely, which, as noted above, is virtually impossible. It should therefore be the sole discretion of the individual concert practitioner and/or performing artiste whether or not to enforce such a regulation.

Although 29% of concert attendees supported the proposition of providing padded barriers on crowd barriers at rock concerts, as suggested by Crowd Management Strategies (2002), just 10% had actually encountered such a provision and only two interview respondents indicated their involvement with implementing such a device. The padding of front-of-stage barriers, particularly at large rock concerts where the force of the crowd pushing forward is great due to the vast capacity of the audience, will reduce the number and seriousness of injuries sustained by those who come into contact with the barrier. The fact that this simple and relatively cost-friendly device is generally ignored by the industry again indicates the general lack of interest and commitment by the industry in terms of striving to promote concert safety.

The implementation of padding front-of-stage barriers to reduce the injuries caused to those who are pushed up against them should not be reviewed in terms of increasing rock concert safety alone. As Ambrose (2001) and Respondent A noted, crowd surges and crushing are not just apparent at, and limited to, of rock concerts, but can occur at any staged entertainment which hosts a large audience and features a single centre of attraction. From this indication it was ascertained that barriers used at any type of large concert or entertainment which hosts a large capacity audience should be padded to promote audience safety as a matter of course.

Respondent D possibly provided the most valid and important comment overall by sternly enforcing that the management of crowds should be recognised and treated as a social science. The literature review supports this notion, suggesting that in order to develop a safer concert environment by understanding how to control crowds effectively, practitioners and academics should unite in order to consider the wider implications of the science, such as crowd psychology, the laws of dynamics, venue design and the licensing of trained security teams. Only when the industry attempts to understand the psychology of rock concert audiences, will it be able to develop and implement effectively, devices and methods designed to alleviate the dangers caused by audience participation of the cultural activity associated with rock concerts. Respondent D also suggested that practitioners should gain a recognised qualification, indicating to local authority officers their level of expertise. This would therefore result in concerts being promoted by experts only, thus significantly increasing concert safety everywhere. Maybe then, and only then, when concert practitioners really become aware of the cultural importance of the rock concert experience, as perceived by concert attendees, and learn how to create a safe-as-possible environment without jeopardising the future of the activity, will related rock concert tragedies cease to exist and become a figment of history alone.

With regard to the perception of audience members held in view of the methods and devices that concert practitioners have previously employed in order to increase rock concert safety, only Respondent F replied that the audience had portrayed a negative reaction. This was because the crowd had regarded the provision of additional security personnel as "an infringement of their rights" as concert attendees, which suggests that the security team had not been properly trained (as outlined earlier). This implication is further enhanced by the comment made by Respondent C, who offered that the audience members at his venue were generally appreciative towards the security team's appropriate attitude, therefore indicating that Respondent F's represented venue's security personnel are perhaps not trained to deal with the specific needs of a rock concert audience. Respondent C also commented that the audience members at his venue are often unaware of the presence of safety methods/devices, which further indicates the venue's unique professionalism towards promoting concert safety. This notion also suggested that the results obtained from the questionnaire, asking respondents if they had previously encountered any such methods/devices, might have been inaccurate due to the possible unawareness that such provisions had been implemented.

In exception to candidate F, of those who provided a reply when asked to account for the audience's general reaction to the implementation of safety methods/devices, all candidates stated that the audience's reaction had been generally positive. This indication if further enhanced by the questionnaire respondents' responses to question eleven as, of those who answered the question, the majority implied that the device(s) that they had encountered had appeared to work effectively. The realisation that concert attendees generally possess a positive attitude towards the safer accommodation of their cultural activity, strongly suggests that such devices have provided an important addition to creating a solution to the problem of concert safety. Without the audience's support in respect of such devices, situations such as those arising due to the prohibition of the cultural activity may have consequently arisen.

Is it Economically Viable to Allow the Conductance of this Cultural Activity?

From the findings, a question arose which challenged the notion of whether or not the implementation of the previously discussed rock concert safety measures would be economically viable to implement. If the concert attendees' enjoyment of the concert experience should be reduced as a result of such methods being implemented, it is likely that they would not attend future concerts that implement these measures. In light of this query, would it be worth spending the incurred amounts of capital on achieving this result?

Smaller capacity venues are the most vulnerable in terms of the economics of increasing rock concert safety. Primarily, as Respondent A highlighted, small venues often have small expenditure budgets, and therefore little capital to spend on elaborate safety improvements. Secondly, smaller venues tend to promote up-and-coming artistes who generally perform many concerts at different venues throughout a relatively small time period. Therefore, if the concert attendance is reduced in terms of enjoyment at a particular venue, attendees are likely to attend the same artiste's concert staged at a venue elsewhere.

Arena and festival sized venues have much less restrictive budgets and are therefore more able to implement safety methods to a great degree. The type of performing artistes that appear at these types of venue generally have a high-profile, are well-known, and have large audience followings, and generally only perform a small number of live concerts per tour, and possibly only one or two festival appearances per year. Therefore, so long as the concert attendees are still able to watch the performance and participate in their cultural activity, no matter the extent to which imposing safety devices are implemented, they will still pay to attend the concert.

As it was indicated earlier, different types of venue require the implementation of different types of rock concert safety measures, dependent upon the individual venue's capacity size and whether they are located indoors or outdoors. The only safety measures and devices accounted for by the findings that would really affect the crowd's enjoyment of a concert would be the implementation of a segregation system, a limit on the actual moshpit capacity, a limit on the age of moshpit participants, and the prohibition of crowd surfing. The three latterly mentioned devices all effectively display elements of prohibition or prevention, which, as Respondent C indicated, are not welcomed by concert attendees. However, if such devices are deployed in conjunction with adequate and fully-informative education which explains the reasons justifying the implementation of such regulations and devices, and highlights the dangers evident if such measures were not taken, concert attendees are likely to be much more accepting and supportive of such measures than they would have been, had they not been provided with any form of explanation.

In terms of economic expense, the cost of providing specialised first-aid, located within close proximity to the moshpit, which is adequate enough to treat the specific needs of a rock concert audience, is dependent upon the individual venue. At a small venue, the relative cost will be small and may only require that security personnel are trained in first-aid; all first-aid personnel are educated of the specific types of injury incurred at this particular type of event, and possibly an increase in the actual level of first-aid provision would suffice. The same nature of improvement will also be required at larger concert venues, the cost of which will be higher due to the increased number of first-aid personnel required, although the relative cost in terms of scale will still be low.

Due to this type of safety measure not being invasive in terms of the audience's perception of enjoyment, and due to the indication that 62% of concert attendees supported the concept of providing specialised first-aid in order to increase rock concert safety, concert attendees will consequently not be at all discouraged from attending a venue that takes this level of precaution. Therefore, in terms of economic viability, the provision of specialised first-aid at rock concerts, staged at any type of venue, would be relatively inexpensive and would be welcomed by concert attendees.

The implementation of an audience segregation system, which separates the moshpit from the rest of the audience, or divides the audience into smaller, more manageable sections, would be both expensive to install and expensive to operate as it would inevitable require the employment of an increased number of security personnel. This type of device, in reference to a statement made by one questionnaire respondent, is also likely to 'spoil' the atmosphere of the moshpit and reduce the enjoyment of the concert attendance experience.

In a small venue which has a small expenditure budget, the implementation of a segregation system would neither be economically viable, nor necessary, as the smaller audience capacity is easier to manage and control. From the findings it was ascertained that this type of device could, however, at a festival or arena sized venue, effectively reduce the effects of crowd surging and crushing, and therefore greatly increase crowd safety. Although the cost of installing and operating such a system may be great, the huge reduction in the risk of serious injuries and fatalities occurring positively justifies the need to incur such an expense. Therefore, segregation systems should not just be considered for large rock concerts, and indeed any other type of event with hosts a large audience and a single centre of attraction, but it should become a mandatory requirement.

In consideration of the audience perception regarding this type of device, the performing artiste and other attractions supplied at large rock concerts/ festivals, will always dominate the decision to attend. Again, so long as the necessary education is provided concerning the reason for this device's deployment, and the expected artiste still performs the concert, the audience's enjoyment should not be decreased to the level that discourages attendance.

The enforcement of an age and capacity limit on moshpit participants at venues which do not implement the use of segregation systems would be very difficult to regulate, unless the capacity of the venue as a whole is reduced and an age limit is placed upon the entire audience. Although these enforcements would reduce the number of safety-related injuries at rock concerts, this would result in a loss of potential income to concert promoters, merchandisers and venue bars. At concerts with segregation systems, such enforcements would be easier to regulate, but would further result in a reduction of audience enjoyment, which may lead to a loss of future ticket sales. Although these enforcements would ultimately help to increase rock concert safety and would cost nothing to actually implement, the economic viability of such measures is debatable.

The installation of a CCTV surveillance system, although expensive to install and operate, would help to increase significantly rock concert safety at venues with large audiences where dangers can occur and remain unnoticed. Although a CCTV surveillance system would not be economically viable for smaller venues to install and operate, due to their small expenditure budgets and the fact that hazards within smaller audiences are easier to detect, it would be greatly advantageous to large venues. A further advantage of this device includes the notion that if cameras were positioned suitably, such a system would not decrease the enjoyment of concert attendance.

Alternatively, where venue expenditure budgets are too restrictive to allow for the installation of a CCTV surveillance system, raised platforms intended for the purpose of audience monitoring can be provided to offer the same nature of service. At small venues, a simple step could be built into the stage-side of the front-of-stage crowd barrier, on which the venue's security personnel can be positioned throughout the entire performance to monitor the crowd. The cost of this device, relative to the increase in concert safety, would be small and would not necessitate the need for employing additional staff. At larger venues, raised platforms, balconies and FOH (front-of-house) positions can be used, employing the services of 'spotters' (who need not be qualified), who can then report, via radio communication, any identified incidents to the head of security. This nature of service, when adapted to the requirements of the specific venue, should be easy to budget for by any concert promoter and/ or venue and, as it would help to significantly increase rock concert safety, is therefore economically viable.

The provision of a properly trained security team, the members of which have advance knowledge and expertise in how to manage and control a rock concert audience in specific, would help to increase greatly rock concert safety at little or no extra cost to the concert practitioner. Security personnel who have been educated and specifically trained to recognise, understand and accommodate the psychology and dynamics of this particular crowd profile, would be able to detect potential hazards and would know how to deal with them properly and effectively. This type of provision would not decrease the crowd's enjoyment of the concert, as security teams are a standard feature of any rock concert. If anything, the team's positive and responsive attitude may even create a more positive concert atmosphere, as security personnel are otherwise normally perceived as neglectful and unnecessarily forceful. As it would require little extra capital to educate and properly train security teams in this nature, this type of provision would be both highly effective and economically viable.

The installation of a ventilation system would only be economically viable for an indoor, arena-sized venue as, within audiences at smaller venues, it is easier for moshpit participants to exit the moshpit environment more quickly than it is within a large capacity, highly concentrated audience. This type of provision would help to increase concert safety and would also cause an increase in the audience's enjoyment, preventing the crowd from becoming overheated and suffocated. Although the installation of a ventilation system would be costly to provide, venues of this size should be able to budget for it, as, in addition to increasing concert safety, the increase of audience enjoyment could potentially lead to a further increase in ticket sales.

The provision of drinking water at rock concerts was highlighted as a problematic area. Often water is difficult to access and is often charged at a high price. In exception to the cost of disposable plastic/paper cups, the provision of water is free and should therefore be freely available to audience members at all times. This provision would help to increase greatly concert safety at all types of venue, by reducing the likelihood of dehydration, often caused by the hot, airless atmosphere at rock concerts, and the consumption of alcohol.

The assistance from performing artistes in controlling audience behaviour can be employed to significantly increase concert safety and should cost the concert practitioner no extra expense. This type of artiste co-operation would not reduce the audience's enjoyment of concert attendance, as, due to the indication that crowd members regard performing artistes in an iconic fashion, instructions concerning audience behaviour are more likely to complied with by audience members out of respect, than if the request was made by an unknown, authoritative figure.

The provision of education concerning the inherent dangers of moshpit participation and how to behave safely and responsibly is both economically viable and important for increasing concert safety by raising awareness. Education of this nature can be provided at no extra expense to the concert practitioner, by making public announcements from the stage, or at a very small cost, by posting public notices at various locations within the venue. This type of measure would not decrease the enjoyment of concert attendance and is therefore economically viable.

The prohibition of crowd surfing, although economically cost-free to the concert practitioner/venue, is very difficult to regulate and can cause a reduction in the enjoyment of a concert by crowd members. Many venues, however, have made the decision to prohibit the activity, meaning that concert attendees are becoming familiar with this type of regulation so the possibility of losing potential ticket sales as result of this enforcement is small. However, due to the activity being virtually impossible to prevent and control, concert safety cannot be significantly increased due to the prohibition of crowd surfing, therefore, the decision to prohibit it should be that of the concert practitioner/ venue and should not become a legal enforcement.

The implementation of padding on crowd barriers at rock concerts can be employed at a relatively low expense, to protect the safety of audience members who participate in the moshpit environment. Such a provision would be effective and efficient at any venue of any size. For venues which possess their own crowd barriers, this would induce a simple one-off payment, and at venues which hire crowd barriers, this would induce the same or a slightly higher cost. Either way, the provision of padding on all crowd barriers would be a highly beneficial addition to audience safety and would be economically viable.

Although the different methods by which to increase concert safety have been discussed separately, it is important to enforce that the implementation of just one or two of these devices is not enough to significantly increase concert safety. Concert practitioners, when creating a safer environment for rock concert attendees, should consider the implementation of all mentioned measures, selecting as many as is feasibly and economically possible in order to create a safe environment.

Conclusions

In retrospect, from the information collated by this research project, the answer to the query "How can perceived anti-social behaviour be accommodated at rock concerts?" already exists. It is now the responsibility of the live music industry to approach the issue of concert safety with true dedication and seriousness, for the lives of concert attendees are in their hands. This project has produced a detailed, revised and collaborated edition of existing knowledge and new ideas in the form of a single document. It can now be used as an aid towards initiating the process of creating an enjoyable and safe experience for all involved with the promotion and experience of the live rock concert industry.

Just as the Discussion section analysed and discussed separately the four main areas in relation to the findings derived in conjunction with this investigation, so has this concluding section been divided into the same four corresponding sections.

What are the perceptions of the management and crowd in relation to rock concert safety?

In the research and analysis performed by this project, it has been discovered that the cultural activity indulged in by many rock concert attendees, sometimes perceived as anti-social by non-participants, is a highly important component to the total experience of rock concert attendance. The results found that the majority of concert attendees perceive the cultural activity as positive but are also aware of its minor inherent dangers. The majority of concert attendees also prefer to be able to participate in the cultural activity. This notion was further accentuated by the indication that many concert attendees, upon discovering that the cultural activity is prohibited at a particular venue, would be prepared to resort to rebellious and/or illegal action. Some are also prepared to leave the concert or would not even attend the concert in the first place. This indicated that many concert attendees place the ability to 'mosh' at a higher advantage than actually watching the performance of the artiste! The results further suggested that those concert attendees, who indicated purely negative perceptions of the cultural activity, were possibly induced to thinking this way as a result of sustaining a serious injury due to the effects of 'moshing'.

From the results, it was ascertained that the majority of concert practitioners are aware of the inherent dangers presented by the cultural activity, but generally regard it as an 'acceptable risk', recognising its importance to the culture of rock concert attendance. The practitioners who hold negative views of the activity and administer prohibition policies to prevent the activity it was suggested, fail to recognise the significance of the cultural activity due to their ignorance in understanding the crowd psychology evident at rock concerts.

The results also indicated that concert attendees are generally unaware of the 'real' dangers of sustaining serious injury and/or fatality by participating in a large capacity audience. They can often, innocently, hold misguided safe perceptions of the activity, as it has become a 'norm' to participate.

In summary, both the indications that this cultural activity is perceived as highly important to rock concert attendance, and that serious injuries and even fatalities can occur within such environments, enlightens the need for the provision of adequate education concerning these two areas, to concert attendees and practitioners alike, and the desperate need to increase rock concert safety.

Should the cultural activity - 'moshing' - be accommodated at rock concerts?

Although, from the concert management perspective, the prohibition of this cultural activity creates a significant reduction in the number of rock concert-related tragedies, denying concert attendees the right to participate effectively denies them the right to enjoy the concert experience in the culturally normal, anticipated way. It was discovered that many rock concert practitioners do choose to prohibit the activity, however, although those interviewed who do not enforce such a regulation are generally aware of the importance, both culturally and atmospherically, of this cultural activity.

The results found that many concert attendees would feel angered at such a regulation and many would rebel against this action, further enhancing the need to accommodate the cultural activity at rock concerts. It was also discovered that concert attendees would be prepared to leave the concert or not attend at all on learning that the cultural activity was/would be prohibited. This indicates that concert promoters will inevitably lose potential ticket sale income if they decide to enforce such a regulation, which could mean the difference between breaking-even on a concert promotion, or making a loss. The indication that some concert attendees are prepared to resort to illegal action (such as rioting) in response to encountering a prohibition of their cultural activity, again accentuates the need to accommodate it, for the best possibly purpose of all parties concerned.

As the dominant majority of past rock concert tragedies have been caused as a result of crowd surging and crushing – not the cultural activity itself – this indicates the need to both accommodate the activity and to significantly increase concert safety to prevent such tragedies from repeating in the future.

How can rock concert safety be improved, without prohibiting the cultural activity and spoiling the concert environment?

The indication that an excessive number of rock concert tragedies have been caused due to lax or improper concert safety standards, highly enforces the need to increase concert safety, without prohibiting the cultural activity 'moshing' (for the reasons outlined earlier). Currently, however, this recognition is generally being ignored and not devoted serious commitment by the industry as a whole. Preventable accidents are continuing to occur and will continue to do so until the industry really accepts the degree of seriousness of this matter, and the extent to which a solution exists purely 'in their hands'.

This project has uncovered a number of methods, devices and practices that can be implemented at rock concerts to enhance and stabilise rock concert safety. Some devices, it appeared, were best suited to *either* small capacity venues *or* larger ones but not both. Other devices, it was discovered, would work effectively at *both* small *and* large capacity concerts.

It was discovered that the provision of specialised first-aid assistance, located within close proximity to the moshpit, which is designed to treat the specific needs of a rock concert audience, should always be provided, irrespective of the audience size and the type of venue. Public Entertainment Licences should also be amended to account for the level of first-aid provision needed at this specific type of event, rather than at music concerts in general (as other types of entertainment do not create as many injuries).

The employment of crowd barriers, which separate the moshpit from the rest of the audience, or divide the audience into smaller sections, could be effectively implemented at large audience capacity rock concerts, to significantly reduce the effects of crowd surges and crushing. The implementation of a moshpit segregation system would also enable a limit to be placed upon the capacity of the moshpit itself, and an age limit to be placed upon moshpit participants. Such limits would be difficult to regulate at smaller concerts, which do not feature segregation systems, unless the capacity of the audience as a whole were reduced, and an age limit were placed upon the entire audience. These limits would effectively help to increase concert safety by reducing the probability of crushing and by making sure those participating in the cultural activity wanted to be there, and that participants were physically and mentally strong enough to cope with the dangerous nature of the activity.

The installation and operation of CCTV surveillance at large capacity rock concerts could help to significantly increase concert safety. In large capacity audiences, it is otherwise difficult to monitor the entire audience, but this type of device would help by enabling the detection of hazards (such as segments of the crowd collapsing), that otherwise would remain unnoticed and therefore could result in tragedy. Alternatively, raised platforms could be employed at smaller capacity venues to provide the same nature of service, but at a lower cost to the concert practitioner. In either case, a system which monitors the entire audience should be employed at all rock concerts with no exception, as this method can help to greatly reduce related injuries, preventing them from escalating out of control.

It is extremely important that, to enable the promotion of rock concert safety, a properly trained security team is employed for every rock concert at every type of venue. The results indicated that security team members often behave boisterously and neglectfully towards rock concert audiences, as they are unaware of, and do not understand the crowd psychology and dynamics present at this type of event. It is important that security personnel are trained and educated properly so that they can control effectively and considerately, a crowd of this profile, enabling hazards to be detected and dealt with properly, to reduce the inception of avoidable accidents. It would also be a great advantage to concert safety if security teams were additionally trained in first-aid. This would ensure that any incident requiring urgent medical attention could be dealt with without delay.

At large audience capacity concerts, there is a great danger of becoming dehydrated and suffocated within the moshpit, due to oxygen being sparse within this high density populated environment, temperatures being high, and water being difficult to access. To reduce the likelihood of becoming dehydrated, water should always be provided, and should be quickly and easily accessible and free to obtain at all concerts. At large audience capacity rock concerts, a ventilation system should be installed and operated, providing moshpit participants with cool, fresh air, reducing the likelihood of audience members collapsing due to heat exhaustion and suffocation.

A highly effective method by which to increase rock concert safety is to gain the assistance from performing artistes in monitoring and controlling the audience. Performing artistes are generally perceived with respect by audience members, meaning that requests made by them to the audience are more likely to be complied with, than if made by an authoritative figure. Such co-operation from performers could even be made a contractual agreement, as they are in a high position – both physically and authoritatively – to help reduce related hazards.

Another effective method by which to promote and increase rock concert safety is to educate concert attendees of the 'real' dangers inherent within the moshpit, and how to cope with them by acting responsibly and helping those in danger. This type of awareness would encourage attendees to behave more responsibly and attentively, meaning that they would be able to detect dangers and also reduce to likelihood of dangers arising. This nature of education can be achieved by public announcements made from the stage, notices posted around the venue, a poster campaign highlighting the dangers of moshpits, and a reduction in mediated images which promote the cultural activity as positive. Education should also be provided to all parties involved with the promotion of rock concerts (i.e. the promoter, stage manager, security personnel, first-aid personnel, etc.), concerning the crowd psychology and dynamics evident at rock concerts, so that they can learn how to control crowd behaviour properly.

The provision of padding on all crowd barriers at rock concerts and other types of event would significantly reduce the severity of injuries sustained by those audience members pushed up against such barriers, particularly at the front-of-stage.

In general, rock concert attendees were very supportive of the previously outlined safety methods, which both accommodate the cultural activity 'moshing' and promote concert safety. Currently, however, such devices are generally not practised by the industry with serious devotion and commitment. Until concert practitioners really recognise the seriousness of this issue and actively attempt to tackle it, concert tragedies will continue to occur.

Is it economically viable to allow the conductance of this cultural activity?

The economic viability of the previously outlined rock concert safety measures will ultimately determine their validity in terms of whether or not they can actually be implemented. It is also important that the enjoyment of attending a rock concert is not reduced by the implementation of such methods, otherwise concert attendees may be less willing to pay to attend a concert staged at the respective venue. Small capacity venues are particularly at risk to this notion, due to their tight expenditure budgets and the fact that they cannot promote well-established artistes who attract concert attendance, regardless of the concert environment.

The costs incurred in conjunction with providing specialised first-aid services, specially trained security teams, padded barriers, drinking water, assistance from performers in monitoring and controlling crowd behaviour, and education concerning the inherent dangers of moshpit environments and how to comply with the rules of 'moshpit etiquette' would not be substantial enough to disregard the implementation of such measures. Further, in support of these measures is the fact that they would not reduce the quality of enjoyment experienced when attending rock concerts. All of these measures would help to significantly increase audience safety at rock concerts and would be economically viable to implement at any type or size of venue.

The implementation of a segregation system would only be worthwhile at large capacity venues, due to the cost of installation and operation of such a device, and the immense density of the audience. Although this type of device may reduce the quality of the concert atmosphere, the performing artistes promoted at large venues will always encourage attendance, regardless of the concert environment. Further still, so long as the reasons justifying the implementation of a segregation system are communicated to the audience, crowd members are likely to be more supportive and understanding of this device than previously anticipated.

The enforcement of moshpit participant age and capacity limits, although increasing concert safety, are likely to reduce the enjoyment of rock concert attendance and may result in a loss of trade to the concert practitioner. Unless these regulations are controlled by a segregation system, their implementation is not as economically viable and the other analysed measures.

The installation of a CCTV surveillance system would not reduce the enjoyment experienced by audience members, so long as cameras are discreetly positioned. The provision and operation of this particular safety device, however, would only be economically viable for large capacity venues, due to the respective expense incurred. Smaller venues can, however, adopt a similar method by which to monitor the audience, by employing raised platforms on which security personnel and/or 'spotters' can be located. The provision of this service would not incur a great expense and is therefore economically viable for all types and sizes of venue.

The provision of a ventilation system would also only be economically viable for large capacity, indoor venues, due to the considerable expense incurred during installation. However, in addition to enhancing safety, this device can also help to increase the enjoyment of the concert experienced by attendees, meaning that large capacity venues should seriously consider the implementation of this measure.

In essence, almost all of the concert safety measures uncovered and analysed by this investigation, would be economically viable to introduce at all or some types of venues. This indication further enhances the need for the concert industry to recognise the *need* to increase concert safety, reasoning the fact that little extra expense or effort, relative to the consequential effect, will be incurred during this process.

In overview of this investigation, it has been discovered that rock concert safety needs desperately to be greatly increased, but should also accommodate the cultural activity - 'moshing'. A range of methods by which to achieve this have been uncovered, analysed, validated and justified by this research. It is now the responsibility of the industry to recognise this issue and tackle it with commitment and dedication. It is simply not enough to implement a select few devices in view of increasing concert safety. Instead, concert practitioners need to implement as many devices as possible so that the rock concert environment can be made as safe as is feasibly possible. Until the industry really attempts to tackle this issue, however, rock concert-related tragedies will continue to occur.

REFERENCES

Ackroyd, S. & Hughes, J. (1992) **Data Collection in Context**. 2nd ed. Essex: Longman Group UK Limited.

Ambrose, J. (2001) **The Violent World of Moshpit Culture**. [s.l.]: Omnibus Press.

Bell, J. (1996) **Doing Your Research Project: a guide for first-time researchers in education and social science**. 2nd ed. Buckingham: Open University Press.

Bignell, J. (1997) **Media Semiotics: an introduction**. Manchester: Manchester University Press.

Bilton. T. *et al.* (1996) **Introductory Sociology**. 3rd ed. Hampshire: Macmillan Press Ltd.

Bowdin, G. *et al* (2001) **Events Management**. Oxford: Butterworth-Heinemann.

Collins (2002) **Dictionary & Thesaurus**. Glasgow: HarperCollins Publishers.

Collins, M. & Cooper, I. (eds.) (1998) **Leisure Management: issues and applications**. Oxon: CAB International.

Crozier, W. (2000) **Music and Social Influence**. In: Hargreaves, D. & North, A. (eds.) *The Social Psychology of Music*. Oxford: Oxford University Press.

Davidson, J. (2000) **The Social in Music Performance**. In: Hargreaves, D. & North, A. (eds.) *The Social Psychology of Music*. Oxford: Oxford University Press.

Department of Culture, Media and Sport (1997) **Guide to Safety at Sports Grounds**. 4th ed. London: The Stationary Office.

Frosdick, S. & Walley, L. (eds.) (1997) **Sport and Safety Management**. Oxford: Butterworth-Heinemann.

Frosdick, S. (1997) **Managing Risk in Public Assembly Facilities**. In: Frosdick, S. & Walley, L. (eds.) *Sport and Safety Management*. Oxford: Butterworth-Heinemann.

Grainger-Jones, B. (1999) **Managing Leisure**. Oxford: Butterworth:Heinemann.

Hamm, C. (1995) **Putting Popular Music in its Place**. Cambridge: Cambridge University Press.

Haralambos, M. & Holborn, M. (1995) **Sociology Themes and Perspectives**. 4th ed. London: Collins Educational.

Hargreaves, D. & North, A. (eds.) (2000) **The Social Psychology of Music**. Oxford: Oxford University Press.

Health & Safety Executive (1999) **The Event Safety Guide: a guide to health, safety and welfare at music and similar events**. [s.l.]: HSE Books.

Highmore, M. (1997) **Safety Risks in Stadia and Sports Grounds**. In: Frosdick, S. & Walley, L. (eds.) *Sport and Safety Management.* Oxford: Butterworth-Heinemann.

Kemp, C. (2000) **Music Industry Management & Promotion**. 2nd ed. Huntingdon: ELM Publications.

Kraus, R. & Curtis, J. (1990) **Creative Management in Recreation, Parks, and Leisure Services**. 5th ed. Missouri: Times Mirror/Mosby College Publishing.

Longhurst, B. (1995) **Popular Music & Society**. Cambridge: Polity Press.

Mason, J. (1996) **Qualitative Researching**. London: SAGE Publications Ltd.

May, T. (1998) **Social Research: issues, methods and process**. 2nd ed. Buckingham: Open University Press.

Meltzer, R. (1987) **The Aesthetics of Rock**. New York: Da Capo Press.

Negus, K. (1996) **Popular Music in Theory: an introduction**. Cambridge: Polity Press.

Punch, K. (1998) **Introduction to Social Research: quantitative & qualitative approaches**. London: SAGE Publications Ltd.

Rogers, *et al.* (1995) **Social Psychology: a critical agenda**. Cambridge: Blackwell Publishers Inc.

Shuker, R. (1994) **Understanding Popular Music**. London: Routledge.

Silverman, D. (2000) **Doing Qualitative Research: a practical handbook**. London: SAGE Publications.

Smith, P. & Bond, M. (1998) **Social Psychology Across Cultures**. 2nd ed. Hertfordshire: Prentice Hall Europe.

Torkildsen, G. (1999) **Leisure and Recreation Management**. 4th ed. London: E & FN Spon.

Warne, C. (1997) **Crowd Risks in Sports Grounds**. In: Frosdick, S. & Walley, L. (eds.) *Sport and Safety Management*. Oxford: Butterworth-Heinemann.

Waters, I. (1994) **Entertainment, Arts and Cultural Services**. 2nd ed. Essex: Longman Group UK Ltd.

Web references

Barron, J. (1994) **Are the Kids Alright?: moshing tragedies abound at recent rock shows**. [online]. Available from: http://www.poprocks.com/journ/mosh.htm [Accessed 21 November 2002].

BBC (2002) **Promoters to Blame for Fan's Death say Limp Bizkit's Manager**. [online]. Available from: http://www.bbc.co.uk/radio1/artist_area/limpbizkit/ [Accessed 8 October 2002].

Crowd Dynamics [n.d.] **Crowd Management Information**. [online]. Available from: http://www.crowddynamics.com/Main/Crowd%20Control.htm [Accessed 15 November 2002].

Crowd Management Strategies (2001) **The Rock and Roll Wall of Shame**. [online]. Available from: http://www.crowdsafe.com/thewall.html [Accessed 15 November 2002].

Crowd Management Strategies (2002) **Mosher Friendly Guidelines**. [online]. Available from: http://www.crowdsafe.com/mosh.html [Accessed 10 October 2002].

Dotmusic (2000) **Concert Safety Investigated After Roskilde**. [online]. Available from: http://www.dotmusic.com/news/july2000/news14555.asp [Accessed 15 November 2002].

Dotmusic (2000) **Moshing Too Dangerous for Festivals**. [online]. Available from: http://www.dotmusic.com/news/July2000/news14443.asp [Accessed 17 October 2002].

Dotmusic (2000) **Roskilde Tragedy**. [online]. Available from: http://www.dotmusic.com/news/July2000/news14421.asp [Accessed 8 October 2002].

Goodwin, S. [n.d.] **An Evaluation of Crowd Safety Management and Controls Deployed for 'Mosh Pits' at Rock Concerts**. [online]. Available from: http://www.livemusiceducation.com/crowd%20surfing.htm [Accessed 8 October 2002].

Malavenda, P. (1995) **Moshing: Freedom of Expression or Liability?** [online]. Available from: http://www.geocities.com/Heartland/Village/3335/Moshing.htm [Accessed 21 November 2002].

Roadogz (2002) **Crowd Management @ BDO in Aussie**. [online]. Available from: http://www.roadogz.com/stories/downunder/crowdmanagement.htm [Accessed 17 October 2002].

Upton, M. [n.d.] **Risk Assessment for Casual Rock Concert Events**. [online]. Available from: http://www.crowddynamics.com/Concert%20Risks.htm [Accessed 1 October 2002].

Holly Marshall

Holly is a recent graduate from the Buckinghamshire Chilterns Univeristy College BA (Hons) Music Industry Management and Live Production Degree course, graduating with a first class honours degree. Holly worked on the crowd safety perceptions project at Knebworth and the National Bowl and now works for the Derek Block Agency. the case study is an edited chapter of her thesis.

APPENDIX A
DEFINITION OF TERMS

Crown Surfing
Where individuals are lifted above the crowd and are transported horizontally overhead by the crowd members holding them aloft and passing them in the direction of the stage.

Moshing
A term used to describe what the seventies punk rock culture called slam dancing. It is a ritualised, intense form of crowd dancing with physical contact, during which participants move together, literally slamming and bumping into each other. The act of moshing takes place in the 'moshpit', an area or circle in which individuals perform the ritualised form of dance. It is generally located towards the front of the crowd behind the front of stage barrier, however, it can start spontaneously anywhere within the crowd and should therefore be regarded as an activity not a place.

Pogoing
A form of dance where individuals jump up and down as high as they can and bump into others dancers. Pogoing can be performed both inside an outside the moshpit.

Skanking (also referred to as a 'circle pit')
Originally a term for slam dancing, it describes a moshpit activity where a circle forms within the crowd. The crowd members move in a circular route, with an open space within the centre of the circle, and continue to slam into each other. Usually initiated by a request from the performer, it can resemble a North American Indian war dance, or in extreme cases, a whirlpool. The size and duration of this rotating circle is dependent on the number of people drawn into it.

Stage Diving
Where a performer or crowd member literally dives from the stage into the crowd. The intention is then that the crowd will catch and support the individual, holding them above their heads while the individual crowd surfs.

Due to the inclusion of front of stage barrier systems and pit security teams, stage diving is made impossible at concerts with large capacities so members sometimes resort to jumping from high places within the venue onto the crowd instead, such as from building supports.

APPENDIX B
CROWD MANAGEMENT AT THE
'BIG DAY OUT' IN AUSTRALIA
Roadogz 2002

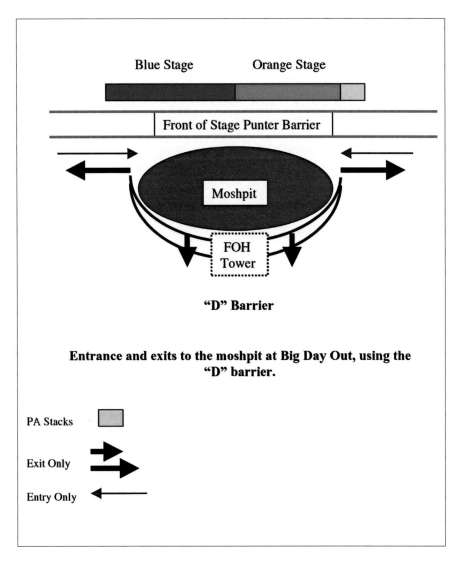

Entrance and exits to the moshpit at Big Day Out, using the "D" barrier.

APPENDIX C
ADDITIONAL GRAPHS FROM SURVEY RESULTS

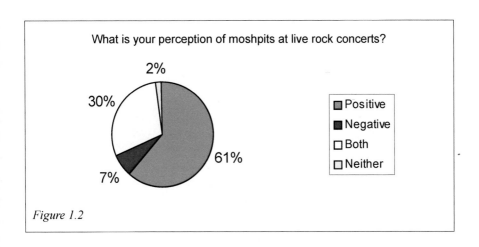

What is your perception of moshpits at live rock concerts?

- Positive
- Negative
- Both
- Neither

Figure 1.2

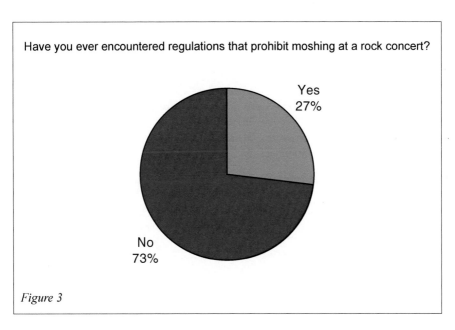

Have you ever encountered regulations that prohibit moshing at a rock concert?

Yes 27%

No 73%

Figure 3

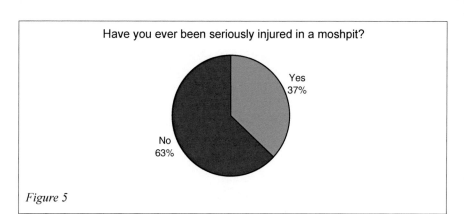

Figure 5

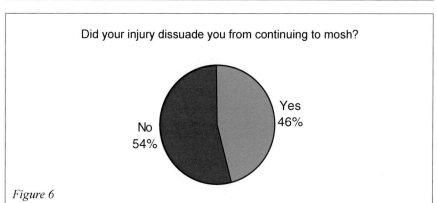

Figure 6

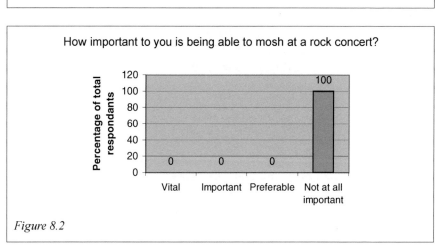

Figure 8.2

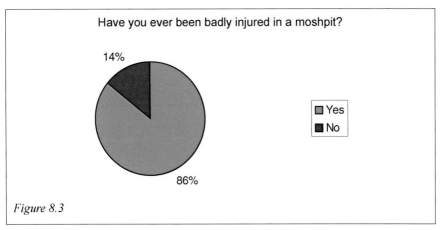

Figure 8.3

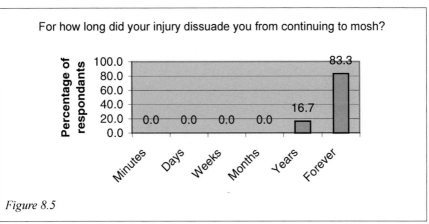

Figure 8.5

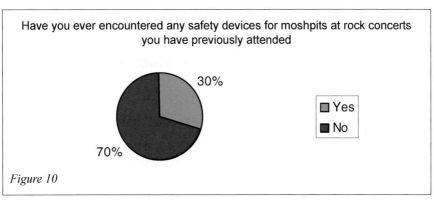

Figure 10

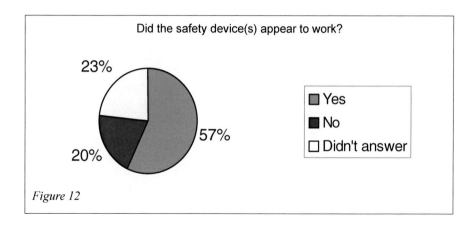

Figure 12

FURTHER READING

Frosdick, S and Walley, L (1999). **Sport & Safety Management**. Butterworth Heinemann

Hannam, C (1997) **An Introduction to Health and Safety Management for the Live Music Industry**. Production Services Association

Huntington, J (2000). **Control Systems for Live Entertainment**. Focal Press

Menear, P and Hawkins T (1988) **Stage Management and Theatre Administration**. Phaidon, Oxford

Vasey, J (1999). **Concert Sound and Lighting Systems (3rd Ed)**. Focal Press

HSE (2000) **Managing Crowds Safely**. A guide for organisers at events and venues

HSE (1999) **The Event Safety Guide**. A guide to health, safety and welfare at music and similar events. HSE, London.

Mullis, A & Oliphant, K (1997) **Torts** Macmillan Press, London

Brazier, M (1993) **Street on Torts** Butterworth Heinnemann London

Trespass and Protest: Policing under the Criminal Justice and Public Order Act 1994 Home Office Research Study 190 1998.

Institution of Structural Engineers (1999) **Temporary Demountable Structures**. Guidance on Design, Procurement and Use. ISE, London.

HSE (1999) **Safe Use of Lifting Equipment**. HSE, London.

HMSO (1999) **Guide to Safety at Sports Grounds**. Fourth edition. HMSO, London

Wertheimer P. (1980) **Crowd Management** *Report of the Task Force on Crowd Control and Safety*. City of Cincinnati.

HMSO (1989) **The Hillsborough Stadium Disaster. Interim report** HMSO, London.

John J. Fruin, (1993) **The Causes and Prevention of Crowd Disasters**. (Originally presented at the First International Conference of Engineering for Crowd Safety, London).

Anthony DeBarros, (2000) **Concertgoers push injuries to high levels**. Published in USA Today, August 8th, 2000.

Au, S.Y.Z., Ryan, M.C., Carey, M.S. (1993) **Key principles in ensuring crowd safety in public venues**. In: Smith, R.A., Dickie, J.F. (eds.) *Engineering for Crowd Safety*, Amsterdam. Elsevier Science Publishers.

Au, S.Y.Z., Ryan, M.C., Carey, M.S., Whalley, S.P. (1993) **Managing crowd safety in public venues: a study to generate guidance for venue owners and enforcing authority inspectors**. HSE Contract Research Report No. 53/1993, London: HMSO.

Department of the Environment Advisory Committee on Pop Festivals (1973) **Pop Festivals Report and Code of Practice**. London: HMSO.

Dubin, G.H. (1974) **Medical care at large gatherings: a manual based on experiences in rock concert medicine**. U.S. Department of Health Education and Welfare

Hanna, J.A. (1995) **Emergency preparedness guidelines for mass, crowd-intensive events**. Emergency Preparedness Canada.

Home Office Emergency Planning College (1992) **Lessons learned from crowd-related disasters**. Easingwold Papers No.4, Easingwold: Emergency Planning College.

Leiba, T. (1999) **Crisis intervention theory and method**. In: Tomlinson, D., Allen, K. (eds.) *Crisis Services and Hospital Crises: mental health at a turning point*. Aldershot: Ashgate.

NHS (1999) **National Service Framework for Mental Health - modern standards and service models**. London: Department of Health.

Turner, B.A., Pidgeon, N.F. (1997) **Man-made disasters**. 2nd Edition. Oxford. Butterworth Heinemann.

Ackroyd, S. & Hughes, J. (1992) **Data Collection in Context**. 2nd ed. Essex: Longman Group UK Limited.

Ambrose, J. (2001) **The Violent World of Moshpit Culture**. [s.l.]: Omnibus Press.

Bell, J. (1996) **Doing Your Research Project: a guide for first-time researchers in education and social science**. 2nd ed. Buckingham: Open University Press.

Bignell, J. (1997) **Media Semiotics: an introduction**. Manchester: Manchester University Press.

Bilton. T. *et al.* (1996) **Introductory Sociology**. 3rd ed. Hampshire: Macmillan Press Ltd.

Bowdin, G. *et al* (2001) **Events Management**. Oxford: Butterworth-Heinemann.

Collins (2002) **Dictionary & Thesaurus**. Glasgow: HarperCollins Publishers.

Collins, M. & Cooper, I. (eds.) (1998) **Leisure Management: issues and applications**. Oxon: CAB International.

Crozier, W. (2000) **Music and Social Influence**. In: Hargreaves, D. & North, A. (eds.) *The Social Psychology of Music*. Oxford: Oxford University Press.

Davidson, J. (2000) **The Social in Music Performance**. In: Hargreaves, D. & North, A. (eds.) *The Social Psychology of Music*. Oxford: Oxford University Press.

Frosdick, S. (1997) **Managing Risk in Public Assembly Facilities**. In: Frosdick, S. & Walley, L. (eds.) *Sport and Safety Management*. Oxford: Butterworth-Heinemann.

Grainger-Jones, B. (1999) **Managing Leisure**. Oxford: Butterworth:Heinemann.

Hamm, C. (1995) **Putting Popular Music in its Place**. Cambridge: Cambridge University Press.

Haralambos, M. & Holborn, M. (1995) **Sociology Themes and Perspectives**. 4th ed. London: Collins Educational.

Hargreaves, D. & North, A. (eds.) (2000) **The Social Psychology of Music.** Oxford: Oxford University Press.

Health & Safety Executive (1999) **The Event Safety Guide: a guide to health, safety and welfare at music and similar events.** [s.l.]: HSE Books.

Highmore, M. (1997) **Safety Risks in Stadia and Sports Grounds.** In: Frosdick, S. & Walley, L. (eds.) *Sport and Safety Management.* Oxford: Butterworth-Heinemann.

Kemp, C. (2000) **Music Industry Management & Promotion.** 2nd ed. Huntingdon: ELM Publications.

Kraus, R. & Curtis, J. (1990) **Creative Management in Recreation, Parks, and Leisure Services.** 5th ed. Missouri: Times Mirror/Mosby College Publishing.

Longhurst, B. (1995) **Popular Music & Society.** Cambridge: Polity Press.

Mason, J. (1996) **Qualitative Researching.** London: SAGE Publications Ltd.

May, T. (1998) **Social Research: issues, methods and process.** 2nd ed. Buckingham: Open University Press.

Meltzer, R. (1987) **The Aesthetics of Rock.** New York: Da Capo Press.

Negus, K. (1996) **Popular Music in Theory: an introduction.** Cambridge: Polity Press.

Punch, K. (1998) **Introduction to Social Research: quantitative & qualitative approaches.** London: SAGE Publications Ltd.

Rogers, *et al.* (1995) **Social Psychology: a critical agenda.** Cambridge: Blackwell Publishers Inc.

Shuker, R. (1994) **Understanding Popular Music.** London: Routledge.

Silverman, D. (2000) **Doing Qualitative Research: a practical handbook.** London: SAGE Publications.

Smith, P. & Bond, M. (1998) **Social Psychology Across Cultures.** 2nd ed. Hertfordshire: Prentice Hall Europe.

Torkildsen, G. (1999) **Leisure and Recreation Management.** 4th ed. London: E & FN Spon.

Warne, C. (1997) **Crowd Risks in Sports Grounds.** In: Frosdick, S. & Walley, L. (eds.) *Sport and Safety Management.* Oxford: Butterworth-Heinemann.

Waters, I. (1994) **Entertainment, Arts and Cultural Services.** 2nd ed. Essex: Longman Group UK Ltd.

Web references
Barron, J. (1994) **Are the Kids Alright?: moshing tragedies abound at recent rock shows.** [online]. Available from: http://www.poprocks.com/journ/mosh.htm [Accessed 21 November 2002].

BBC (2002) **Promoters to Blame for Fan's Death say Limp Bizkit's Manager**. [online]. Available from: http://www.bbc.co.uk/radio1/artist_area/limpbizkit/ [Accessed 8 October 2002].

Crowd Dynamics [n.d.] **Crowd Management Information**. [online]. Available from: http://www.crowddynamics.com/Main/Crowd%20Control.htm [Accessed 15 November 2002].

Crowd Management Strategies (2001) **The Rock and Roll Wall of Shame**. [online]. Available from: http://www.crowdsafe.com/thewall.html [Accessed 15 November 2002].

Crowd Management Strategies (2002) **Mosher Friendly Guidelines**. [online]. Available from: http://www.crowdsafe.com/mosh.html [Accessed 10 October 2002].

Dotmusic (2000) **Concert Safety Investigated After Roskilde**. [online]. Available from: http://www.dotmusic.com/news/july2000/news14555.asp [Accessed 15 November 2002].

Dotmusic (2000) **Moshing Too Dangerous for Festivals**. [online]. Available from: http://www.dotmusic.com/news/July2000/news14443.asp [Accessed 17 October 2002].

Dotmusic (2000) **Roskilde Tragedy**. [online]. Available from: http://www.dotmusic.com/news/July2000/news14421.asp [Accessed 8 October 2002].

Goodwin, S. [n.d.] **An Evaluation of Crowd Safety Management and Controls Deployed for 'Mosh Pits' at Rock Concerts**. [online]. Available from: http://www.livemusiceducation.com/crowd%20surfing.htm [Accessed 8 October 2002].

Malavenda, P. (1995) **Moshing: Freedom of Expression or Liability?** [online]. Available from: http://www.geocities.com/Heartland/Village/3335/Moshing.htm [Accessed 21 November 2002].

Roadogz (2002) **Crowd Management @ BDO in Aussie**. [online]. Available from: http://www.roadogz.com/stories/downunder/crowdmanagement.htm [Accessed 17 October 2002].

Upton, M. [n.d.] **Risk Assessment for Casual Rock Concert Events**. [online]. Available from: http://www.crowddynamics.com/Concert%20Risks.htm [Accessed 1 October 2002].

Websites
www.dotmusic.com
www.crowdsafe.com
www.glastonburyfestivals.co.uk
www.festivalnews.com
www.ilmc.com

ENTERTAINMENT TECHNOLOGY PRESS

FREE SUBSCRIPTION SERVICE

Keeping Up To Date with

Health and Safety at Live Events

Entertainment Technology titles are continually up-dated, and all major changes and additions are listed in date order in the relevant dedicated area of the publisher's website. Simply go to the front page of www.etnow.com and click on the BOOKS button. From there you can locate the title and be connected through to the latest information and services related to the publication.

The author of the title welcomes comments and suggestions about the book and can be contacted by email at:
chris.kemp@bcuc.ac.uk

Titles Published by Entertainment Technology Press

ABC of Theatre Jargon *Francis Reid* **£9.95**
This glossary of theatrical terminology explains the common words and phrases that are used in normal conversation between actors, directors, designers, technicians and managers.

Aluminium Structures in the Entertainment Industry *Peter Hind* **£24.95**
Aluminium Structures in the Entertainment Industry aims to educate the reader in all aspects of the design and safe usage of temporary and permanent aluminium structures specific to the entertainment industry – such as roof structures, PA towers, temporary staging, etc.

The Exeter Theatre Fire *David Anderson* **£24.95**
This title is a fascinating insight into the events that led up to the disaster at the Theatre Royal, Exeter, on the night of September 5th 1887. The book details what went wrong, and the lessons that were learned from the event.

Hearing the Light *Francis Reid* **£24.95**
This highly enjoyable memoir delves deeply into the theatricality of the industry. The author's almost fanatical interest in opera, his formative period as lighting designer at Glyndebourne and his experiences as a theatre administrator, writer and teacher make for a broad and unique background.

Introduction to Rigging in the Entertainment Industry *Chris Higgs* **£24.95**
An Introduction to Rigging in the Entertainment Industry is a practical guide to rigging techniques and practices and also thoroughly covers safety issues and discusses the implications of working within recommended guidelines and regulations.

Focus on Lighting Technology *Richard Cadena* **£17.95**
This concise work unravels the mechanics behind modern performance lighting and appeals to designers and technicians alike. Packed with clear, easy-to-read diagrams, the book provides excellent explanations behind the technology of performance lighting.

Lighting for Roméo and Juliette *John Offord* **£26.95**
John Offord describes the making of the production from the lighting designer's viewpoint - taking the story through from the point where director Jürgen Flimm made his decision not to use scenery or sets and simply employ the expertise of Patrick Woodroffe.

Lighting Systems for TV Studios *Nick Mobsby* **£35.00**
Lighting Systems for TV Studios is the first book written specifically on the subject and is set to become the 'standard' resource work for the sector.

Lighting Techniques for Theatre-in-the-Round *Jackie Staines,* **£24.95**
Lighting Techniques for Theatre-in-the-Round is a unique reference source for those working on lighting design for theatre-in-the-round for the first time.

Lighting the Stage *Francis Reid* **£14.95**
Lighting the Stage discusses the human relationships involved in lighting design – both between people, and between these people and technology. The book is written from a highly personal viewpoint and its 'thinking aloud' approach is one that Francis Reid has used in his writings over the past 30 years.

Practical Guide to Health and Safety in the Entertainment Industry
Marco van Beek £14.95
This book is designed to provide a practical approach to Health and Safety within the Live Entertainment and Event industry. It gives industry-pertinent examples, and seeks to break down the myths surrounding Health and Safety.

Production Management *Joe Aveline* £17.95
Joe Aveline's book is an in-depth guide to the role of the Production Manager, and includes real-life practical examples and 'Aveline's Fables' – anecdotes of his experiences with real messages behind them.

Sixty Years of Light Work *Fred Bentham* £26.95
This title is an autobiography of one of the great names behind the development of modern stage lighting equipment and techniques.

Sound for the Stage *Patrick Finelli* £24.95
Patrick Finelli's thorough manual covering all aspects of live and recorded sound for performance is a complete training course for anyone interested in working in the field of stage sound, and is a must for any student of sound.

Stage Lighting for Theatre Designers *Nigel Morgan* £17.95
An updated second edition of this popular book for students of theatre design outlining all the techniques of stage lighting design.

Technical Marketing Techniques *David Brooks, Andy Collier, Steve Norman* £24.95
Technical Marketing is a novel concept, recently defined and elaborated by the authors of this book, with business-to-business companies competing in fast developing technical product sectors.

Theatre Engineering and Stage Machinery *Toshiro Ogawa* £30.00
Theatre Engineering and Stage Machinery is a unique reference work covering every aspect of theatrical machinery and stage technology in global terms.

Model National Standard Conditions *ABTT/DSA/LGLA* £20.00
These *Model National Standard Conditions* covers operational matters and complement *The Technical Standards for Places of Entertainment*, which describes the physical requirements for building and maintaining entertainment premises.

Technical Standards for Places of Entertainment *ABTT/DSA* £30.00
Technical Standards for Places of Entertainment details the necessary physical standards required for entertainment venues.